The Decline of the
World Communist Movement

About the Book and Author

International Communism today is split on a number of ideological and political issues and is incapable of the kind of unified action implied by the term "movement." So argues Heinz Timmermann in this assessment of the current state of world Communism.

Dr. Timmermann discusses the historical concept of a world Communist movement in connection with the USSR and China. Focusing on Communism in the West, he examines such diverse groups as the Communist parties in Italy, France, Portugal, Cyprus, Chile, and Japan. Communist parties in the West are increasingly adjusting their policies to better fit their own cultures, and the author links this independence to the emphasis the Soviet Union's Communist Party has been placing on the specifically Russian character of the October Revolution and Soviet state interests.

Apparently, Moscow is now showing some flexibility in its response to tendencies toward differentiation and pluralism within the system of Communist parties. Gorbachev is less concerned with ideological orthodoxy than with Communists effectively supporting Soviet foreign policy. The author argues that by acceding to the concept of "unity in diversity," Gorbachev is signaling that the Soviet leadership is willing to look beyond the myth of a world Communist movement.

Dr. Heinz Timmermann has been on the staff of the Federal Institute for East European and International Studies in Cologne since 1969.

Published in cooperation with
the Federal Institute for East European
and International Studies, Cologne

The Decline of the World Communist Movement

Moscow, Beijing, and Communist Parties in the West

Heinz Timmermann

translated by
Julius W. Friend

Westview Press / Boulder and London

A Westview Special Study

This Westview softcover edition is printed on acid-free paper and bound in
softcovers that carry the highest rating of the National Association of State
Textbook Administrators, in consultation with the Association of American
Publishers and the Book Manufacturers' Institute.

Published in 1987 in the United States of America by Westview Press, Inc.;
Frederick A. Praeger, Publisher; 5500 Central Avenue, Boulder, Colorado 80301

Library of Congress Cataloging-in-Publication Data
Timmermann, Heinz.
    The decline of the world Communist movement.
    (A Westview special study)
    Bibliography: p.
    Includes index.
    1. Communism--1945-   . 2. Communist parties.
3. Soviet Union--Foreign relations--1945-   .
4. China--Foreign relations--1949-   . I. Title.
II. Series.
HX44.T537 1987   324'.1   87-6263
ISBN 0-8133-7381-6

Composition for this book was provided by the author.
This book was produced without formal editing by the publisher.

Printed and bound in the United States of America

The paper used in this publication meets the requirements of the
American National Standard for Permanence of Paper for Printed
Library Materials Z39.48-1984.

6   5   4   3   2

6-12-89

Contents

Foreword

Richard Lowenthal

The political idea of a world Communist movement is older than the creation of the Soviet power: it was conceived during World War I by Vladimir Ilyich Lenin when he was in Zurich waiting for an expected series of Communist revolutions to end the war. He had no way of knowing which revolution would break out first. After returning home and founding the Soviet state with his Communist party, he still expected revolutions in Europe. He thought Germany would be the next nation to revolt and expressed his belief that revolutionary Russia would have to learn from the revolutionary West. Lenin was a great Russian, but not a "Great Russian," as his successors were to be.

Lenin's European hopes failed after the Hungarian revolution was crushed with the help of foreign troops, the Munich revolt was squashed, and Soviet forces were defeated when they did not stop after repelling a Polish attack, but followed orders and tried to conquer Poland in the name of the Soviet revolution. Lenin then understood that the immediate postwar revolutionary prospects were over and concluded that for an indefinite time a world Communist movement must be organized on Soviet principles. In fact, the principles had already been approved at the second congress of the Communist International in August 1920, even while Soviet troops were still trying to conquer Warsaw.

It is true that Lenin had some doubts in the last years of his life. At the fourth congress of the International in 1922--the last he visited--he worried that the principles approved at the second congress had been "too Russian" to be understood by the European comrades. In one of his very last papers he stated that "Russia, China, India, etc." representing the majority of mankind, would ultimately ensure the worldwide victory of Communism. (The plan for an armed revolution in Germany in the fall of 1923, which was stopped just in time by the leader of the German Communists, was conceived when Lenin was already too ill to know of it.) What thus remained when Lenin died was a strict organization for "world Communism"--without a political concept.

Stalin, who had in fact taken over before Lenin died, was a Georgian and not a Russian, but he was a "Great Russian." I mean by this that he had a fundamentally different concept of the Soviet revolution from Lenin's. He did not believe that Soviet Communism could only be achieved with the cooperation of the people of more advanced countries but that it could and must be achieved by the extreme effort of the Russian people--and in his eyes, it eventually was achieved in this way. Of course, this was a very different kind of "Communism" from that which Lenin, let alone Marx, had had in mind. But it had the double advantage of existing, and existing as Stalin's work, of already commanding the belief of millions of people inside Russia, and even more outside. Yet I am not suggesting that Stalin only cared for his own power. Of course, he believed in power and was utterly ruthless, but he also believed that his ruthlessness, with its hecatombs of victims, was creating a kind of "Communist" greatness for Russia. And by the end of World War II large numbers of Russians and Westerners, forgetting the road Stalin had taken before Hitler's attack, agreed with him.

In the long pre-war period of Stalin's rule, from 1924 to 1941, no Communist party came to power in any country, and only two of them made serious efforts in that direction: Yugoslavia and China, the same two which later succeeded in establishing Communist governments, only to break with the Soviet Union still later. Stalin was not urging them to fight for power--he was urging them to sing his praises and to support policies in their countries that would be useful to the Soviet Union. This was the rationale behind his effort to get the Chinese Communists to cooperate modestly with Chiang Kai-shek when he was fighting to create a more modern China and behind his decision, after Chiang had moved against them, to make them concentrate on resistance to Japan--however far away Japan might be. This was also the rationale for making the German Communists turn against the Social Democrats, calling them "social fascists," because the SPD favored better relations between Germany and France while Stalin relied on the German military to be pro-Soviet.

During the early part of the war, Stalin was still ordering French and British Communists to oppose their governments' resistance to Hitler and instructing the exiled German Communists to attack an alleged capitalist clique opposing Hitler. Of course, he turned them around when Hitler turned against him. From then on, Communists in all the occupied Western countries were instructed to support and if possible lead the resistance, working both for broad cooperation and for special military groups of their own. Even the Yugoslav Communists were urged--without success--to cooperate with Serb nationalists, who had been arresting them for years. Further east, however, where Poland had only recently been occupied (as agreed) by Hitler's and Stalin's troops, it was necessary to create pro-Soviet Polish units in the Soviet Union and send them back to what had been their homeland, or rather a reduced part of it.

This book does not deal with the evolution of those Eastern European countries that were to become parts of the Soviet bloc, but a single case must be mentioned. Tito's Yugoslavia emerged from the war under native Communist leadership, and Soviet units simply marched in and recognized its existence. A few years later, this same country had reason enough to break with the Soviets and stamina enough to survive the break. It was a singular error on Stalin's part to believe that he could overthrow that tough national hero by raising his little finger; yet he stuck to his unstated but clear rule of not sending troops against the leader of a country linked to yesterday's allies. In the early postwar years Stalin made a number of _political_ attempts to extend his new territory beyond the wartime agreements, but he was _not_ prepared to use _military_ action for that purpose.

This brings us to the creation of the Cominform in 1947--a Soviet-controlled organization of leaders of countries in the newly created Soviet bloc, and of Communist party leaders from Western European countries. While ideas for such an organization had apparently been discussed in Moscow for some time, the actual cause for its creation was the American Marshall Plan's proposal for the joint reconstruction of Eastern and Western European countries (including the Soviet Union) using American money. The plans for reconstruction were to be prepared jointly by the recipients. The Soviet Union had rejected the plan as a hostile attempt to influence its power sphere and had forbidden the leaders of two countries in that sphere, Poland and Czechoslovakia, to take part in it, as they had desired. But while that had been decided before the Cominform was created (on Polish territory!), the Cominform's actual first conference had to deal largely with western Communist problems--the need for the French and Italian Communist parties to stop cooperating with their governments in rebuilding their countries, as they had done previously, and to start a bitter campaign against the Marshall Plan and all its supporters.

It was Stalin's last major campaign in the Western world. While the East German and West German Communists were not represented in the Cominform (because the two new German states were only finally created two years later) their fate was very much influenced by it. For the West German authorities were promptly invited to join the Marshall plan and eagerly accepted. Because their practical acceptance required a new currency, an agreement was proposed to the Soviets that would have made possible East German participation. But the agreement was finally rejected by the Soviets. A new currency for West Germany alone, though, would not have had a stable basis without a West German state, however provisional. By the middle of 1948, when all preparations were ready, Stalin decided on a final attempt to disorganize both Western currency reform and parliamentary preparation for a West German state by stopping all Western traffic to Berlin. Yet that blockade, expected to force Berliners either to starve or choose the Soviet side, was foiled in less than a year by the firmness of Berliners under their Social Democrat mayor, Ernst Reuter, and the effectiveness of American and British airplanes bringing supplies--a countermove planned by U.S. general Lucius D. Clay. When the blockade was ended and the powers had reached a de facto agreement on the partition of Germany in 1949, Stalin's last serious attempt to shift the new borders of Europe was over--and over without a shot.

This was also the end of the period in which Western European Communist parties mattered as factors in Stalin's policies. The West German party proved very small in the first West German election, and later won no parliamentary seats at all. The large Italian and French parties could no longer serve in their governments, which they had left in May 1947, and after September 1947 were enlisted in the

Cominform campaign against the Marshall Plan. They lost part of their trade union power when the unions divided into separate organizations over the same problem. The Greek Communists, who had conducted a bitter civil war for years, were finally called back by Stalin when British troops were replaced by American troops on the opposite side after 1947. The East-West borders in Europe have remained stable ever since--with the Western powers equally respectful of the Soviet bloc in East Germany in 1953, Hungary in 1956, Czechoslovakia in 1968, and Poland in various crises.

But in his last years Stalin still had great decisions to make about Asia. He never came to understand that the former colonies of the Western powers had really become independent, and he could therefore give no meaningful instructions to Communist parties in countries like India-- that development came after his time. But he was, of course, aware of the rise of the Chinese Communists during the war with Japan. He did not expect and probably did not want total victory for the Communists, but counted on some uneasy arrangement between Chiang Kai-shek and Mao Zedong, which might give him influence over both. While entering the war against Japan at the last moment and sending his troops to Manchukuo, North Korea, and the Kuriles, he was still dealing separately with Chiang and Mao; it seems that he only accepted the rise of a Communist China in about 1947. By then, of course, the Chinese Communist party was by far the most important such organization outside Russia; and while he was determined to keep China dependent on the Soviet Union, Stalin realized that he could not keep it in the kind of manifest inferiority he had devised for his Eastern European comrades. The difficult negotiations with Mao in 1949/50 gave Stalin control over some economic and military positions, which Khrushchev later had to abandon, but no ideological control. It was the Korean war of 1951 that was to force the Chinese Communists to intervene for their own security and Stalin's honor. The war was started by the Communist rulers of North Korea on Stalin's advice and with the advantage of a superior army. But the reaction of the United Nations and the arrival of American troops were unforeseen. It was possible to repair the damage done by the senseless war only after Stalin's death, but the lesson of the need for greater independence remained not only with Mao but with all Chinese Communists.

Nikita Khrushchev's policy toward the world Communist movement was determined by two early decisions of his: a decision to make use of a realistic discovery, which he then overplayed, and by a bold decision on domestic policy, the international consequences of which he could not control. The realistic discovery was the rise of the ex-colonial "Third World" and the chances it opened to Soviet influence and the growth of Communist organizations. The bold decision was, of course, the public admission of part of the truth about Stalinism: its uncontrollable consequences were shock and bitter disagreement in the world Communist movement.

Both decisions became fully visible within two to three years after Stalin's death, and the realistic discovery came first. By 1955, if not before, Khrushchev had understood the range and potential importance of the ex-colonial countries. India, Burma, and other former colonial countries were no longer regarded, as in Stalin's time, as still "really" under British or other former colonial control and their Communists were no longer urged to treat men like Nehru and U Nu as enemies. Instead, as Khrushchev stated in a public speech at the party congress in February 1956, they were treated as potential allies in the cause of peace against the forces of capitalism and imperialism. In reality, this policy was already in practice before that speech. It is true that for some of the parties concerned, this made their position more secure but also less interesting and less independent. They were no longer encouraged to attack their non-Communist rulers--least of all if they were developing important economic relations with the USSR (as was the case particularly with India). In addition, Khrushchev hinted on the same occasion that outside the range of the imperialist powers, the victory of the Communist idea need not require the bitter revolutionary struggle that it had required in Russia and China. Moreover, Khrushchev had taken an early occasion to liberate Communist China from some of the Soviet privileges on which Stalin had insisted; he truly believed in a world Communism of natural friends.

But Khrushchev also believed in a Soviet Communism freed from the mass terror against Communists Stalin had practiced in 1936-1938. (And when he said so at a secret session of the 1956 party congress, he gave hope to Stalin's surviving victims, their families, and the young Soviet generation.) But he also caused intense concern to large numbers of Soviet officials whose careers had bloomed in Stalin's later years--and to large numbers of outside Communists trained to base their propaganda on the justification of all of Stalin's acts. The immediate effects included a difficult rearrangement of the Polish Communist leadership, a crisis in Hungary (leading to a massive uprising, partly led by Communist critics, that was ended only by Soviet troops and the execution of the leading critic), a public appeal by the Italian party leader Togliatti for the greater independence of the non-Soviet Communist parties, and serious public criticism by Mao Zedong of the method (though not yet the substance) of Khrushchev's frankness.

Study of that period, the series of international party conferences that followed it, and the break between Soviet and Chinese Communism in 1964, has shown the Soviet-managed "world Communist movement" to be the "myth" Dr. Timmermann describes in this book.[1] It is not that the movement suddenly ended after the conferences of 1957 and 1960 and the break of 1964; in the midst of all those upheavals, the Soviets succeeded in getting the originally independent revolutionary Castro regime in Cuba to become an ally. (At first it was a difficult ally, particularly in 1962 after the arrival and departure of Soviet missiles directed at the U.S.--then an increasingly tame one.) The ups and downs of more or less Communist states in Africa have not stopped to this day. But in the course of time, the character of those dependent associates has become more and more different not only from the type of comrades that Lenin hoped to win, but also from those that Khrushchev believed he had won--as a brief final look at the Brezhnev era will show.

Brezhnev was a product of Stalin's era--one of those who moved up when their former superiors were killed. But he was neither as ruthless nor as gifted as Stalin. Nor did he believe in any original interpretation of Communist power: Khrushchev's version of Communism was just a joke to Brezhnev. He believed, of course, in Russian power and very much in his own power--to be achieved as comfortably as possible.

He took office after Khrushchev's fall in late 1964, after the failure of Khrushchev's Cuban adventure when

---

1. I first dealt with this problem in my book Communism-- The Disintegration of a Secular Faith (New York: Oxford University Press, 1964).

both the Western governments and Soviet experts were wondering whether a more stable and less costly relationship could not be achieved between powers that had respected each other's territory ever since 1949. He received General de Gaulle's 1966 visit and noticed signs of West German interest in better relations. He also took note of the NATO Harmel report (1967) which outlined the best all-round concept for East-West stability that the West had to offer. He learned that the American president Lyndon Johnson, who was needlessly involved in the Vietnamese war, believed that the war was a first step by the Chinese Communists towards a major expansion in Southeast Asia, while Johnson saw Russia as a power satisfied with the status quo. Brezhnev steadily continued to support the Vietnamese with arms without making much noise about it.

A moment of crisis came in 1968 with the Czechoslovak attempt to create a more liberal form of Communism, with more freedom for the press and literature and more rights for workers. After some hesitation, Brezhnev's leadership decided to declare this a counter-revolutionary plot, which allegedly would be supported by West German troops. The West German government was in fact negotiating with Moscow and its allies for better relations. A joint invasion by Soviet, Polish, East German, Bulgarian, and belatedly, Hungarian troops ended the Czech hope, without intervention by any Western power. The price of this cheap victory--in Brezhnev's eyes clearly a minor price--was a major step by the Italian Communist party toward an increasingly independent stance. The Spanish Communist leaders who had experienced the events as exiles in Czechoslovakia and returned to a free Spain a few years later were in their majority determined to work for equal independence. The invasion of Czechoslovakia also produced the first turn of the French Communists toward independence, at least on the Czech issue. It was the starting point of what came to be known for some years as Eurocommunism. However, Eurocommunism soon lost its potential importance outside Italy, when the young Spanish party split and lost its potential importance, while under a new leader the French party, then still important, soon returned to a blind loyalty to Moscow instructions--and suffered a severe reduction of its importance as well.

The next "revival" of the "world Communist movement," as apparently conceived by Brezhnev and/or his expert Ponomarev, occurred in Africa and soon moved further east, ending in the tragedy of Afghanistan. To understand it, we must recall that after the Czech crisis, Brezhnev was ready for constructive negotiations with President Nixon and his advisor Henry Kissinger, and with West Germany, soon to be governed by Willy Brandt. The negotiations with the U.S. produced the first major limitations on nuclear weapons on both sides in many years. Talks with the Federal Republic not only brought the first normal relations between Bonn and the Communist governments of Eastern Europe (which the Germans knew were long overdue) but also (equally overdue) Western recognition of the East German state. Firm rules were established for the security of traffic between West Germany and West Berlin and for that of West Berlin itself (that last subject could be settled only by the former "allied four powers," and it was). The crowning result of both sets of negotiations was the 1975 Helsinki conference, where West and East Europeans, Americans, Canadians, and Soviets sought to establish common international principles. The conference also introduced the membership of the two German states in the United Nations.

Yet at this very moment, when Brezhnev appeared as a hero of peace, he observed a serious temporary weakness in the United States and fell for the fatal temptation to exploit it. The final defeat of the U.S. in Vietnam had more or less coincided with the domestic Watergate scandal that brought about President Nixon's fall, and the new president had to start with greatly diminished authority in Congress. It was under that impression that Brezhnev, more or less overnight, began two forms of unprovoked and aggressive policies. One was the creation of a series of new intermediate range nuclear missiles. These missiles were unable to reach the United States and their deployment did not conflict with the recent agreements. But they were able to attack all of Western Europe as well as Chinese and other Far Eastern targets. The other aggressive policy consisted of a series of measures to create governments of a more or less Communist type in various parts of Africa and the Near East, culminating in the Soviet occupation of Afghanistan. Nothing had happened that threatened the Soviet Union in either direction. The only conceivable motive for both new measures must have been Brezhnev's belief that having achieved military balance with the West by negotiation, he now had a chance to win military superiority by exploiting a phase of American political weakness--and his initial refusal to start new negotiations on intermediate range missiles underlined this foolish attitude.

xvii

There is no need and no room in this context to discuss the futile negotiations on intermediate missiles nor to address the respective contributions of both sides to their failure. What matters for our subject is the sad, if not tragic, fate of the latest expansion of the "world Communist movement"--in Africa and Afghanistan. It seems that only one of the African movements, Angola's, was started at least in part by trained Communists; the Ethiopian movement, the biggest of the others, was formed by a group of power-hungry military men without any previous ideological background. The Angolans, a small but comparatively educated minority group, were fighting for control of the country after the departure of Portuguese troops against two larger, more regionally rooted and less educated groups. Cuban soldiers were sent to their aid in Soviet ships; and to this day, they continue to fight with Cuban support against these rivals, one of which is now backed by South Africa! The extreme misery of Ethiopia, due largely to repeated years of drought in large parts of the country, is internationally known. So is the utter weakness of Mozambique, which at times has even asked for aid from neighboring South Africa. No enemy who wanted to turn the idea of a world Communist movement into a horror story could have conceived the African achievements of Mr. Brezhnev's government.

As for the tragedy in Afghanistan, which had been on peaceful terms with the Soviet Union for many years, it is still not clear how the original overthrow of the previous government was initiated by two rival Communist organizations that soon succeeded both in fighting each other and in being fought by considerably larger Islamic movements. Only after all these groups had become involved together did the Soviet government decide to intervene, both to decide between the rivals and to take over military control of the country--or so it believed. This "Communist movement" is by now more or less recognized in the Soviet Union as a tragic failure, from which the Soviets would like to withdraw by some kind of honorable agreement--if only that were possible....

When Gorbachev, the present general secretary, took over control of the Soviet Union, he clearly was aware of many of the weaknesses of its system and policies--but not of all of them. In the declaration of principle he made on January 15, 1986, he discussed many problems in an original and critical manner. But the seventh and last section of this speech, dealing with the role of the capitalist powers in the underdeveloped countries, differed from the rest. It described the capitalist world as the source of all poverty and misery in the Third World and the Soviet Union as the Third World's only source of support. Maybe Gorbachev had not yet got around to studying the Communist role in parts of Africa and in Afghanistan, and the final section of his speech had been written by Ponomarev....

By now he must know--and what he must know about the world Communist movement of today may be summed up very simply. Leaving aside the Soviet Union itself and the countries of the Soviet bloc, and leaving aside independent Communist states like China, there are three types of Communist organizations. Without denying its origins, one type has developed an increasingly independent way of thinking--and it is in fact a challenging and challenged but basically normal and productive part of the modern world. The Italian Communist party is a case in point. The second type consists of Communist parties that have more or less stopped thinking and, while enjoying the freedoms of democratic countries, are slowly but surely fading away. The French Communist party is perhaps now the most important of this group, but there are many smaller and less familiar ones. But there is still a third type, not in the more or less stabilized Communist world and not in the Western or the well organized parts of the Asian world-- but in a world of militant misery, victims of total phantasy at the foundation and total hopelessness at the end--for they do not even know what has been done to them.

Dr. Timmermann's sober and scholarly book documents the evolution of world Communism from Lenin's original hopes through Stalin's ruthless practices and Khrushchev's illusions to the incoherent activities of Brezhnev and Gorbachev's critical search for a return to reality. The reader will find the threads of this journey in this book by an author who has made world Communism his subject for many years.

PART ONE

Introduction

A Complex of Contradictions

At its Twenty-seventh Party Congress in the spring of 1986 the Communist party of the Soviet Union (CPSU) replaced its old party program dating from the Khrushchev era with a new version, entirely rewritten.[1] Particular attention was given to clauses that had shown themselves unrealistic or utopian. Left unchanged was the thesis of an historical inevitability whereby the new societal form of socialism would supercede "decaying and dying capitalism." The new program, like the old, named as the vanguard of this global process of change the "international Communist movement" which unites the Communist parties.

Now as before, the Soviets see the Communist movement as the main propulsive force in the struggle for peace and socialism in the world, central to the main forces of our time that quicken the world revolutionary process. Constituent elements of this process are the world socialist system (i.e. the collectivity of states under Communist rule), the workers' movement in capitalist countries (with the Communist parties as their vanguard), and the national and social-revolutionary liberation movements in the Third World (with the revolutionary-democratic parties of the "socialist-oriented countries" in the van). The new program names a fourth main element of the progressive forces, "the democratic mass movements" in the West. For the first time it lists the "new social movements"--the ecology movement, the peace movement, women's liberation, etc.-- alongside pro-Soviet front organizations and trade unions.

In its own view the CPSU continues to play a central role in the process of world change. The revised program states "the CPSU is a component of the international Communist movement. It considers its activity in perfecting socialist society and in leading the way to Communism as an extraordinarily important task, whose solution is in the interest of the world socialist system, of the international working class, and of all mankind."

The CPSU did not repeat its earlier claims to be the model for and leader of the Communist party system. However, it proclaimed that it would in the future undertake all efforts to preserve "the unanimity and cooperation of the fraternal parties." The revised program affirms CPSU intent consistently to defend "the revolutionary ideals and the Marxist-Leninist fundamentals of the world Communist movement," against "dogmatism" and "sectarianism" on the left as well as against "revisionism" and "reformism" on the right. "Proletarian internationalism," that doctrine whose principles and patterns of action were formed in the Comintern period, assumes greater importance in this revised version.

Today, after the experiences of the Gulag and Moscovite expansionism, it is not merely difficult to bring the practice of Soviet-oriented Communism into harmony with the revolutionary ideals outlined by Marx. It is even doubtful whether one may still speak of the existence of a comprehensive and particularly of a compact "world Communist movement," as the CPSU and its followers still do. For the word "movement" commonly suggests a body whose individual components are animated by the same or similar basic values, patterns of action, and goals.

This has long not been true of world Communism, and the Communist party system today presents a contradictory picture, at first blush a paradoxical one. On the one hand, the oddly assorted group of fifty-one Communists from thirty countries who on a March day in Moscow in 1919 stood godfathers to the newborn Communist International (Comintern) has grown to an impressive conglomerate. As the Soviets describe it, the Communist world spans five continents and numbers circa one hundred Communist parties. Fifteen of them are members of the "world socialist system" which unites the ruling parties, with some seventy-five million members. In addition, some eighty-five nonruling parties have roughly five million members. In the first category the biggest parties are the Chinese (CPCh) with forty million members and the CPSU with nineteen million. The

Italian Communist party heads the list of non-ruling parties with 1,540,000 members, followed by the French party (PCF) with 608,000, the Japanese (JCP) with 466,000 and the Indian party with 445,000 members.

After World War II, Communism did indeed become a world system, as a result of war and revolutions in China, North Korea, Vietnam, and Cuba. The expression "world" became truer still when the system later gathered in the Marxist-Leninist vanguard parties in the "socialist-oriented countries," particularly in Africa (Angola, Mozambique, Ethiopia)--parties which had no ties to the Comintern and its traditions. The CPSU does not forget to point repeatedly to this expansion when it wishes to document the momentum and attraction of Communism as a movement that possesses ideals and political dynamism. One may still count circa eighty Communist parties that more or less closely follow Soviet leadership on international Communist questions.

But the Communist party-system that emerged from the Comintern family has fallen apart. Ideology, once an integrating and mobilizing factor, has become a cause of splits and reciprocal polemics. Even Communists today will remark with ironic detachment "Marxism-Leninism as a state religion has had its day, and no one believes in it any more."[2] Without denying the importance of the October revolution and the Comintern period as parts of their history and identity, many Communist parties have widened their field of reference to include political forces outside the world Communist movement. The League of Yugoslav Communists (LCY) has concentrated its attention on the non-aligned movement; the Chinese party gives equal weight to relations with Communist parties and "other parties of the working class," i.e. Social Democrats and Socialists. The Italian party (PCI) looks first to its relations with parties of the Socialist International-- successor to that Second International so constantly and bitterly fought by the Comintern.

Moscow's military interventions in socialist states--in Hungary in 1956, Czechoslovakia in 1968, in "socialist-oriented" Afghanistan in 1979, and armed clashes between socialist states (the Soviet-Chinese skirmishes on the Ussuri river in 1969; the Chinese "punitive action" against Vietnam in 1979) considerably sharpened divergences in the Communist state and party system. After the united fraternal parties of the Second International had suddenly split into enemy camps in 1914, large parts of the workers' movement carried over to the Third International the hope that socialist brother states without an exploiter class profiting from national conflict would be exempt from internecine war. These hopes were now shown up as myth.

All of this raises the question whether there still is a "Communist movement" as it existed in the Comintern, Cominform, or even during the period of world Communist conferences in 1957, 1960, and 1969. Even such prestigious former Comintern parties as the PCI have replied in the negative. With its eyes fixed on real socialism of the Soviet type, the PCI has proclaimed that "the phase of development which found its conclusion in the October revolution has exhausted its propulsive force."[3] The PCI thus denies the continued existence of a specific "world Communist movement," and considers that it is today part of a comprehensive "international workers' movement," under the aegis of a "new internationalism."

The CPSU has made a large contribution to this development by opposing all those parties which were unwilling to regard Soviet society as exemplary or allow themselves to be used as tools of Moscow's foreign policy. The condemnation of Tito in 1948, the Moscow-Beijing conflict in the 1960s, and the polemic against Eurocommunism in the 1970s are all rooted in this earth. Placing the interests of the Soviet state above the interests of the other Communist parties, and thus nationalizing the Communism that sprang from the October revolution, the CPSU inevitably promoted the tendency in the fraternal parties to fit themselves to their national situations and go their own way.

Internationalism, "New" or "Proletarian"?

A multiplicity of socialisms has thus developed, some quite distinct from the Soviet model: self-determination in Yugoslavia, the post-Maoist version of socialism in China, Eurocommunism in Western Europe (and Japan). They have in common a rejection of the "general laws" for socialist revolution and the building of socialism postulated by Moscow, and indeed see the choice of different roads as "raising development toward socialism to its highest power."[4] Nor are they ready to uphold the Soviet Union as "the bulwark of peace and social progress," or support without hesitation the Soviet line in foreign and security policy. What the Chinese have called "hegemonism," the Japanese "great power chauvinism," and the Italians "sphere of influence" activism has caused them to judge

Moscow's policies from case to case and by political criteria, not on commonly held ideological bases as before. These parties unanimously condemn Soviet intervention in Afghanistan, for example.

In reality, the Italian Communists (and more or less explicitly the Yugoslavs also) have gone a step further. They not only reject Moscow's claims to leadership, but now deny the existence of any "world Communist movement" as a system of revolutionary vanguard parties existing on a higher plane than other progressive forces. With their "new internationalism" replacing the "proletarian international- ism" that serves Soviet state interests, they consider them- selves part of a larger "international workers' movement," which includes the parties of the Socialist International just as much as the national and social revolutionary lib- eration movements in the Third World.

The Chinese, Yugoslav, Italian, Spanish, Japanese and many other parties were firmly opposed to the project of a fourth world Communist conference launched by Moscow in 1981. The last such conference had taken place in 1969. These world meetings of Communist parties formed the only really important venue that still assembled all Communist parties, after the dissolution of the Comintern in 1943 and the Cominform in 1956. Who was to call them, who should take part, who would draft their theses? These were the questions put by a senior Italian Communist in June 1986, after Polish Communist chief Jaruzelski had renewed the call for a conference of all Communists on the theme "peace and disarmament." What about the Chinese party with its forty million members, half of the world's Commu- nists? How would Social Democrats and Socialists be in- cluded, if this was to be a Communist conference?[5] Ob- viously, these Italian questions were intended to discredit the idea as untimely, counter-productive, and liable to cause splits. But what are the basic concepts and patterns of action of those parties which combine full independence from the Moscow center with the vision of a "new inter- nationalism"?

New Points of Reference

Since the end of the 1970s the Chinese Communist party has again become active in the Communist party sys- tem, and one cannot exclude an eventual resumption of the relations with the CPSU that were broken off in 1966. The Chinese make it clear, however, that today there can no

-5-

longer be any "directing center" or "leading party," "paternal party" or ready-made "model" for socialism. The Communist parties must instead let their relations be guided by "the principles of independence, of complete equality, mutual respect, and non-interference in each other's internal affairs."[6] The value of socialism is in its practice, said the reform-minded Chinese secretary general Hu Yaobang to a gathering of PCI officials in Rome in June 1986, and therefore we must respect each other and learn from each other.[7]

The new internationalism of the Chinese party is firmly anchored in Beijing's overall foreign policy and reflects increased Chinese self-confidence. This policy pays little attention to types of society or class structure and more to Chinese state interests (here paralleling Soviet practice), which is to say that it is just as unideological and power-oriented as earlier theories of "intermediate zones," the "Three Worlds," and the "anti-hegemonist unity front." However, the reactivation of Chinese interest in the Communist party system is not without problems for the Soviets. Arguing for the complete independence of all parties and treating the existence of Communist divergences as unavoidable, even a stimulus, they provide an example for an alternative method of cooperation among parties, thus undercutting the CPSU's pretentions to leadership.

For the Yugoslav party, pioneer of independence from Moscow, the new internationalism of the Chinese has a special interest--its intent to let independent forces widen the margin of maneuver between the two super-powers, thus genuinely furthering the aims of the Third World states and the non-aligned movement. Belgrade considers that the Communist parties are not always the leaders of the battle for national independence and socialist traditions. The Yugoslavs think that the worldwide process of emancipation is now characterized by a disappearance of the "Communist monopoly" on socialist initative.[8] Belgrade unites this idea with severe criticism of the Soviet notion that the nonaligned countries are reserves for Moscow's socialist community of states, to be regarded as "natural allies."

Eurocommunism is without doubt a failure, if one saw in it the beginning of a development to bring together the Italians, French, and Spaniards into a dynamic bloc of gradualist Communist parties which would win increasing influence in their own countries and in the European Community. The French Communist party several years ago began a process of decline that may prove irreversible, sliding from twenty percent of the electorate in 1978 to 9.8 percent in 1986. There is even opposition in the party, castigating the inability of Secretary General Georges Marchais and his associates to fit the program, policies, and internal structure of the PCF to the conditions of a rapidly changing industrial society. The main points of attack are a mistaken strategy based on an outmoded analysis of societal conditions, an undifferentiated polemic against the Socialists, the retreat of the party into its oppositional fortress, and the enduring intellectual and practical dependence on Moscow. It is very doubtful whether the party's function as a protest movement can halt its decline--and in Jean-Marie LePen's National Front it has strong competition on the right.

The Spanish Communist party (PCE) is caught up in an on-going process of splintering and decay. The relative success of an ideologically heterogeneous "United Left" ticket in the June 1986 elections (4.6%; seven of 350 deputies) will scarcely end this. A very large share in this decline can be ascribed to Santiago Carrillo, deposed as secretary general in 1982, who refused to unite a program for the reform of society with democratization of the party's own structure. His authoritarian style caused the party to disintegrate when he prevented any consensus-oriented party discussion about the nature of the PCE and its political line.

The Italian Communist party has avoided the errors of its Eurocommunist fraternal parties and thus kept its position as the second strongest party of Italy, with about thirty percent of the vote. At its party congress in April 1986 it continued its process of "westernization," or as it says "secularization," significantly characterizing itself in the congress slogan as a "modern reform party." The mark of this was an unrestrained freedom of internal discussion, with an agenda that tackled problems caused by change in values and social approaches in industrial society, and made a commitment to European Community integration and for "Europe's self-assertion" inside the Atlantic alliance.

The congress theses qualified the PCI as an "integrating party of the European Left,"[9] and as such the PCI is coming ever closer to Western European social democracy, itself in the process of change. Its ties to the Social Democrats are underlined by PCI leader Alessandro Natta's meeting in Bonn in March 1986 with Willy Brandt, chairman of the SPD and the Socialist International.

The direction in which the PCI is going becomes even clearer when the party emphasizes, with a glance at Moscow, that it considers itself "neither a member of an ideological camp nor of an organized movement, either on a European or on a global plane."[10] This tendency of the most influential Communist party in Western Europe to look with favor toward the parties of the Socialist International throws a significant light on the decay of the "world Communist movement," which Lenin founded in 1919 as a revolutionary counter-movement to a social-democratic Second International he thought reformist and opportunist.

Have the New Soviet Leaders Changed Their Views?

A number of signs indicate that the new Soviet leadership under Gorbachev is reacting flexibly to growing tendencies toward differentiation and pluralization in the Communist party system, despite the presence of strong traditionalist sentiment in the CPSU apparatus. They evidently feel that the settlement of these ideological differences does not occupy center stage; they are far more interested in effective political aid in their detente offensive against the West.

In his report to the Twenty-seventh CPSU Congress Gorbachev omitted the tired litanies still present in the new version of the party program cited above; he did not mention Moscow's claim to world leadership of the movement. Noting that the Communist movement has entered a "qualitatively different stage of development," facing "many new realities, tasks, and problems," he asked that differences of opinion among Communist parties not be dramatized, that they should instead look toward "the common final goals, peace and socialism." Unity, he said, was possible only in diversity, and had "nothing in common with uniformity, hierarchy, with the interference of one party in the affairs of another, with the claim of one party to monopolize the truth."[11]

The replacement of the Comintern veteran Boris Ponomarev as Central Committee secretary and chief of the International Department by the career diplomat and U.S. expert Anatoliy Dobrynin is a clear indication of Gorbachev's intention better to fit the international apparatus of the CPSU to the needs of Soviet diplomacy, and to avoid sterile disputes over ideological principles.

An Impossible Unity

This pragmatic and flexible concept of cooperation in the world Communist movement recalls the ideas of the late PCI leader Palmiro Togliatti, who wished to reshape the Communist party system into a "polycentric" one, arguing for "unity in diversity." Doubtless the leaders of some East European ruling parties--in Budapest, Bucharest, and East Berlin-- would be pleased if these new beginnings of Gorbachev's also applied to them. That does not seem to be the case, for the new general secretary has tried to check the tendencies to fragmentation in the socialist community that arose during the Moscow succession crises. Gorbachev will grant the East European Communists freedom of action only insofar as they are ready to support the basic concepts of Moscow's foreign and security policy, make positive and priority contributions to the programs for economic modernization, guarantee domestic stability, and do not overstep the boundaries of the Moscow system.

But those parties to which the appeal for closer cooperation was directed--the Chinese, Yugoslavs, Italians and the like-minded, who represent half of the world's Communists--have long since departed the narrow camp of Moscovite world Communism. They will hardly allow Moscow to reintegrate them into an organized movement, however loose. For them the Communist party system is no longer a priority point of reference. Gorbachev's invitation to return, at least to a Togliatti-style "unity in diversity," comes twenty years too late. Viewed thus, the existence of a world Communist movement today turns out to be a myth.

The following chapters will discuss in current perspective the basic aspects of the origins and development of the Comintern, its degeneration into Moscow's instrument, the gradual decay of world Communism, new trends under Gorbachev, and Chinese positions. They will point out those Communist currents and trends which even in the Comintern period diverged from the official line (sometimes rather sharply), and which could possibly have given history another course, had they prevailed. These tendencies, long suppressed by the Soviet-inspired majority in the world Communist movement, were in many ways the forerunners of that process of growing autonomy and pluralization which has characterized the Communist party system since the 1960s.

A second section will take a closer look at the history and policy of some important western Communist parties. The problem of these parties is to strive for revolutionary transformation in a non-revolutionary environment without becoming identified with socialism of the Soviet-Communist type. It is hardly an accident that most of them have lost ground to social-democratic or socialist parties, and some are menaced by historic decline. Undoubtedly the change in values that has accompanied social change in the West has made a major contribution to this development. But one must also not overlook another factor. The end of the myth of the world Communist movement has complicated the problem, particularly for those parties whose strategies show their inability to draw the lesson of the dying myth.

Parts of this book are updated and expanded versions of articles the author has published during the last two years. Part I, chapter 1 appeared in Gerhard Simon, ed., Weltmacht Sowjetunion. Umbrüche-Kontinuitäten-Perspektiven (Cologne: Wissenschaft und Politik, 1987); Part I, chapters 2 and 3, and Part II, chapter 2 appeared in Berichte des Bundesinstituts für ostwissenschaftliche und internationale Studien no. 55 (1986); no. 28 (1985); no. 35 (1986). Part I, chapters 5 and 6, and part II, chapter 7 appeared in Osteuropa, 35, no. 3 (1985); 34, no. 2 (1984); and 36, no. 6 (1986).

The author wishes to thank Wolfgang Berner (Cologne) for much professional advice and many suggestions, J.W. Friend (Washington), for his useful suggestions and the competent translation, and Karen Forster (Boulder) and Barbara Langer (Cologne) for all-around technical help in preparing this book. Part I, chapter 6 was translated by Karen Forster.

NOTES

1. For the new version of the party program, see Pravda, March 7, 1986. For the original version, see Pravda, November 2, 1961.

2. Cesare Luporini, in la Repubblica, January 14, 1986. Luporini, a historian and theoretician, is a member of the PCI Central Committee.

3. Resolution by the PCI Direzione, l'Unità, December 30, 1981. For a similar resolution by the PCE Central Committee, see Mundo Obrero, January 8, 1982.

4. Alexandr Grlickov, "National und International," Sozialistische Theorie und Praxis 4, no. 4 (1977). Grlickov, a member of the LCY Central Committee, is one of its most important theoreticians in the field of international relations.

5. Antonio Rubbi, la Repubblica, July 1, 1986. Rubbi, a member of the Direzione, is chief of the Central Committee Foreign Section. Jaruzelski made the proposal in his report to the Tenth Congress of the Polish United Workers' Party (PZPR) in June-July 1986. See Trybuna Ludu, June 30, 1986.

6. Secretary General Hu Yaobang, in his report to the Twelfth Congress of the Chinese Communist Party in September 1982. See Beijing Review, 19, no. 37, September 14, 1982.

7. Radio Beijing, June 25, 1986.

8. Cedomir Strbac, "Zeitgenössischer Sozialismus und Internationalismus," Internationale Politik (Belgrade) 34, no. 795, May 20, 1983. Strbac is the director of the Institute for the Workers' Movement in Belgrade.

9. L'Unità, December 15, 1985. This point was left unchanged by the congress.

10. Ibid.

11. For Gorbachev's political report, see Pravda, February 26, 1986.

1

From Comintern to Cominform

World Revolution and Socialism in One Country

The Comintern was founded in particular circumstances, at a time when the Russians believed that the
revolutionary spark struck in Russia would soon leap over
to Western Europe. The victorious proletariat of the
industrialized West would then reassume the leadership of
the revolutionary struggle, relieve the burden of their
Russian class brothers, and help them to develop their
economically backward country. This expectation that the
revolution would quickly spread beyond Russia had
important consequences for the character of the Third
International, some of which still affect Moscow-oriented
Communist parties today.[1]
One result was to strengthen the trend toward
rejecting the Western European social democratic parties,
which Lenin thought a hindrance for the revolutionary
struggle. He held that the leaders of these parties had
betrayed the ideals of internationalism in 1914, becoming
social imperialists and social chauvinists. They had
integrated the working class into the capitalist system and
made themselves its support props. Thus the revolution
could not be made with the social democratic leaderships,
but only against them. The twenty-one conditions agreed on
at the Second Comintern Congress in 1920 contained a
strong emphasis on the uncompromising struggle against
social democracy as the duty of every Communist. Equally
suspect were "centrists" in their own ranks, likely to prove
waverers and potential class traitors in the hard battles to
come. These ideas still influence the official Soviet mind;
they appear in the 1986 Party Program. When they approach

any area of cooperation, especially arms control and disarmament, they think it the duty of all Communists to take their distance from the "reformist" ideology of the social democrats.

The expectation of rapid revolutionary breakthroughs had notable consequences for the structure and strategy of the Comintern itself. It strengthened Lenin's existing inclination to give the Third International a centralized organization in order to make it a powerful instrument for the oncoming global class struggles; the new International would not have that loose form of organization which in Lenin's view had led straight to the bankruptcy of the Second International.

The twenty-one conditions for entry into the Third International anticipated the process later known as bolshevization. Strategy, tactics, organization of the Communist party were all set forth in detail, underlining the character of the Comintern as the disciplined general staff of the world revolution. The political behavior of the member parties was no longer to be revolutionary in theory and reformist in practice, but revolutionary in theory and practice. As Arthur Rosenberg incisively noted, the twenty-one conditions breathed "a spirit of hard exclusiveness, but also one of powerful revolutionary will."[2]

Strict centralization of decision-making in the Comintern had in fact a certain logic, if one were convinced that the revolution would soon spread to Western Europe, and its headquarters move to Paris or Berlin. In this light, foundation of a Communist world party appeared only to anticipate a fusion of parties with equal rights and weight, with the Bolsheviks taking a merely transitional leading role. This role seemed to be legitimized by the impetus to worldwide revolution provided by the Bolsheviks in the October revolution, with the Red Army as a necessary instrument to curb and repress imperialism. (It may be noted that in its early years the Red Army took its loyalty oath to the Comintern.) In those years the victorious Bolsheviks thought they would soon be joined by a row of other victorious Communist parties, which would have a major influence on the course of the International.

Against Communist expectations, the revolutionary tide had begun to ebb by 1920; there remained the general staff of a revolution that had not taken place, or did not survive except in Russia. The country of the October Revolution was left to its own devices, and sought with the New Economic Policy to stabilize its economy and take up diplomatic relations with the capitalist world around it. The Soviet Union now increasingly presented itself as a "normal" state with "normal" national interests. Stalin gave this development theoretical expression in late 1924 with the doctrine of "socialism in one country." This thesis was intended to make the Russian revolution independent of the world revolution--without denying the ultimate dependence of the Russian revolution on revolutions in the countries of the highly industrialized West.

In retrospect, it is clear that the Comintern was really never what it was supposed to be--a union of parties with equal rights and weight designed to aid in the birth of world revolution. One party, the Russian one, had its revolution already behind it when the Comintern was founded; no other party was ever successful for long. This disjunction was not evident for a time, concealed by the equality in principle accorded the non-Russian parties in anticipation of their revolutionary successes. But as the revolutionary wave sank away, the prestige and influence of the Bolsheviks in the Comintern grew immeasurably. Just because the world revolution was not taking place, the Soviet Union became the symbol of all hope for a revolutionary future, and the defense of the Soviet land became the duty of every Communist. "What the 'Future State' had been for the radical workers before 1914, was now Soviet Russia."[3]

In one result of this process, the member parties ("sections") of the Comintern copied the Soviet model in all details--ideologically, politically, organizationally, following the "bolshevization" decreed by Stalin. Support for Soviet foreign policy became an unquestioned duty. Communists were ruled by Stalin's maxim of 1927:

> He is a revolutionary, who without reservations, unconditionally, openly and honestly ... is ready to protect and defend the USSR, for the USSR is the first revolutionary proletarian state in the world, which is building socialism. He is an internationalist, who without reservations, without wavering, without making conditions, is ready to protect the USSR, because the USSR is the base of the revolutionary movement in the whole world.[4]

This statement laid the basis for a dogma still seen as binding on Communist parties loyal to Moscow, whereby the attitude toward the Soviet Union is the touchstone for loyalty to proletarian internationalism. In practice, the dogma turned upside down Lenin's demand that "the nation which defeats the bourgeoisie be ready and able to bring the greatest national sacrifice to the overthrow of international capital."[5] For Lenin, loyalty to the Soviet Union was not the touchstone of internationalism; loyalty to internationalism was instead the touchstone of the revolutionary character of the Soviet Union.

This obligatory attitude to the Soviet Union produced dramatic, frequently contradictory, and ultimately disastrous consequences for the Comintern and its member parties. If further revolutions did not spell life or death for the victory of socialism in the USSR, but were only desirable events, the International must necessarily lose importance in Soviet eyes. Later developments confirmed this; it is noteworthy that Stalin made only brief appearances at and took no part in the Sixth and Seventh World Comintern Congresses in 1928 and 1935, both of which made radical changes in the previous line. Lenin however had participated actively in Comintern discussions and policy until the end, insofar as his physical condition permitted.

In view of the drop in Comintern importance and the uneven development in the individual countries it would surely have been appropriate to switch to a different and less centralized organizational model, giving the national parties a means to take notice of special conditions and traditions in their struggle for social change. Neighboring Communist parties could have come together on a regional basis to try out the tactical means suiting their specific situations, without taking the long road to Moscow prescribed in the Comintern statutes. An example for this was given by the Italian, French, and Spanish Communists in the 1970s, when they moved closer together under the banner of Eurocommunism and attempted to work out suitable strategies fitting their national and regional conditions.

No such road was taken. On the contrary, in spite of the ebb of the revolutionary flood and the concomitant loss in Comintern importance, the fiction was maintained that the world revolutionary process was moving forward without halt, with the centralized International as its engine, regardless of the relative stabilization of capitalism. The fiction was more than doubtful, but it was of a piece with the increasing domination by the Bolsheviks as the "most experienced" and "most tempered" fraternal party--a domination furthered by the use of a centralized organization created to give impetus to world revolution. Under Stalin, the CPSU succeeded in passing off the national interests of the Soviet Union as revolutionary interests affecting the whole of world Communism, thus stifling any independent impulses that arose in the national parties. The CPSU was also able to play a major role in determining the details of their internal policies, including the choice of leaders. Although its ability to do this has sharply decreased, the CPSU still keeps to an idea developed in the Stalin era--demanding that every Communist party place the interests of the entire movement (as defined by the Soviets) above its own particular interests.

The Consequences of Stalinization

There is no room here to explain in detail by what steps and with what methods the Bolsheviks made use of the Comintern and the national parties. But one aspect of this process not only characterized the development of the Comintern but determined the nature of Moscow-oriented Communism until the present day. The role of theory as a motivation for practical action was pushed increasingly into the background, finally becoming merely a supplementary justification for the political line of the CPSU, regardless of whether this line tended to the "left" or to the "right." An important cause of this growing modification in the function of theory, exemplified in a variety of summary judgments on capitalism, social democracy, and fascism, can be found in the gradual choking off of dissent and open discussion in the Comintern. The Comintern congresses were scheduled to follow those of the CPSU, against the protests of some Communist parties which rightly feared that the decisions of the Comintern would be determined in advance by the Soviet party.

Comparison of the Sixth and Seventh Congresses sheds a significant light on the petrification of decision-making in the Comintern. The Seventh Congress in 1935, which with its new assessments of bourgeois democracy, social democracy, and fascism has gone down in history as the congress of the "great turn" to the right, was simultaneously a congress of pure acclamation, lacking any possibility for criticism.[6]

The cause for the new turn itself shows that the decision-making structures of the Comintern had not altered, i.e. the decisions were taken in Moscow alone. The change had not been triggered by the experience of the national parties (e.g. the harassed KPD) burdened with a left-sectarian and isolationist line that left them unable to do much against fascism. Rather it was the Soviet Union which felt alarm, recognizing the threat of an encircling coalition of authoritarian, fascist, and strongly anti-Communist regimes. To break this ring, Communist parties were now to cooperate with social democrats and even bourgeois forces to stop the spread of fascism and German National Socialism to all of Europe.

In the circumstances, this policy was certainly the only rational one, and in fact gave the national parties a means to combat the spread of fascism with flexibility and a chance for success. This was the incontestable merit of the Seventh Congress. But this policy had been produced in the same old way, inside the old decision mechanisms of the Comintern which gave Soviet interests priority and made any criticism impossible. Thus no changes were made in the traditional political and ideological system of reference in national parties. The great turn was ceremoniously and solemnly proclaimed at the congress, not discussed in the slightest. The views on the Seventh Congress of today's autonomists, including the Eurocommunists, are highly dubious--indeed mere legend-making, when they call it the congress which conceded them greater scope for action vis a vis the Moscow center. The "scope for action" had been prescribed by the CPSU, even though it matched the circumstances and wishes of the national parties. A change of line could be revoked as easily as it was introduced. This was soon demonstrated in 1939, when the Communist parties had to agree with the Hitler-Stalin pact, admittedly amid considerable confusion.

The Sixth Congress in 1928 however had witnessed passionate and controversial discussion, as had previous congresses when discussing central questions on the nature of and means for the world revolutionary process. This was the congress which took a sharp turn to the left, sanctioning the thesis of "social fascism." To be sure, arguments even in 1928 were not real discussions about the best policy. They arose largely from the split in the CPSU between Stalin's "leftwing" majority and Bukharin's "rightwing" minority--a split which radiated out to the other Comintern parties, giving critics one last chance to be represented and heard. Bukharin had headed the Comintern since 1926. In 1929, he was successively relieved of his position and then excluded from the Politburo. With this, and the exclusion of his followers in most of the national parties, no opposition and thus no discussion could appear in the Comintern.

The Comintern had begun as early as 1921 to slight its own serious mistakes and those of the Bolshevik party, taking little notice of them in forming future strategy and tactics. This process had now been brought to completion; errors were laid to the account of "opportunist" or "dogmatic" groups, whichever suited, when not blamed on "enemy agents" in the party ranks. All criticism was outlawed and suffocated, every change of the CPSU line had to be followed without reservation. The Bolshevik empire, wrote Arthur Rosenberg as early as 1932, "resembles the land of the emperor in Andersen's immortal fairy-tale. The emperor can walk about naked, because everyone is ostracized who cannot see his supposed clothing. So the emperor strides through the Bolshevik empire, and left and right party officials accompany him, excluding anyone who dares to cry out 'the emperor is naked'!"[7]

Autonomist Tendencies in the National Parties

Currents did in fact exist in the Comintern and in the top leadership of many parties that were not quite ready to ignore the emperor's nudity. After the exclusion of "leftist" groups like the followers of Trotsky, these consisted mostly of "rightwing" tendencies, particularly strong in the KPD (with the theoretician August Thalheimer), but also present in the Italian, Polish, and American parties. All these elements had looked to Bukharin. They all gave unreserved support to the Bolshevist experiment despite all its mistakes and imperfections. But they warned that it could not be transferred to the West, quite in the spirit of Rosa Luxemburg, who had already in 1918 motivated her doubts about premature establishment of a new International with the danger that the Bolsheviks would "make a virtue of necessity, solidify theoretically and all of a piece the tactics forced on them by these terrible conditions, and recommend them for imitation to the international proletariat as the pattern of socialist tactics."[8]

In this spirit, the "rightwing" currents in the Comintern objected in general to making Soviet interests an absolute, proposing for example at the November/December 1926 session of the Comintern executive committee that the "defense of peace" be the war cry of the Communist parties, and not the "defense of the USSR," a slogan proposed and ultimately pushed through by the majority.[9] Moreover, the "rightwingers" (anticipating the ideas of later reformers in East and West) argued that the Comintern program should differentiate the strategic line for special conditions in individual countries, and not content itself with the regular repetition of stereotyped formulas to this effect. They made an earnest plea that different capitalist countries and regions should not be considered "only on the basis of their common denominator, but in all their differences," in order to give Communist parties a possibility to choose suitable strategies and their own "special ways" to Communism.[10] Bukharin himself at the Sixth World Congress in 1928 spoke of the "diversity" and "dissimilarity" of the world revolutionary process. He accentuated the profound meaning of this concept with regard to the revolutions in the economically backward and politically dependent countries of the Third World ("colonial" or "semi-colonial countries"). Bukharin referred to the necessity of a "concrete decoding of the process of world revolution," emphasizing:

> We cannot speak only of an abstract revolution in an abstract capitalist society, but must speak of the world revolution, not in an absolute sense, but from the standpoint of the internal diversity of its means of expression, from the standpoint of the variety of its forms, which only in their inclusive whole constitute the general process of world revolution. And we must speak more concretely about the process of world revolution and thereby emphasize its internal dissimilarity. The analysis must thus have a concrete character and must simultaneously be placed in the context of the world motif. [11]

Along with this emphasis on a necessary differentiation in the strategy of the national parties, the "rightwing" currents in the Comintern demanded a realistic estimate of developments in the capitalist countries. Bukharin argued that in an overall Western context capitalism was by no means on the brink of collapse, but within a framework of "general crisis" was demonstrating in some countries "an unfolding of powerful productive forces" and an "upturn in technology."[12] Bukharin therefore warned against the view "that a tendency toward a parasitic degeneration of capitalism is everywhere gaining ground and determines everything."[13]

From this analysis, the "rightwingers" drew the conclusion that Communists must put more emphasis on the struggle for the everyday demands of the proletariat as transitional demands, and therefore keep contact with the social democrats, who still controlled the organizations in which the working masses were enrolled.

Bukharin's followers were violently opposed to the thesis of "social fascism," which discovered a similarity in nature and function between social democracy and fascism, and denied any difference whatsoever among bourgeois forms of domination.[14] The most cogent contradiction of this view came in an analysis by the "Bukharinite" Togliatti, who as leader of the Italian Communist party had experienced the difference between bourgeois democracy and Mussolini's fascism in the flesh.

In remarkable agreement with Thalheimer's Bonapartism thesis (and basically also with Marx' analysis in The Class Struggles in France), Togliatti did not see fascism only as a petty-bourgeois mass movement, as Clara Zetkin had done in 1923, for example, when refuting the thesis that fascism was merely an agency of the bourgeoisie. He saw fascism as a particular form of domination which achieved its own dynamics through its mass appeal, gradually becoming independent of the bourgeoisie and thus distinguishing itself qualitatively from previously known forms of bourgeois domination such as bourgeois democracy, authoritarian governments, or even military dictatorship.[15] After 1945, Togliatti drew on this theoretical recognition for his conception of the PCI, by presenting it as a reform-oriented mass party with a policy of broadly based political and social alliances, in order to deprive fascism of any chance to win back its mass base.

The different views on the condition of capitalism, of the character of bourgeois democracy, the nature of social democracy, and the particularity of fascism all show that until the Sixth Comintern Congress there were alternatives to the Stalinist line. (The line, incidentally, found its strongest support in the then strongest nonruling party, the KPD, dominated by Ernst Thälmann. At the same time, the KPD repeatedly brought forth critically-minded minorities unable to win the day, who ended by being expelled.) Developments in Germany might conceivably have turned out otherwise had the Comintern accepted the distinction between social democracy and fascism, which included the possibility of a common communist-socialist battle against fascism.

The defeat of the rightwingers again makes clear the problems posed by the increasing dependence of the Comintern on the CPSU. For the sectarian turn in the Sixth Congress in 1928 did not take place on the basis of a realistic estimate of the situation in the capitalist countries. Their economic collapse took place after the New York stock market crash in November 1929--in a crisis not predicted by the Comintern, which ended not in the rise of the Communist parties but of Nazism. In reality, the turning at the Sixth Congress was caused by the Soviet power struggle. Commencing with Lenin's departure from the helm, it had repeatedly colored disputes in the Comintern and its member parties, as factions in the Bolshevik party sought to strengthen their own positions by purging the Comintern followers of their domestic rivals.

This had repercussions, exemplified in the hastily concluded plans for a revolutionary uprising in Germany in 1923, closely connected with the factional struggles between Trotsky and Zinoviev on one side and Stalin and Bukharin on the other. In 1928 the stake for Stalin was the pursuit of a policy of "revolution from above" in the Soviet Union, against Bukharin and his followers in the CPSU and the Comintern. The struggle against fascism and imperialism, the preparation of a "third period" of revolutionary struggle in Western Europe only appeared to be at the center of the disputes at the Sixth World Congress. In reality the main thrust was directed against the Social Democrats, (not least because they were perceived as the main exponents of arrangements between Germany and France), and directly against the Bukharinites in the International. For if social democracy was characterized as "social fascist," then all those who harbored "illusions about the nature of the social democrats" or would even "deliver up the working class to fascism and reaction" could easily be stamped as rightwing opportunists in the new revolutionary phase prophesied by the Comintern majority. With this, the CPSU majority robbed itself of any means of forming a united front to fight fascism when it really became a serious danger.

Popular Front and Special Paths

In retrospect it is clear that the decisions of the Sixth Comintern Congress had a strong influence on the further development of world Communism--stronger in any case than those of the Seventh Congress, so highly praised in the Eastern and sometimes also the Western literature on the subject. With the removal of the Bukharinites the CPSU had liquidated the last organized current proposing an anti-Stalin policy in the Comintern. It thereby assured itself an unlimited hegemony in international Communism, which was not disturbed until the aftermath of the CPSU Twentieth Party Congress in 1956. Khrushchev's secret speech then dealt a severe blow to the authority and prestige of the CPSU among the fraternal parties, accelerating and revealing the ongoing process of erosion in the world Communist movement.

This judgment is not intended to depreciate the importance of the Seventh World Congress and the later phases of resistance and national reconstruction for the individual Communist parties; they remain today part of the Communist self-image. At the Seventh World Congress the Communists changed their attitude to bourgeois democracy, at least insofar as they accepted it as the most suitable ground on which to fight for socialism. (This view is still held by the Moscow-oriented parties, while the gradualist Communists now accept the principle of democracy.) After the liquidation of the SPD by the Nazis and the SPÖ by the authoritarian Dollfuss regime, the Communists dropped the thesis of social democracy as fascism's twin brother, a social prop for the bourgeoisie that must be combatted. The Communist parties in France and Spain became mass parties, after they had concluded popular front alliances with the Socialists and other parties and presented themselves as representatives of the interests of the entire nation.

The concept of "national" or "special" ways to socialism adopted by the Communists in Eastern and Western Europe in 1944-1948 went somewhat further. [16] An outstanding example is furnished by the PCI, which at that time upheld the idea of democrazia progressista, a state not yet socialist but no longer the bourgeois state dominated by landholders and monopolies. The PCI took an active part in drafting the Italian constitution (still in force) which guaranteed basic rights and liberties, but simultaneously included the possibility of drastic economic and social reforms that would finally have changed the nature of the system. Togliatti plainly delimited the ideas of his party from the Soviet Communist model, as did Anton Ackermann in East Germany and Wladislaw Gomulka in Poland. Echoing the ideas of the Comintern "rightwingers" in 1928, Togliatti again proclaimed in 1947 that the advance toward democracy and socialism would necessarily take "special forms...in every country," in each case conditioned by differences in capitalist development, as well as by national traditions and peculiarities. The central task of the PCI would be to acquire those ideological, political, and organizational capabilities that would allow it to find "our way, the Italian way" to socialism. [17]

This study cannot enter into the question of whether European Communist concepts of a special path were then more than tactical ideas, tolerated or even inspired by the Soviets as variants of Bolshevist revolutionary strategy. Parts of the membership may have understood the special path as the genuine strategic line, especially those who had entered the Communist parties in the wake of national resistance to Nazism rather than through any special inclination toward the ideology of Marxism-Leninism-Stalinism. The party leaders, however, seem in general to have been thinking of variations in methods and tempo to prepare a revolutionary upheaval. It is significant that they never labelled the Communist special path concept as a "third way" between Soviet-style socialism and capitalism, as did a variety of socialist, Christian and radical-liberals of the time. Even leading PCI figures thought in terms of a double phase, analogous to the developments in the Russian revolution between February and October 1917--"the first phase of democratic struggle and after that the second phase of transition to socialism and on to another grouping of classes."[18]

Thus the innovations of the Popular Front during the 1930s and the phase of rebuilding in the immediate postwar period were not in fact characteristic of the Communist parties, although some aspects of the line in these periods corresponded to the ideas of the Comintern "rightwingers." As traditions these were later accorded much importance by the parties and currents of reform Communism. But in fact the "external relations" which the Communists developed with non-Communist forces in both periods had not affected their "internal relations" in an international Communism dominated by the CPSU. Given their character as Stalinized cadre parties, which they maintained during their phases of political flexibility , they could without difficulty be made to reverse poles, reverting to uncompromising confrontation whenever the political climate in Moscow might change. After 1945, this held true not only for the ruling Communist parties in Moscow's realm, but also for the nonruling mass parties in Western Europe which were physically removed from the grasp of the CPSU.

The dissolution of the Comintern in 1943 brought no change here, although Stalin and company now for the first time criticized the idea of an international center and emphasized the necessity of a variety of ways to socialism.[19] Instead, the International Department of the CPSU Central Committee took over the affair. A major participant was Boris Ponomarev, chief of the International Department from 1955 on, who as a Central Committee secretary (1961-1986) and candidate member of the Politburo (1972-1986) had a major and still enduring influence on Moscow's policies toward the Communist parties. With the founding of the Cominform in September 1947, Moscow's ability to force a radical change of line on the Communist parties again became plain.

The Cominform: The Second Bolshevization

The Cominform period marked the high point of Soviet ideological monolithism in the world Communist movement.[20] The founding of the Cominform was closely related to the opening phases of the cold war, and itself contributed to the hardening of fronts in the East-West conflict. Not the least contribution to this momentum was the report of chief Soviet delegate Andrey Zhdanov to the conference participants in Sklarska Poreba.[21]

Zhdanov developed the following arguments: since the war, the world has been divided into two camps, with the imperialist and anti-democratic camp on one side, and the anti-imperialist camp on the other. Strong in its economic and military potential, the United States, as the leading power of imperialism, had embarked on an open course toward conquest and expansion, with the goal of building American world domination. In this situation the most important task of the anti-imperialist camp was to close ranks and foil the aggressive plans of imperialism. In this task "the leading role falls to the Soviet Union and its foreign policy," for the Soviet Union is in essence "totally alien to any aggressive exploitative feeling" and its foreign policy reflects "the desires of all progressive mankind." In fact, according to Zhdanov the Soviet Union was the central "bulwark of anti-imperialist and anti-Fascist foreign policy."

In the West, Zhdanov's speech was generally interpreted as a sharp challenge to former allies. In reality, in creating the Cominform the Soviets did not intend to initiate a new phase of revolutionary expansion.

Zhdanov himself kept open the possibility of political agreement with the United States, proclaiming the desire of the Soviet Union for "further cooperation between the USSR and countries with other systems." Significantly, the East German Socialist Unity Party was not invited to the founding conference or to subsequent ones; drawing this party into the Soviet-dominated cartel of Cominform members would have contradicted Stalin's policy of seeking agreements with his former allies for a united Germany, neutralized and demilitarized.

This is not the place to examine the question of whether Stalin in 1945 did originally intend to expand Soviet control over all of Europe. If he did have such plans, he deferred them and switched to a defensive strategy after the United States strengthened its engagement in Western Europe in 1947. Despite its increased strength after the victory over Germany, the Soviet Union did not feel itself economically and militarily the equal of the United States, and therefore avoided direct confrontation. In this framework, the Cominform had a defensive character. Especially after the proclamation of the Truman Doctrine in March 1947, the Moscow leadership feared increasing American activities with the goal of rolling back Soviet influence in Europe.

These fears grew after the proclamation of the Marshall Plan in June 1947, which was at first greeted positively both in Poland and Czechoslovakia. According to Zhdanov, the Marshall Plan showed American intent "to rob the peoples of Europe of their independence and subject them to American imperialism." In this polemic the Soviets were not much interested in defending the independence of the Western European countries; according to Moscow's understanding they belonged without question in the American sphere of influence. Their chief concern was what they regarded, according to Zhdanov, as the central task of the Marshall Plan: "to reestablish the power of imperialism in the countries of the new democracies and compel them to renounce their close economic and political cooperation with the Soviet Union." Moscow feared that the economic reconstruction of Western Europe was also intended to draw in the impoverished East European countries, open them to political penetration, and gradually remove them from Soviet control.

In this the Soviets were partially right, because the United States never understood the Yalta division of Europe into spheres of influence as <u>carte blanche</u> for the

Sovietization of Eastern Europe. It is doubtful, however, that the United States then or later really intended to interfere in Moscow's sphere of influence. Whether or not this was so, the Truman Doctrine and the Marshall Plan were interpreted in Moscow as part of a rollback strategy. In Moscow's view therefore the chief task of the Cominform member parties was to contribute, each in its own way, to the protection of Moscow's strategic glacis in Europe. The Communist parties were now to engage themselves not for "socialism in one country," but collectively to defend "socialism in one zone." The ruling parties in Eastern Europe had to close ranks around the Soviet Union and renounce independent initiatives. The Western Communist parties were instructed to take up "the struggle against the new American plans of expansion for the enslavement of Europe," holding high "the banner of defense of national independence and the sovereignty of their countries."[22]

This strategy was of necessity strongly Eurocentric, and this at a time when as part of the decolonization process the main thrust of the revolutionary movement was shifting to the Third World. It was besides a defensive posture, as emphasized by Stalin's reservations on the Greek civil war. (Ten years earlier, the Soviet Union had engaged itself more deeply in the Spanish Civil War, both politically and militarily.) This Cominform line was accompanied by a "second bolshevization"[23] of the Communist parties, and had drastic consequences still visible today. In Eastern Europe it led to their merger with the state apparatus, so that they lost contact with societal reality, and thus crumbled when faced by reform-minded mass action--as in Hungary in 1956 and in Poland in 1980-1981.[34] For the Western Communists, the new discipline meant at best decades of opposition (PCF, PCI), and in most cases descent into political impotence.

Of even more consequence for future developments was the reversal by the CPSU of the relationship between the importance of independent initiatives and Soviet aid for the revolution. Moscow began to see the Soviet armies as the decisive factor in the success of social transformations in Eastern Europe, according only marginal importance to the contribution of national efforts. This viewpoint did have the advantage of corresponding to the actual facts, since the Eastern European states had been changed into "peoples' democracies" by Soviet-inspired revolutions from above. But the Cominform went further, disastrously, freezing this process into a universally valid, theoretical mould. Parties like the Yugoslav CP which had achieved liberation through their own struggle and thus slipped out of Soviet control now fell victim to condemnation.

From then on the doctrine taught that authentic socialist revolutions could only take root and be secure when they based themselves on political, economic, and military aid by the Soviet Union. Here one finds the theoretical roots of the "socialist internationalism" that sprouted from "proletarian internationalism," i.e. of the Soviet pretensions embodied in the Brezhnev doctrine of limited sovereignty whereby the established system in socialist states may if necessary be upheld by armed intervention.

The Cominform period did not, however, only mark a high point of monolithism in world Communism; rather, by overexpanding the pretensions of the Soviet leadership, it carried within itself the germs of decay of the Communist party system. When the Cominform expelled the Yugoslav party, which had won national liberation by its own forces and combined it with social revolution, thus earning much respect from the fraternal parties, proletarian internationalism had been "irreparably compromised," as authoritative PCI representatives now put it.[25] Fernando Claudín goes to the heart of this when he analyzes the lessons drawn by many Communist parties outside Moscow's physical reach about Stalin's instrumentalization of both Comintern and Cominform for Soviet state interests:

> The conquest of autonomy became the prime condition for developing any policy, whether revolutionary or reformist, which permitted realistic action. The policy dictated by Moscow had the unproductive property of being neither revolutionary nor reformist, but only abstract and unworkable. [26]

Mythology from Above and Below

It is clear in retrospect that in the Comintern period (with effects reaching into Cominform times) "the desire on above for mythology ⟨met with⟩ the desire for mythology from below," and Arthur Rosenberg was not wrong in seeing in this "the secret of its existence."[27] This does not mean that the Communist party system rooted in the Third International was constantly perfecting itself in theory while expanding quantitatively, as the accounts of the Moscow-oriented Communist parties have it today. Indeed, the development of this party system displays a multiplicity of contradictions, changes of line, and even radical breaks. The consequence of these breaks was a change in the character of the Comintern, from its aspirations to be an authentic revolutionary movement to its finality as an instrument of Soviet state interests--a change which ultimately led to the decay of world Communism.

A symptom of this development in the Communist movement was the degeneration of theoretical analysis into justificatory ideology for Moscow's current line. A conspicuous example is the thesis of the possibility of "building socialism in one country," which created the theoretical presuppositions for the domination of world Communism by the CPSU. Another is the essentially undifferentiated maintenance of Lenin's thesis of "decaying and dying capitalism," even in periods when capitalism displayed unbroken force and vitality. This thesis is reminiscent of the notion of the inevitable collapse of capitalism and the effect which it had on the social democrats of the Second International. This historical determinism strengthened the Communist parties in their expectation that concurrently with the swift development of the Soviet Union, revolution in the West would mature, falling like ripe fruit from the tree of socialism in one country. The theory of collapse also induced the Communist parties to use noisy radical slogans, accompanied by passive expectation and a close dependence on the CPSU. Since the global balance was inevitably changing in favor of socialism led by the Soviet Union, unreserved support for the Soviet Union had clear priority over development of models of transition based on national or regional conditions. It is significant that the CPSU retains this forced optimism in the analytical section of the party program revised in 1986, that imperialism is "decaying, dying capitalism, marking the eve of revolution."[28] However, other Communist parties, like the PCI, find capitalism today in a dynamic phase of profound structural change and dramatic technological revolution, which they must seek to influence from within by their own ideas. [29]

If the Soviet-oriented appreciation of history suffers from a refusal to recognize radical breaks in the development of the world Communist movement, it seems that Western historiography also needs some correction in its periodization. For example, the bolshevization of the mid-1920s was more a symptom than a cause of the final Stalinization of the Comintern. The real cause was the fact that the revolution expected in the West in the early 1920s did not arrive, and the national parties thus almost necessarily fell under the domination of the Bolsheviks. "Bolshevization" was thus only a consequence of a birth defect in the Comintern. There is a similar problem in the Seventh World Congress. In some Western research this congress has been overvalued (despite the important changes it brought about in the appreciation of bourgeois democracy, social democracy, and fascism), possibly because it has been so much emphasized in the Eastern literature, which after 1956 understandably had every reason to underline its relevance. This congress of perfected Stalinism was not a decisive turning point in the history of the Communist International. The Sixth Congress--frequently treated as marginal--had far greater consequences, in that it finished off the Bukharin "right-wingers," the last organized current, i.e. the last with independent ideas. Witnessing the final victory of Stalin, it permitted the suffocation of any more than local resistance against the unrestricted domination of the CPSU in the world Communist movement, a situation that lasted into the 1950s.

All this raises a number of questions for the future. One may ask how the CPSU succeeded in dominating the Communist party system for so long, yoking it to the pursuit of Soviet interests. Undoubtedly the main reason is that the Communist parties supported Soviet interests with the tacit assumption that they were not serving the interests of an ordinary state, but rather the bulwark of the revolution, encircled by imperialism and threatened in its existence.

Defense of the Soviet Union and the socialist camp thus served their own interests as revolutionary parties, since the USSR represented both a base for future revolutions and at the same time a symbol that they too had a chance to defeat the bourgeoisie with their own force. The active engagement of the CPSU in the Spanish Civil War (which seemed to emphasize its revolutionary character), the victory over Nazi Germany (to a great extent attributed to the superiority of the Soviet socialist system), the defense of the people's democracies against the perceived rollback intentions of imperialism, and finally Soviet support for national and social revolutionary liberations movements in the Third World-- all this long helped to hold the Communist parties, despite growing doubts, to their basic conviction that the country and the party of the October Revolution ultimately embodied the main force for peace and socialism. For many parties, this basic conviction has now changed to sharp criticism of the Soviet Communist social system and/or of Soviet foreign policy.

But one might reverse the question, and ask why the CPSU did not dissolve the Comintern much earlier instead of holding on to it so long. Arthur Rosenberg raised this interesting question as early as 1932, arguing as follows: after the ebb of the revolutionary tide in the early 1920s the Soviet Union increasingly became a "normal" state, interested in "normal," correct relations with other states. The Comintern could only be a hindrance for such correct relations, since its existence meant that the CPSU had a hold on the Communist party of a country with the consequent ability to interfere in its domestic affairs.[30] Though the existence of the Comintern was thus a handicap for the external relations of the USSR, it held fast to it. The reasons were essentially two: most importantly, the myth of the world revolutionary movement led by the Soviet Union, representing the interests of all Communist parties was (and is) an essential device for the Soviet leaders in legitimating their own system from within. Secondly, the leaders of the CPSU evidently thought the usefulness of Communist parties in propagating Moscow's foreign and security policy (especially in a period of icy East-West relations) outweighed the problems caused for Soviet relations with the West.

NOTES

1. On this and other questions in this chapter, see my contribution "The Fundamentals of Proletarian Internationalism," in Lawrence L. Whetten, ed., The Present State of Communist Internationalism (Lexington, Mass.: D.C. Heath and Company, 1983), pp. 3-17.
2. Arthur Rosenberg, Geschichte des Bolschewismus (1932; reprint ed., Frankfurt: Europäische Verlagsanstalt, 1966), p. 176.
3. Ibid., p. 212.
4. Josef Stalin, Gesammelte Werke, vol. 10 (East Berlin: Dietz Verlag, 1952), p. 45. Emphasis in original.
5. Wladimir Lenin, "Ursprünglicher Entwurf der Thesen zur nationalen und kolonialen Frage" (for the Second Comintern Congress), Werke, vol. 31 (East Berlin: Dietz Verlag, 1964), p. 136ff.
6. Noted by Barbara Timmermann in her dissertation "Die Faschismus-Diskussion in der Kommunistischen Internationale (1920-1935)," (University of Cologne, 1977), p. 95ff.
7. Rosenberg, Bolschewismus, p. 214.
8. Rosa Luxemburg, "Zur russischen Revolution," in Gesammelte Werke, vol. 4: August 1914-January 1919 (East Berlin: Dietz Verlag, 1974), p. 364.
9. Cf. Anna di Biagio, "Il Pervonacal'nyj Proekt Tezisov di Bucharin al VI Congresso del Komintern," Quaderni della Fondazione Giangiacomo Feltrinelli no. 17 (1981): 10ff.
10. Karl Radek, "Zur Frage des Programms der Kommunistischen Internationale (Vorläufige Bemerkungen), in Materialien zur Frage des Programms der Kommunistischen Internationale (Hamburg: Carl Hoym, 1924), pp. 7-13.
11. Internationale Pressekorrespondenz 8, no. 89 (August 23, 1928): 1683. Original emphasis. This was Bukharin's justification for the draft he had presented for the Comintern program; his position in the CPSU had by that time been so weakened that he had to make important theoretical concessions to the Stalinist majority at the Sixth World Congress.
12. Ibid.: 1686.
13. Internationale Pressekorrespondenz 8, no. 91 (August 28, 1928): 1713.
14. Cf. Barbara Timmermann, "Die Faschismus-Diskussion," p. 253 ff.

15. Cf. Ercoli (Palmiro Togliatti), "Zur Frage des Faschismus," in Die Kommunistische Internationale 10, no. 29/30 (July 25, 1928): 1677-1692.

16. Cf. "Ziele, Formen und Grenzen der 'besonderen' Wege zum Sozialismus," publications of the Arbeitsbereich Geschichte und Politik der DDR am Institut für Sozialwissenschaften der Universität Mannheim vol. 2, (Mannheim, 1984).

17. See Il Partito (Rome: Editori Riuniti, 1964), pp. 11-125 for Togliatti's speech.

18. Direzione member Paolo Bufalini, in a roundtable discussion, Rinascita 35, no. 8 (1978): 18. Emphasis in original.

19. For the resolution on dissolution of the Comintern, see Hans-Joachim Lieber and Karl-Heinz Ruffmann, eds., Der Sowjetkommunismus. Dokumente vol. 1, (Cologne: Kiepenheuer und Witsch, 1963), p. 350.

20. Cf. my article "The Cominform Effects on Soviet Foreign Policy," Studies in Comparative Communism 18, no. 1 (1985): 3-23.

21. Andrej Shdanow, Über die internationale Lage (East Berlin: Dietz Verlag, 1952), p. 9. Zhdanov was the leader of the Soviet delegation to the founding conference of the Cominform.

22. Shdanow, Internationale Lage, p. 37ff.

23. Fernando Claudín, Krise der kommunistischen Bewegung (West Berlin: Olle und Wolter, 1978), p. 9.

24. Manuel Azcárate, "La URSS y el Movimiento Comunista," in El sistema sovietico hoy (Madrid: Fundación Pablo Iglesias, 1984): 179ff.

25. Giuseppe Boffa, "L'internazionalismo del Pci," Critica Marxista 19, no. 1 (1981): 7. Boffa, an expert on Eastern Europe, is a member of the PCI Central Committee and president of its Center for the Study of International Policy.

26. Claudín, Krise, p. 363.

27. Rosenberg, Bolschewismus, p. 212.

28. Pravda, March 7, 1986.

29. Cf. the draft theses for the Seventeenth PCI Congress, l'Unità, December 15, 1985.

30. Rosenberg, Bolschewismus, p. 207ff.

2

Differentiation and
Pluralization Under Khrushchev

After the Twentieth Congress of the Communist party of the Soviet Union (CPSU) many Communists believed that world Communism might have reached a turning point. They thought after Khrushchev's condemnation of Stalin's crimes that a new era of reform and liberalization was dawning in the USSR, which would also affect the relations of the CPSU to the world Communist movement. This belief was held by certain groups of reformers who under Stalin had opposed the leadership of their own parties--as in Poland, Hungary, France, and Scandinavia. It also inspired the leaders of the Italian Communist party; Togliatti himself expected a new beginning for world Communism, desiring to give it new force in "polycentrism." This was to be accomplished in close cooperation with the party of the October revolution, not against it or by ignoring it. A widespread conviction held that the CPSU, despite all deformations under Stalin, had not lost the flexibility and readiness for reform in internal and external affairs that stemmed from its revolutionary dynamic.

There were indeed attempts by Khrushchev to define anew the function and patterns of action of the Communist parties in the phase of global "transition from capitalism to socialism," and to bring the forms and character of their cooperation into accord with Moscow's new foreign policy line. These attempts were limited to the period between the Twentieth Party Congress in February 1956 and the Moscow world conference of November 1957. The discussions and decisions of the Twentieth Congress suggested that the Soviet leaders were ready for a more flexible style of cooperation with the Communist parties, which would grant the individual parties greater autonomy. The world conference in essence signaled the end of this reform trend, positing as it did a series of ideological-political principles valid for all Communist parties. But precisely this attempt to defend unity and "separate true Communists from revisionist traitors"[1] rendered the decay of the international Communist movement inevitable, though this was not immediately clear. Not until the advent of Mikhail Gorbachev did any CPSU leader begin to draw conclusions from these events.

Khrushchev's Conception of World Communism

Even before the Twentieth Congress Moscow had appreciably enlarged its freedom of action in foreign affairs. One need only recall the armistice in the Korean war, the Geneva summit in 1955, and Khrushchev's active diplomacy with important Third World countries. Relaxation in relations with China (dissolution of the "mixed companies" during Khrushchev's visit to Beijing in 1954, for example) and Khrushchev's spectacular trip to Belgrade in 1955 suggested that the Soviet leaders were intent on giving new form to their relations with Communist states and parties.

The Twentieth Congress itself was marked by Khrushchev's endeavor to overcome the internal stagnation of the Soviet Union with dramatic theoretical innovations, and in international affairs to move from Stalin's defensive positions to the offensive. Thus alongside the condemnation of Stalin, the revision of his central dogmas was to give the Soviet Union new impetus within and without.[2] One of these dogmas was the thesis of the unavoidability of wars between capitalism and socialism, which Stalin's successors replaced with the theory of peaceful coexistence. Certainly this innovation strengthened the intent to avoid armed conflict between East and West, given the destructive power of nuclear weapons. But it also implied a new and militant dynamic. Local and regional advances below the threshold of war with the U.S. again seemed possible.[3]

The Soviets also dropped Stalin's dogma that neutral states, especially those freed from colonial domination, should be regarded as part of the "imperialist system." Khrushchev reclassified them as part of the new "zones of peace" in the Third World. After the 1955 Bandung Conference the main thrust of the revolutionary movement was deemed to have shifted to the countries that had recently been or still were colonies. With this change of emphasis

Khrushchev created the theoretical basis for stronger Soviet influence in the developing countries.

Finally, the Twentieth Party Congress abandoned the thesis of capitalist encirclement of the Soviet Union in favor of the idea that world capitalism had entered into a new third stage in its general crisis, while the international socialist camp was exerting an ever greater influence on events in the world.[4] In 1961 the party program went even farther, noting "an increasing superiority of the forces of socialism over those of imperialism," and declaring that "imperialism is decaying and dying capitalism; we are on the eve of socialist revolution. The world capitalist system is in its totality ripe for the social revolution of the proletariat." [5]

This revolutionary optimism and confident belief in the strength of Communist ideas distinguishes Khrushchev from his predecessor and all of his successors. Equally optimistic was his assumption that the Communist parties could and would play the role he intended for them in his offensive strategy. Stalin had emasculated the Communist parties by obliging them to defend the Soviet Union under any and all conditions, with the absolute precondition that they conform to the Soviet model of society. Gorbachev seems interested in the non-bloc parties only insofar as they actively support his foreign policy initiatives. In both cases the interests of the Soviet state determine the relation of the CPSU to its fraternal parties. But Khrushchev at least retained a residual universal vision of a socialism which ascribes an authentically revolutionary mission to the Communist parties. His idea, reminiscent of Bukharin, was that in an international class struggle characterized by peaceful coexistence each party would contribute by its own strategy to shifting the world balance of power toward socialism.

This line, first sketched out vaguely at the Twentieth Party Congress, was based on the conviction that "there can be no serious conflict between the interests of Soviet power and the interests of world revolutionary expansion by independent Communist states and movements."[6] This line basically evokes Lenin's ideas, to the extent that Khrushchev believed in principle in the concordance of interests of all Communist parties, in power or not.

But Khrushchev, unlike Lenin, did not want to yoke the parties to the organizational discipline of a centralized world party which would distribute instructions for action. After all, experience had shown that no party had been guided to power by Comintern instructions, while in the Cominform period the western Communists were everywhere on the defensive. Khrushchev's conception of the offense instead promoted autonomy so that the parties might fit themselves flexibly to national conditions and thus further the world revolutionary process. These considerations allowed him to take a more favorable view of the special paths chosen by Yugoslavia and China. Stalin had regarded them with suspicion (or fought them) precisely because both were examples of revolutions by parties which had freed themselves from the Moscow center.

Thus it was no accident that the Twentieth Congress "undertook for the first time since Lenin to systematize the experience of Communism as an international movement,"[7] and to draw theoretical lessons for the Communist parties from its positive results. The outcome relativized the meaning both of October 1917 as a model for revolutions and of the USSR as a model of society; the CPSU was recognizing the possibility of different roads to socialism and variant means of building socialism. This referred to the experience of the Chinese and the Yugoslavs, including the conquest of power through partisan combat. But it also gave validity to the aspirations of leaders in Eastern Europe to enlarge their scope of action at home. Khrushchev's innovations also extended to the policies of the parties in the West. Legitimation of the peaceful road to power included the possibility of using parliament "not as before as a tribune to prepare revolutionary action, but as the instrument for the transition to socialism itself." [8]

In these revisions of Stalinist dogma Khrushchev supposed that just because of this political and organizational differentiation the Communist movement must necessarily let itself be guided as before by common principles, in order not to lose sight of the common revolutionary goal. This in turn demanded recognition of the dogmatic authority of a leading party. It seemed quite natural to Khrushchev that only the CPSU could take this role--not only because of its history as the party of the October revolution, but also because of its weight as the strongest power in the "anti-imperialist camp." The Chinese too shared this view, until they came to the conclusion that the CPSU under Khrushchev was "unworthy" to lead and must be replaced by the Chinese party.

The Failure of the Khrushchev Line

In this as in other areas, Khrushchev's analysis and its underlying strategic line of realigning the international Communist movement turned out to be too optimistic and thus unrealistic. The proofs came in the Polish and Hungarian crises of 1956, the second break with the League of Yugoslav Communists in 1957, the conflict with the Chinese Communists which broke into the open in 1960, and finally the divergences with the Italian party. The Stalin-Tito rift in 1948 had already made it clear that a common Marxist-Leninist ideology was not suited to bridging over differences about the national conditions and interests of the individual parties. On the contrary, when used as an instrument to legitimize special roads to Communism, a variously interpreted ideology rekindled smouldering conflicts of interest, most fiercely in the argument between Moscow and Beijing.

There is no space here to go into the causes, course, and outcomes of the different conflicts. Instead some of the contradictions of Khrushchev's new course will be presented briefly--contradictions which emerged more clearly after the Twentieth Party Congress, much accelerating the process of erosion in the world Communist movement.

Dogmatic Authority. The Soviets continued to presume that Soviet socialism should be considered exemplary, if not perhaps the sole model. This, plus their claim to ideological leadership in world Communism, collided with the reductive effect of the CPSU leaders' declaration that Stalin's crimes were an emanation of the cult of personality and were thus "a stage in the life of the Soviet land that has been surmounted."[9]

The Chinese, Yugoslavs, and Italians were not content with such a superficial explanation. Partly with an eye to the future, they demanded a more searching analysis of the causes and the inner mechanisms of a system that had made Stalin's despotism possible. It was just the lack of such a causal analysis that provoked PCI secretary general Togliatti to remark in June 1956 that the Soviet leaders, by the style of their criticism had "doubtless lost a bit of their prestige,"[10] a comment which showed notable reservations about supporting Soviet claims to ideological leadership.

National Roads. The Twentieth Congress did indeed legitimize the pursuit of national roads to socialism. The concrete expression of this can be found, for example, in the Moscow declaration on resumption of party relations between the CPSU and the League of Yugoslav Communists in June 1956. It declares that the development of socialism proceeds differently in different countries, and that neither side may force its views about the ways and means of this development on the other.[11]

This revision was rapidly devalued by the Soviet leaders. By September 1956 they had already made it clear to their bloc partners that Yugoslavia was an isolated case which could not serve as a precedent for any other Communist state or party.[12] Probably Khrushchev's concessions to Tito were only intended to bring the Yugoslav heretic back into the Soviet dominated bloc, thus removing a dangerous and destabilizing ideological and political influence on developments in Eastern Europe.[13]

Immediately after the crisis in Poland and the Hungarian uprising the Soviets labeled every national road as "revisionism" or even "nationalism," while Beijing cheered them on. The world conference of parties in 1957 then formulated "general laws of socialist revolution and building socialism" which directly contradicted the logic of different roads to socialism and much reduced the scope for developing special roads.[14] At the same time the conference enunciated a formula concerning the dialectic between the particular and the general rules for Communist parties which was so vague that the scholastics of world Communism are still arguing about it.

Differentiation. The Twentieth Congress put all parties on the same plane by leaving to them the choice of the way to socialism and the means of building it. However, it left unchecked the existing tendency to give priority to the ruling parties united in the "world socialist system" over the nonruling parties. Whereas the Twentieth Congress discussed in detail the experience of the Soviet Union and other socialist countries, the conditions for peaceful roads to socialism in the developed capitalist states were not closely analysed, while the results of the Popular Front period and the new paths after 1945 were passed over in silence.

The world conference of Communist parties in 1957 produced the concept of socialist internationalism to describe collaboration in the Communist state system, a principle later raised to constitutional status in the countries of the socialist community. Theoretically a special case of proletarian internationalism, socialist internationalism became for the Soviets the glue binding together the states of the Warsaw Pact, and acquired greater importance than proletarian internationalism.

A significant organizational expression of the priority accorded the state parties was the division of the 1957 world conference into two separate phases. Only the nucleus composed of the twelve ruling parties (without the Yugoslavs) issued the final declaration with its "general laws" that were meant to bind all Communist parties. The plenum of the sixty-four party delegations present limited itself to accepting a "peace manifesto," a rather generally phrased appeal to halt the danger of war.

The division in 1957 of the CPSU Central Committee department for International Relations into one for ruling parties (under Yuriy Andropov) and another for nonruling parties (under Boris Ponomarev) probably belongs in this same context. By reorganizing its foreign apparatus to show its preferences, the CPSU encouraged that regionalisation of the Communist movement which it later criticized so sharply in the Western European Eurocommunists.

Recentralization. Recognizing the necessity of taking into account the "national peculiarities and conditions" of the individual parties, the Twentieth Congress did decide to dissolve the Cominform and stop publication of its newspaper.[15] This was not only a concession to Tito but corresponded also to the wishes of other autonomy-minded parties such as the PCI. In contradiction to this, Khrushchev soon after made known his intention to give the Communist movement a new Moscow-centric structure, best exemplified by the world conferences that promulgated a general line. Also, a new CPSU-inspired periodical began publication in 1958 in Prague, Problems of Peace and Socialism (English title: World Marxist Review). Khrushchev's attempt to assert the validity of democratic centralism for world conferences (with the CPSU as the leading party) marks the high point of these tendencies toward recentralization.

Reactions in the Communist Party System

The Communist parties in all their variety agreed on two points in their reaction to the Twentieth Congress. Characteristically, even this consensus mirrors the contradictory nature of Khrushchev's new dispositions. All parties were pleased by Khrushchev's offensive strategy and by the autonomist role assigned them, at least for action in their national contexts. An end to the thesis of capitalist en-

circlement implied for Communists everywhere the hope
that after the obligatory defense of the Soviet Union as the
"bulwark of the world revolution" they could now concentrate more on strategies of change in their own back
yards.

On the other hand, the parties just as unanimously
condemned (if out of different motives) the style and means
employed by Khrushchev in opening the way to destalinization. The arguments went something like this: with all his
positive and negative traits, Stalin as leader of the CPSU,
the most influential party in world Communism, has over
the decades stamped his mark on the Communist party system. The reappreciation of his actions is therefore not just
Moscow's internal affair, but must be conducted by all the
Communist parties. At the very least the CPSU should have
consulted the fraternal parties before it undertook such a
radical re-evaluation of Stalin's line, confronting all Communist parties with more or less serious problems.

Thus it was not only the lessons of Soviet degeneration under Stalin that caused many Communist
leaders to begin "thinking with their own heads," as the
Spaniard Santiago Carrillo later put it. It was rather the
surprising, almost clandestine staging of this turning point
in the congress that turned many already sceptical parties
against Khrushchev. His procedure stood in striking contradiction to Soviet assurances of confidential and equal cooperation in the world Communist movement. What the French
Communist historian Roger Martelli called the "shock of the
Twentieth Party Congress," surely an initial success in
mobilizing the Soviet people, turned out to be ambivalent
at the least for the Communist parties.

In retrospect, one sees that Khrushchev's idea of
placing the Communist movement on a new basis by flexibly
combining domestic autonomy with a common international
strategy was doomed to rapid failure. This was evident at
the latest by the end of 1957, when the first world conference of parties in its proclamation of binding "general
laws" sought to put new chains on the individual parties,
again fettering them to the Soviet line.

However, this idea was no longer feasible. By damning
Stalin Khrushchev had in fact jeopardized his own plan to
resolve the contradictions in world Communism. Stalin's
idea had been to make "the primacy of Soviet raison d'état
an essential ideological article of faith."[16] This was no
longer possible after the Twentieth Congress. The congress
thus became a ferment working for the renationalization of

Communist strategies which would affect each party differently according to its own traditions and conditions. The consequences are still visible today.

In Eastern Europe furious conflicts arose immediately between the Stalinists and those groups pushing for drastic reform in the spirit of national autonomy. After the violent suppression of the reform movement in Hungary in November 1956, Moscow was able to stabilize the immediate situation in its strategic glacis, but the real problems of the Eastern European societies were not solved, as shown by the liquidation of the Prague spring in 1968 and of <u>Solidarnosc</u> in 1981.

The Chinese had basically been pleased by Khrushchev's destalinization. But they had expressed strong doubts about the superficiality of his analysis and simultaneously pleaded that the services of the dictator in unifying world Communism should not be forgotten amid the criticism. [17] In any case, the Chinese party saw its own reputation and importance among the parties rising with the loss of Soviet authority and used its strength to assert a greater influence in world Communist affairs--first in accord with the Soviets, then against them.

Destalinization also had decisive consequences in the western Communist parties. At the end of 1956 the PCI resolved to take its stand on "the Italian road to socialism," and began to champion the line of the Twentieth Congress. The Spanish party rid itself in April 1956 of its Stalinist leadership under Vicente Uribe and made a fundamental change in its alliance policy. Where it had earlier sought collaboration only among those forces which had fought alongside it in the Civil War, it now coined the slogan of "national reconciliation," designed expressly to overcome the old alignment of forces. The French party, on the contrary, sought to play down the radical change in Moscow and preserve its own Stalinist identity. (Significantly, it officially recognized the existence of Khrushchev's secret speech only in 1977.) The PCF made several attempts, from 1956 until 1960, to undermine Khrushchev's authority in world Communism. Misunderstanding the reason for Togliatti's criticism of Khrushchev, it first sounded out the Italian party, and later the Chinese and the Albanians as well.

Less known but not less interesting was the reaction of the Japanese party.[18] It held back at first, while Khrushchev wrestled with a critical Japanese demand--that he condemn Stalin for a personal decision in 1950 that forced the Japanese party to adopt a damaging line calling for violent revolution. (The JCP lost its entire delegation in the Diet, where it had had thirty-five of the 466 seats in 1949.) Conflict with the Soviets became certain when in August 1956 the JCP thought to take advantage of weakening Soviet authority after the Twentieth Congress and raised a territorial question, demanding the return to Japan of the Kurile islands of Habomai, Shikotan, Kunashiri, and Etorofu, which had been annexed by the USSR in 1945. Here, on a small scale, appeared the contradictions in national interest dressed in ideological clothing which were to give the Moscow-Beijing conflict its real bitterness. It has remained a central point of controversy between the JCP and the CPSU until this day.

Ideas for a New Start in Party Cooperation

Many of the parties were sceptical of the tendency to redirect and loosen the Communist party system, with its associated loss of Soviet authority. This was especially true of those parties which had no real influence in their own countries but drew their force primarily from adherence to an extensive and centrally directed movement. However, even an influential party like the PCF sided with the advocates of recentralization, and French polemics (for example against Togliatti's polycentrism proposal) were also aimed indirectly at Khrushchev.

But reaction to the Twentieth Congress also produced some remarkable new starts in the Communist movement. There were even--briefly--certain convergences in the views of important parties. Three examples may illustrate this phenomenon.

The Foremost Role of the CPSU. The Chinese, and the Yugoslavs and Italians as well, were apparently ready to continue to grant the CPSU the foremost role in the world revolutionary process. They were impressed by what then seemed the steadily increasing economic and scientific-technical dynamic of the USSR, while its function as a counterweight to the American-dominated camp of "imperialism" also counted heavily. In their view, Soviet precedence presupposed Soviet readiness to place the CPSU in the lead of reform-oriented change, giving every party the right to resolve internal contradictions (such as getting rid of Stalinist leaders) without external interference. In this spirit, all three parties supported reforms in Warsaw and at first also in Budapest. In 1956-1957 the Chinese conducted extensive discussions in their own ranks about "the origins of contradictions among the people."

These partial agreements among Chinese, Yugoslavs, and Italians changed into divergences in 1957, when Mao Zedong insisted during the world conference of Communist parties both on the leading role of the USSR among Communist states and of the CPSU in the world Communist movement. Probably this Chinese position, a surprise and disappointment[19] for the Italians (and the Poles) stemmed largely from Beijing's own national interest. By backing Moscow's leading role, Mao intended to put the Soviets under a moral obligation to give China greater help in building socialism and aid in its defense from external danger.

The Italians, for their part, have since 1956 expressly rejected the notion of a "leading state" and a "leading party" with special rights. And Tito put an end to rapprochement with Moscow when he perceived that Khrushchev was really only interested in bringing the Yugoslavs back into the Soviet camp. Once Belgrade had seen the draft for the final declaration of the forthcoming world conference, the LCY refused to participate in the final discussions, signing only the "peace manifesto."[20]

Polycentrism. Togliatti's proposal to re-arrange the Communist system of parties on a polycentric basis is worthy of note.[21] The PCI chief was not trying to question the predominant role of the CPSU in the world revolutionary process. Rather, he desired to give neighboring Communist parties a way to come together on a regional basis to discuss the means for struggle in their particular situations.

Interestingly, such an idea was considered during the Twentieth Congress, when the member parties of the Cominform decided on its dissolution and reflected on new methods of cooperation. It even appeared in the resolution ending the Cominform, with language reading "each party or group of parties" may according to the special conditions of their countries work out "new beneficial forms to create ties and contacts among Communist parties."[22] This idea was not followed up. Opposed by the dogmatic and centralist French party, it also seemed to some autonomists like the Poles to carry with it the danger of a neo-Cominform tie.

No Monopoly for the CP's. A further thesis--set forward by the Yugoslavs, later more popular with the Italians[23]--was the revolutionary idea that the development toward socialism was no monopoly of the Communist parties, but could also be carried out by forces and movements which had not emerged from the Third International.[24] This thesis then referred chiefly to international social democracy, but might in the future include liberation movements in the Third World. The Italian Communist Adriano Guerra correctly sees in this "an evident break with a certain integralism ⟨stemming⟩ from the Third International" and a start on "a completely new discourse on the possibility and necessity of beginning a process leading to the reunification of the different branches of the socialist movement in Western Europe." [25]

Remarkably enough, this idea caused no controversy among Communists at the time, despite its revolutionary variance from Lenin's conception of the vanguard Communist party and the new perspectives which it opened. Even the PCI was very slow in spelling out its final logic; not until December 1981, after the suppression of Solidarnosc, did it resolve itself to take the spectacular step of abandoning its privileged relations with the CPSU and other Communist parties and put them on the same level as relations with Socialist or other progressive parties.[26]

Study of the short period between the Twentieth Party Congress in February 1956 and the world conference of November 1957 shows an abundance of ideas for new directions in the world Communist movement, developed both by the Soviets and the other parties. At the same time it became clear that the party system could neither be held together ideologically nor restructured entirely anew. Khrushchev had indeed freed the movement from outmoded dogmas, the better to use it in his offensive strategy against the West. But his attempts at a new unitary direction were doomed to failure. Ideology increasingly lost its force as the guideline for common political action in favor of perceived national interest. With the weakening of Soviet authority after the Twentieth Congress, the important parties in fact increasingly employed ideology to draw a line between their own ideas and Moscow's domestic and foreign policies.

Thus Khrushchev despite his dramatic innovations may be regarded as a transitional figure in the development of the Communist party system, rather than as the author of projects and structures pointing to the future. In the last analysis, the Twentieth Party Congress only accelerated a process of inner differentiation in world Communism which had set in long before and had merely been concealed by the ritual of the Stalin cult.

NOTES

1. Richard Löwenthal, Chruschtschow und der Welt-kommunismus (Stuttgart: Kohlhammer, 1963), p. 179.
2. Cf. Khrushchev's official speech, Pravda, February 15, 1956. For the secret speech see i.a. Strobe Talbott, ed., Khrushchev Remembers (London: André Deutsch, 1971), pp. 559-618.
3. Richard Löwenthal, Weltpolitische Betrachtungen (Göttingen: Vanderhoeck und Ruprecht, 1983), p.21.
4. Khrushchev, official speech, February 1956.
5. See Pravda, November 2, 1961 for the party program.
6. Löwenthal, Chruschtschow, p. 173.
7. Ibid. p. 26.
8. Roger Martelli, 1956: le choc du vingtième congrès du pcus (Paris: Editions Sociales, 1982), p. 24.
9. Cf. Pravda, July 2, 1956. This judgment remains the official one.
10. Interview with Nuovi Argomenti, in Roberto Bonchi et al., eds., Il Partito comunista italiano e il movimento operaio internazionale 1956-1968 (Rome: Editori Riuniti, 1968), p. 48.
11. See Stephen Clissold, ed., Yugoslavia and the Soviet Union 1939-1973 (London and New York: Oxford University Press, 1973), p. 261.
12. Clissold, Yugoslavia, p. 263. Cf. also Robert F. Miller and Ferenc Feher, eds., Khrushchev and the Communist World (London and Sydney: Croom, 1984), p. 194ff.
13. Cf. Talbott, Khrushchev, p. 378 ff.
14. See Pravda, November 22,1957 for the twelve-party declaration.
15. See the Cominform journal For a Lasting Peace, For a People's Democracy, April 17, 1956 for the resolution dissolving the Cominform.
16. Löwenthal, Chruschtschow, p. 12.
17. Cf. Young and Woodward, "Khrushchevism in Chinese Perspective," in Miller and Feher, Khrushchev, pp. 162-188.

18. Cf. Manfred Pohl, Die Kommunistische Partei Japans: ein Weg ohne Peking und Moskau (Hamburg: Verband für Asienkunde, 1976), and Central Committee of the Japanese Communist Party, eds., Sixty-Year History of the Japanese Communist Party (Tokyo: Japan Press Service, 1984).

19. Cf. Pietro Ingrao, "Mao a Mosca," in Pietro Ingrao, Tradizione e progetto (Bari: De Donato, 1982) pp. 145-151.

20. Miller and Feher, Khrushchev, p. 198 ff.

21. Nuovi Argomenti interview, pp. 60 and 69. Cf. also Joan Barth Urban, Moscow and the Italian Communist Party: From Togliatti to Berlinguer (Ithaca and London: Cornell University Press, 1986) p. 225 ff.

22. Cf. the resolution dissolving the Cominform in For a Lasting Peace. Also see Togliatti, in l'Unità, December 21, 1961.

23. Löwenthal, Chruschtschow, p. 19.

24. See the Nuovi Argomenti interview, p. 50, and Togliatti's speech to the PCI Central Committee, l'Unità, June 24, 1956. Cf. also Joan Barth Urban, Moscow, p. 232 ff.

25. Adriano Guerra, Il giorno che Chruscev parlò: Dal XX Congresso alla rivolta ungherese (Rome: Editori Riuniti, 1986), p. 94ff.

26. See l'Unità, December 30, 1981 for the resolution.

3

Decay in the Brezhnev Era

Proletarian and Socialist Internationalism

In its relations with the Communist parties, the new Brezhnev leadership adhered essentially to the line traced by the Moscow world conference of 1957. It operated on an assumption which goes back to the founding of the Comintern, that a common interest in the struggle against imperialism exists within the revolutionary workers' movement. Both ruling and nonruling parties unite in the spirit of proletarian internationalism against imperialism as the vanguard of the working class, with common action, aid, and solidarity. Proletarian internationalism is an indivisible concept drawn from common values rooted in Marxism-Leninism, which cannot be split into national or regional departments, as Eurocommunism implies, for example. Each Communist party is of course independent, has equal rights, and is called upon to defend the national interests of its country. At the same time there must be a guarantee that the interests of the national parties will be subordinated to the interests of the world Communist movement in the pursuit of the common goals.

However, the CPSU identified this interest of the whole unambiguously with the interests of the Soviet state, the community of socialist states controlled by Moscow and integrated into the Warsaw Pact, and the Council for Mutual Economic Assistance (CMEA). The Soviets based this de facto claim to leadership in world Communism primarily on the following arguments:

-- The CPSU carried out the October revolution, the decisive break with capitalism and imperialism. As heir and continuator of this great revolution, the CPSU fulfills the task of the revolution in its concrete policy.

--The CPSU has the richest experience in socialist transformation, and thus has gained the deepest insight into the historical laws governing the building of social- ism/communism.

--The Soviet Union has made the greatest progress among socialist countries, and is already engaged in "creating the material-technical basis for Communism."

--Soviet Communism does not have the inner dynamics peculiar to capitalism which would push it toward aggress- ion and expansion; its foreign and security policies are thus by nature peace-loving, in the words of Central Committee member Vadim Zagladin "a synthesis of the urge to peace of all mankind."

--The Soviet Union (and with it the socialist state community) is the decisive factor for change in the world revolutionary process, given the international correlation of power in favor of socialism. It thereby not only opens new perspectives for peace and progress in the world, but also increases the chances for success of nonruling Communists and Third World liberation movements in revolutionary upheaval in their countries.

As the Brezhnev leadership saw it, the main task of all Communist parties was consistently to defend the Soviet Communist model of society and give support without reservation to all aspects of Soviet foreign policy. Crit- icism of the CPSU line from Communist ranks therefore rap- idly evoked severe reproach, and an accusation of anti- Sovietism. Precisely this ideological orthodoxy and lack of political flexibility in the CPSU deepened the differences, divergences, and splits in the world Communist movement. Violent arguments ensued on such central questions as the interpretation of proletarian internationalism, the relation between national and international, the way to socialism and how to build socialism, as well as on the forms of organizational cooperation in the world Communist movement.

The CPSU sought to check this process of erosion with a double procedure. For their East European hegemonic domain, the basis of Moscow's position as a world power, the Soviets created the concept of socialist internationalism, in theory a special case of proletarian internationalism, and now for the Soviets the more important of the two. The states and Communist parties united in the Warsaw Pact work closely together in accord with the principles of socialist internationalism. Their cooperation covers all areas of political and social life:

ideological, domestic political, and party organizational questions (including the tasks of building socialism and communism), as well as problems of foreign policy coordination, economic integration, and military cooperation.

Socialist internationalism takes into account "respect for the special situations as well as for the specific interests" of the individual Warsaw Pact states. At the same time, it postulates the collective responsibility of the socialist state community to defend "socialist achievements" against "reactionary schemes" at home and abroad, including in extreme cases military intervention in those socialist countries where domestic developments are seen as incompatible with the principles of Marxism-Leninism. Leonid Brezhnev gave his name to the doctrine applied in 1968 in the suppression of reform Communism in Czechoslovakia, a theory of the limited sovereignty of socialist states. In many Communist parties--from the Chinese traditionalists to the gradualist Italocommunists-- the Brezhnev doctrine was decisively rejected, and contributed much to accelerate the process of decay in the world Communist movement.

The CPSU urged the adoption of regular world conferences by the Communist movement as a timely instrument for coordinating cooperation. There were three such conferences, held in Moscow in 1957, 1960, and 1969. Their final documents are still accorded the character of binding agreements (or, at a minimum, guidelines) by the CPSU and its followers. When one looks at the substantive results of these conferences and the weight of the disagreements among the participants (and also the non-participants), the value of the conference resolutions for the CPSU has a clearly diminishing trendline. The 1957 document on the general line, with its decalogue of general laws for socialist revolution and building socialism, still corresponded fully to Soviet conceptions. The final declaration in 1960 was already strongly marked by the Moscow-Beijing conflict, evident in its combination of divergent positions on central questions: peaceful versus non-peaceful paths to socialism; peaceful coexistence versus the unavoidability of warlike conflict between socialism and capitalism/imperialism; steps toward normalization of relations with the League of Yugoslav Communists versus condemnation of the Yugoslav way as a right-revisionist "chief danger" for the world Communist movement, etc.

-51-

At the world conference in 1969 a number of important parties were missing altogether: not only the Chinese, but also the North Vietnamese, North Korean, Albanian, and Yugoslav parties. The CPSU was unable to convince the remaining parties that they should support its main objective, a collective condemnation of the Chinese party. Neither could it prevent mention of the intervention in Czechoslovakia, with all its implications for the relations of Communist states and parties. Soviet plans for a fourth world conference, first mooted in 1981, have made no progress. They encounter the resistance of important parties like the Yugoslavs, the PCI and the JCP, which as parties bent on autonomy and independence expressly reject the idea on principle, now and for the future.

It was therefore no coincidence that Moscow coined the expression "really existent socialism" to refer to the Soviet Union and the socialist community precisely during the high tide of Eurocommunism in the 1970s. With this formula, intended as a fighting slogan, the CPSU leaders combined an intent to decry the programmatic and political innovations of the Eurocommunists as utopian at best, and also to characterize the Soviet Communist type of society as the basic model and only realistic possibility for the building of socialism/communism.

A symptom of this attitude is the fact that the formal concessions made by the Soviets to the autonomists did not result from any Soviet insight but had to be extracted under pressure. Examples are the passage in the final declaration of the 1960 conference concerning the independence and equal rights of all parties;[1] the remark in the main document of the 1969 conference that the Communist movement has "no directing center;"[2] and the abandonment of the usual liturgical flourish on "proletarian internationalism" in the final document of the East Berlin European party conference in 1976. Instead all participants declared, in a compromise formula only half-heartedly accepted by the CPSU, that they wished "to develop their internationalist, comradely, voluntary cooperation and solidarity...on the basis of the great ideas of Marx, Engels, and Lenin"--i.e. no longer on the basis of a Marxism-Leninism boiled down by the Soviets to "general laws." [13] The Soviet inflexibility nourished the differences, divergences, and splits in the Communist party system and excluded any idea of a fourth world conference.

The "New Internationalism" of the Autonomists

The autonomists are ideologically divided in several ways, and have developed a number of variations of socialism. One can mention self-management socialism in Yugoslavia, the Maoist version of socialism in China, Castroism in Latin America, reform Communism in Eastern Europe and Eurocommunism in Western Europe, with some strong points in other parts of the world. Beyond these nationally conditioned conceptions of socialism, however, the autonomists have important common interests, which have repeatedly brought them together for tactical or lasting alliances inside the world Communist movement.

The least common denominator of these interests is a defense against Soviet efforts to interpret proletarian internationalism to mean the priority of the general interests of the Communist movement against the national interests of the individual parties--a formulation first set forth in the Comintern program of 1928.[4] In the eyes of the autonomists these general interests are abstract and irrational constructs, designed to promote the hegemonic ambitions and nationalism of some parties, or to emasculate others and condemn them to the role of sects. The CPSU has used the formula to assert its ideological and political leadership in the movement and to discipline fraternal parties by carrying the organizational principle of democratic centralism into the realm of inter-party relations.

Since there are of necessity many conceptions of socialism, say the autonomists, there can be neither a center nor a leading party or state in the world Communist movement. Instead, every party, with all respect for internationalist solidarity with fraternal parties, is in the first instance responsible to its own working class, for the pursuit of "different ways raises the development of socialism to its highest power," as the Yugoslav Aleksandr Grlickov put it. And here the autonomists can even refer to the Soviet constitution of 1977, which in discussing the determination of Moscow's foreign policy goals speaks of "building Communism in the USSR" and gives the "security of the state interests of the Soviet Union" a clear priority over other--internationalist--goals. [5]

In this spirit the autonomists, including the Chinese party, advocate a "new internationalism" in the world Communist movement, in which the parties are guided by the principles of independence and autonomy, full equality of rights, mutual respect, and reciprocal non-interference in each others' affairs.[6]

This conception does contain the idea of a cooperation of equals, although not in the framework of a structured (or centrally controlled) party system elaborating general lines in world conferences. On the other hand, it points the way out of the world Communist movement, since the parties which desire this system also want parallel relations to the parties of the Socialist International as well as to liberation movements in the Third World. In the place of the traditional, hierarchically ordered system of progressive forces with the Communist parties as their self-elected vanguard, the "new internationalism" of the Chinese, Yugoslav, Italian and other parties posits a complex of formations, differing on ideology and policy but all of anti-imperialist inspiration. The social democratic and socialist parties are seen as the main discussion partners, not only for foreign and security policy, as traditional Communists would have it, but in a much wider context, for policies affecting the society, the economy, and relations with the Third World.

The rise of autonomist tendencies in the world Communist movement did not lack for setbacks and contradictions, as shown by the development of Castroism and Maoism. The Cuban Communist party moved much closer to Moscow at the end of the 1960s, primarily for economic reasons, after it had developed its own revolutionary model for Latin America, under the strong influence of Ernesto "Che" Guevara, and had come into conflict with the CPSU. The model called for a revolution kindled on the hearth of a guerrilla uprising--i.e. abandoning revolutionary mass mobilization and refusing peaceful coexistence and the peaceful road to power pursued by the working class.

The Chinese party performed several radical changes of course in its relations with the Moscow-oriented world movement. The basic constant was the Chinese effort to preserve their independence in foreign and security matters, and to give China a place in world affairs befitting its history, its self-confidence, and its importance.

Viewed in this light, there is an evident explanation for all the variations in Beijing's conflicts with Moscow in the Communist movement. They manifested themselves in the concept of a common leadership in world Communism (until circa 1957), the drive for ideological and political hegemony (until the beginning of the 1960s), and the attempt to split the world movement and transfer its leading center from Moscow to Beijing (until the beginning of the 1970s). After a period of considerable indifference the Chinese party has now in its post-Mao phase returned to inter-party activity on the basis of "new internationalism." (It resumed relations with the LCY in 1978, with the PCI and PCE in 1980, with the PCF in 1982 and with some East European state parties in 1986.) The Chinese party's internationalism has as little to do with ideology and as much with power as its former theories of "intermediate zones," "the four enemies," the "Three Worlds" and the "anti-hegemonist unity front." Like the CPSU it is primarily interested in national interests.

The return of the Chinese party to an interest in world Communist affairs poses problems for the CPSU, since it emphasizes the legitimacy of special roads, and by offering an alternative to Moscow's model for inter-party relations further undermines Soviet pretensions to leadership. Autonomists like the PCI and Yugoslavs who formerly had been violently attacked by the Chinese feel their efforts toward independence upheld.

The Yugoslav Communists came early to this line. After their exclusion in 1948 from the Cominform, they had argued vigorously for a new internationalism, and directed their efforts in the non-aligned movement to that end. The PCI, forerunner of Eurocommunism, became an important ally of the Yugoslavs. Under Togliatti's leadership after 1956 it cautiously advocated new forms of cooperation in the world movement, first "polycentrism," later "unity in diversity." Togliatti argued, for example, for the replacement of world conferences by regional ones—some of which took place—in order to consider specific political problems, and for political seminars to discuss new theoretical questions as they arose.

After the Soviet action in Afghanistan in 1979 and the crackdown in Poland in 1981, Enrico Berlinguer's PCI moved away from "unity in diversity," an idea which supposes a basic ideological-political consensus distinguishing Communist parties from all non-Communist ones. With its phrase on the loss of "propulsive power" by real socialism Soviet style, the PCI abandoned privileged relations with the CPSU and the Communist party system and brought them to the level of its relations with other "progressive" parties—e.g. Social Democrats and Socialists.[7] A clear convergence exists here with the Yugoslav, Chinese and many other parties, which also maintain close contacts with the parties of the Socialist International.

The Brezhnev CPSU could still mobilize a large majority of parties--the state parties of Eastern Europe (except autonomist Rumania), and a series of rather small parties, especially in Latin America, in the Arab-Islamic world, and in Northern Europe. The decay of the world Communist movement in its traditionally structured Moscovite form accelerated, however, during the Brezhnev era; the movement continued to retreat from stewardship of common revolutionary tasks toward a championing of Soviet state interests and superpower ambitions.

This decay has indirectly affected Soviet ability to mobilize the Communist parties to support a foreign and security policy which is ideologically motivated (at least according to Soviet propaganda). The CPSU has found it more difficult to construct an identity of interests by appealing to common ideological and programmatic values, thus enlisting non-Soviet Communists in the service of the Soviet line. The new orientations of the PCI are typical of this dropping of traditional ideological ties. Enrico Berlinguer, speaking after the Moscow-inspired coup in Poland in December 1981, emphasized that his party would no longer automatically follow Soviet foreign policy; for domestic and organizational reasons this would be downright "suicidal." The PCI would in future determine its attitude on Soviet actions from case to case, depending on given Soviet positions or actions.[8]

It becomes clear from this concrete example that the gulf between "proletarian internationalism" Soviet style and the "new internationalism" of the autonomists became unbridgeable during the Brezhnev era. It is hardly coincidental that since then doubts whether it makes political sense to insist on the existence of a "world Communist movement," with common values, patterns of action, and goals, have found their most emphatic expression among Communist parties.

NOTES

1. See _Pravda_, December 6, 1960. The formula responded to a demand by the Japanese CP. Cf. Tetsuzo

Fuwa, Stalin and Great-Power Chauvinism, (Tokyo: Japan Press Service, 1983), p. 47. Fuwa is the chairman of the JCP presidium.

2. Pravda, June 18, 1969. The passage refers to a proposal by the PCE. Cf. Manuel Azcarate and Carlos Alonso Zalvidar, "Le Parti communiste d'Espagne et le PCUS," in Lilly Marcou, ed., L'URSS vue de gauche (Paris: Presses Universitaires de France, 1982), p. 241.

3. Pravda, July 1, 1976.

4. Protokoll des 6. Weltkongress der Kommunistischen Internationale 1928 (Hamburg and Berlin: Carl Hoym, 1929), p. 99.

5. See the supplement to New Times 25, no. 47 (October 1977): 5 for this phraseology in the Soviet constitution.

6. Cf. Beijing Review 25, no. 32 (September 1, 1982): 32 for this passage in General Secretary Hu Yaobang's report to the Twenty-third Chinese Party Congress.

7. Cf. l'Unità, December 30, 1981 for this resolution by the PCI Direzione, later approved by the Central Committee also.

8. L'Unità, January 24, 1982.

4

Gorbachev's Strategy

The new Soviet leadership under Mikhail Gorbachev appears to have drawn certain lessons from past experience. It has come to see that Soviet patriotism mobilizes the populace far more effectively than a now threadbare Marxist-Leninist ideology. The large-scale celebrations staged in 1985 on the fortieth anniversary of the victory over Nazi Germany provide a recent example. Gorbachev has also evidently recognized that given the dwindling cohesive force of Marxism-Leninism, further efforts by Moscow to use ideological means to bind the western Communists to the Soviet line are senseless and even counterproductive. Moreover, the Chinese Communist party, reengaged in the Communist party system since 1980, offers an attractive alternative model to the Soviet form of leadership, combining the independence of all Communist parties with relations of equal rank to Socialist and Social Democratic parties as well.[1]

Gorbachev has thus made a virtue of necessity by giving flexibility to the internationalist strategy of the CPSU, seeking to adjust it to growing tendencies toward differentiation and pluralization in the Communist party system. Basically, he cares less about preserving an ideological orthodoxy supposed to energize the world revolutionary process than he does about reaching political agreement on the concrete foreign policy of the CPSU. His intent is to collect the broadest possible support from all progressive forces from Moscow's diplomatic offensive against the West.

Party Relations: Less Ideology, More Politics

This new alignment of international party relations is to be sure still controversial within the leadership and apparatus of the CPSU, and thus subject to contradictions. These appear in differences of accent in the documents of the Twenty-seventh CPSU Congress, and become especially apparent when the new version of the CPSU program of 1961 is juxtaposed with the general secretary's political report and the final congress resolution.[2] Obviously there are still many people, especially in the foreign apparatus of the CPSU Central Committee, who like Comintern and Cominform veteran Boris Ponomarev wish to hold fast to the classical Soviet-determined definition of proletarian internationalism, and oppose any slackening of Soviet claims to be the model for and leader of the Communist party system. These traditionalists were largely successful in drafting the section on party relations in the new version of the CPSU program.

Gorbachev was perhaps most ready to make concessions here, in order to win a free hand to make changes in a draft begun under Chernenko and thus further his priorities on economic, foreign, and security policy. The version of the program issued by the Twenty-seventh Congress concedes that "the Communists of each country ⟨may⟩ analyze and estimate the situation by themselves; independently determine their strategic course and their policy." The program also provides that in case of disagreements between fraternal parties they would "conduct comradely discussions, in order to better understand the viewpoint of the other, and to work out mutually acceptable appreciations."

However, when it is a question of "the revolutionary core of Marxism-Leninism, of the nature and role of real socialism," then the CPSU "will also in the future consistently defend its principled positions." It will hold fast to proletarian internationalism and conduct a determined struggle against "bourgeois ideology, revisionism and dogmatism, reformism and sectarianism."

These patterns of Soviet thought and behavior toward the fraternal parties are typical of the Brezhnev period. By placing the accent on the preservation of ideological orthodoxy they complicate relations with the fraternal parties and restrict the number of potential non-Communist alliance partners. Thus they pose difficulties for pragmatic Soviet actions designed to enlarge the scope of foreign policy by winning international Communist support.

Gorbachev and his followers are now moving in a different direction. Certainly Gorbachev does not intend to abandon the idea of the Communist party as vanguard of the process of radical societal change. The special historical mission of the party in transition from capitalism to socialism is still considered inevitable. True to this spirit, the general secretary maintains the conception of a still existent "international Communist movement" set apart from other progressive forces (a motif appearing in the revised CPSU program). The CPSU is "unconditionally a component of this movement," said his political report to the congress. He thereby countered all those who like the Italian party, the Yugoslavs, and the Chinese, think that this idea of a vanguard movement is now out of date, and speak out for a "new internationalism" granting equal rights and weight to all progressive forces.

Gorbachev did however depart from the revised program in his political report. He made no mention of a traditional claim that his predecessors asserted and defended by arms, that Moscow remains the center of orthodoxy in world Communism. Noting that the Communist movement has now entered "a qualitatively different stage of development" and faces "many new realities, tasks, and problems," he asked that differences of opinion among the fraternal parties not be dramatized; parties should instead keep their eyes fixed on the continuing "common final goals: peace and socialism." Gorbachev declared:

> In our opinion the diversity of our movement is not a synonym for its disunity. In the same way, unity has nothing in common with uniformity, hierarchy with the intervention of one party in the affairs of another or with the pretensions of one party to possess a monopoly of the truth. The strength of the Communist movement can and must lie in its class solidarity, the equally privileged cooperation of all fraternal parties in the struggle for common goals.

The final resolution of the Twenty-seventh Party Congress adopted Gorbachev's ideas almost word for word,[3] thereby giving them the character of specific tasks for the CPSU leadership in the coming period of office. These new appreciations do not merely signal a flexible adaptation by the CPSU to growing tendencies of differentiation and pluralization in the Communist party system. They mark the emergence of the CPSU leadership from the politically sterile defensive position into which it had maneuvered itself, as a result of conflicts in secondary theaters of ideological warfare (for instance, in its relations with the PCI). They demonstrate the general secretary's intention to bring the character of party relations into harmony with new political thinking on foreign policy.

One of the more interesting expressions of the new trend is that the project for a new world Communist conference, suggested by Moscow in 1981, was not raised at the Twenty-seventh Party Congress. The world conference became the only important forum for all-Communist affairs after the dissolution of the Comintern in 1943 and the Cominform in 1956. The new CPSU party program refers indirectly in its section on "the CPSU in the international Communist and workers' movement" to "regional or larger international consultations...which may be convoked when needed." Behind the scenes, CPSU leaderships under Brezhnev, Andropov, and Chernenko have repeatedly since 1981 used fraternal parties close to Moscow to beat the drums for such a conference, sounding out the chances for broad participation through inter-party channels. The CPSU leaders themselves held back for tactical reasons, largely because they did not wish to draw direct criticism from parties which consider the project anachronistic because of the profound conflicts among Communists, and therefore reject it.[4]

Gorbachev put an end to the pulling and hauling on a new world conference. In a long conversation in May 1985 with Gianni Cervetti, a member of the PCI Direzione and chairman of the Communist fraction in the European parliament, the CPSU general secretary labelled the project "completely untopical," and let it be understood that he considered this type of overall Communist conference outmoded. Gorbachev emphasized that the time of the Comintern is over. The CPSU, like the PCI, desires "numerous and fruitful relations" with the largest possible number of progressive forces in Europe... without too many formalities and with the goal of mutual understanding."[5]

Unity in Diversity Among Progressive Forces?

The notable new orientations of Gorbachev's CPSU toward the Communist parties are in many ways reminiscent of positions developed during the 1960s, especially by the PCI--and often in sharp contrast to the CPSU. Indeed, Gorbachev used an interesting echo of Togliatti in explaining the revisions made, speaking of "dialectical unity in the entire organism of forces struggling for peace and progress."[6] Earlier, before his ascension to the top job in the CPSU, he had told representatives of the PCI that "Berlinguer's criticisms (of the Soviet Union) were not without value."[7]

These new views are notably connected to a new estimate of the "progressive forces" in the West. In Moscow's eyes the Western Communists have lost much of their importance vis a vis these other forces; indeed, the preferential relations of the CPSU with the Communist parties often prejudice its ties with "progressive forces." It is not coincidental that the CPSU ideologues have picked up the notion of "new internationalism," supposed to characterize future cooperation among progressive forces.[8] Until recently they had rejected this concept, developed by the Italians and Romanians as champions of the autonomists in conscious contrast to Soviet style proletarian internationalism.[9]

This idea of a "new internationalism" has led the CPSU to re-evaluate social democracy. The new version of the CPSU program eliminated the views of the 1961 document,[10] where the "rightwing Socialists" still ranked as in Comintern times as the "most important ideological and political prop of the bourgeoisie in the workers' movement." But now the social democrats are classified as a part of the "international Communist and workers' movement," with this gloss:

> However deep the divergences may still be between the different currents of the workers' movement, they are no obstacle to a fruitful and systematic exchange of opinion, for parallel or common actions against the danger of war, to normalization of the international situation, to abolition of the remains of colonialism, in the interests and rights of the workers.

This courtship of the parties of the Socialist International does not signify any search for ideological convergence, a fact underlined by the obligation in the revised program (and also in the updated statutes of the CPSU)[11] for a determined struggle against "revisionism" and "reformism." It is rather a part of Moscow's endeavor to win the widest possible following for the Soviet detente offensive against the U.S. The same ambition holds for the

"democratic mass movements" in the West, among which
Moscow now counts the "new social movements" which have
arisen in the past few years alongside pro-Soviet front
organizations and the union movements. These "mass
movements" were named for the first time in the revised
program as a fourth current of the forces favoring peace
and progress, together with really existent world socialism,
the international Communist and workers' movement and
the national and social-revolutionary liberation movements
in the Third World, the three traditional chief components
of the anti-imperialist struggle. The new Soviet leadership
thereby underlines its intention to cultivate a relationship
with mass and alternative movements, over and above
relations with the governments of the West and their
parliamentary opposition, "to help the peoples to intervene
themselves in the questions of war and peace."[12]

Quantitatively, the Twenty-seventh CPSU Party
Congress was in Soviet eyes an undoubted success in
international party relations. The number of guest delegations had increased considerably, with 153 instead of the
123 present at the Twenty-sixth Congress in 1981. All the
Communist state parties were present except the Chinese
(invited) and the Albanians (not invited), while all of the
non-ruling parties invited did appear. Besides this, thirty-
three social-revolutionary and national-democratic parties
and movements were represented, plus twenty-three
socialist and social democratic parties (among them fifteen
members of the Socialist International), and two non-
socialist parties of special importance to Moscow, the
Indian Congress party and the small farmers' Center party
of Finland.

The question here is, do Soviet declarations of intent
merely imply greater tactical flexibility designed to
preserve the Soviet claim to leadership in the Communist
party system and still win over non-Communist "progressive
forces" for Moscow's aims? Or do they signal real readiness
at the top of the CPSU to discard an outmoded type of
behavior stemming from the late Comintern period and
actually take steps in the direction of "new
internationalism," in the sense employed by the
autonomists?

The answer to this question is relevant to other areas
of Soviet policy also, but the question remains open for the
moment. Nevertheless, there are some indications that the
new accents in Gorbachev's policies are more than tactical
variations. What are the reasons that caused Gorbachev's

rethinking of party relations (and other areas), and what political aims do they imply?

Harmonizing Foreign Policy and Internationalism

One reason has already been mentioned: that Moscow too has recognized that Marxism-Leninism has lost its earlier cohesive force and no longer exercises any attraction on the gradualist Western European Left. Unlike his predecessors, Gorbachev no longer seeks to win the various currents in the workers' movement for the goals of Soviet foreign policy by reminding them of common roots, or appealing to purported common values and inferring from them a principled identity of interests in international policy. Instead of the class question, he is campaigning on common interests in the basic questions of mankind's survival, above all in reference to problems of disarmament, the environment, and policies toward the Third World.

In this change of language Gorbachev is evidently trying to bring the character of party relations into harmony with Moscow's new patterns of thought and action.[13] To be sure, the new version of the CPSU program still gives express emphasis to the revolutionary and combative character of Soviet foreign policy. At the same time, Gorbachev used the Twenty-seventh Congress to mix a negative estimate of the NATO camp (equals "imperialism") with a remarkable stress on strategic rethinking in foreign policy. Thus he argued for the conclusion of mutually acceptable compromises aiming at longterm cooperation between East and West. The preservation of peace, he said, takes priority over the class question, for a global conflict would in the nuclear age lead to the destruction of the human race.

Gorbachev even maintained that in the interaction of competition and contest between the two systems "a world totality is taking shape, contradictory, but clinging together in dependence." Although he repeatedly referred to Lenin in order to present his line as the logical further development of the original Leninism, the idea of mutual dependence (vzaimozavisimost') in a world totality actually breaks with the ideas and positions of the Soviet Union's founding father.

For relations with the state parties of the "socialist community" of the Warsaw Pact and CMEA system, Gorbachev's new approach amounts to a pragmatism oriented toward efficiency and success. The intent is to stress the economic factor in relations with these states and enlist them in increasing measure in the modernization of the Soviet economy. All-around cooperation among the Communist parties of the fraternal countries was accentuated in the CPSU program--for the first time--as the most important "propulsive force" for the unity and solidarity of the socialist community. But the program speaks simultaneously of "consideration of the situation and interests of each country," and the final resolution of the Twenty-seventh Congress goes further, referring to the "increasing importance of mutual enrichment through reflections, ideas, and experiences of socialist construction," as well as to the necessity "to find mutually acceptable solutions even to very complicated problems." Evidently the Soviet leaders have in mind a concept of more organic, less crisis-prone and better coordinated relations between the USSR and the members of the socialist communities, which would grant them more freedom of action, to the extent compatible with the Moscow general line.

It is interesting that when speaking of the socialist states (the "world socialist community") as a whole, Gorbachev's political report went beyond the general language of the revised program and the final declaration expressing a desire for closer cooperation. He said:

> In our opinion it is worthwhile to examine more closely relations inside the socialist world as a whole. We do not believe that the ⟨socialist⟩ community is separated by barriers from the other socialist countries. The CPSU advocates honest, open relations with all Communist parties, with all states in the world socialist system, and desires comradely exchanges of opinion with them. In the first instance, we are endeavoring to see what unites the socialist world.

One may thus expect that the new Soviet leaders will intensify the diplomatic offensive directed at countries like China, North Korea, and Yugoslavia, and using a pragmatic and flexible approach attempt to avoid the mistakes of their predecessors, in order to win over the socialist state system as a whole to support Soviet foreign policy. One piece of evidence for increasing pragmatism in these relations is an important change in the relevant area of the Central Committee apparatus--the ideologically-minded

Konstantin Rusakov, former Central Committee secretary and chief of the influential department for "liaison" with the Communist parties of socialist countries, has been replaced by the economic technician and CMEA expert Vadim Medvedev.

Political Influence of the West European Left

The clearest case of CPSU revisionism in foreign relations is found in its relations with western Communists. When the Soviet political expert and ideologist Vadim Zagladin was asked in April 1986, during the PCI Seventeenth Party Congress, for his evaluation of the PCI's self-characterization as an "integrating part of the European Left," (i.e. identifying itself with that Left) he amazed the interviewer with his answer: the CPSU has no objections to the PCI decision to enroll itself in the Western European Left; after all the CPSU considers itself an "integrating part of the European Left."[14]

Zagladin's answer is symptomatic of the new regime's political evaluation of the gradualist Western European mass parties of the Left as a whole--with special emphasis on the SPD and the PCI. In Brezhnev's time the necessity for unity of action between Communists and Social Democrats was stressed, especially in the struggle against "imperialism" and for the preservation of peace. At the same time the CPSU strongly opposed the formation of a "Euroleft" composed of Social Democrats and Communists, with specific political and programmatic ideas for a "third way" between capitalism and real socialism. The Soviets saw in these tendencies an explosive charge which might endanger ideological unity among Communists. In polemical discussions, they admonished the fraternal parties that fundamental differences separated Communists from Social-ists, for example "in the methods and ways of making the transition to socialism, on the content of the concept 'socialism' itself, in the understanding of freedom, dictatorship, and democracy."[15]

Gorbachev has struck a new note since he became general secretary. Among other changes, he has shaken up the International Department of the CPSU apparatus, responsible for relations with non-ruling Communist parties, social democratic parties, "democratic mass movements," and the various parties and movements in the Third World. The replacement of its old chief, Comintern veteran Boris Ponomarev, by career diplomat Anatoliy Dobrynin signals a drastic change of function of the department. Reportedly, its main emphasis is now on development of new ideas and concepts in foreign and security policy. The tasks of preserving ideological orthodoxy to energize the revolutionary process and to oppose dangerous ideological-programmatic "social democratization" in the Western European Communists seem to have taken a back seat. In future, the International Department is supposed to make sure that the political action program of the CPSU for foreign relations is backed by the largest possible number of progressive forces in the West. The chief dialogue partners are the parties of the "Euroleft," and also the wide spectrum of "democratic mass movements" in Western Europe.

Gorbachev has here a competent specialist in Anatoliy Chernyayev, whom he named his chief foreign policy counsellor after the departure of Andrey Aleksandrov in February 1986. Chernyayev, deputy chief of the International Department since 1970, has specialized in the European left, concentrating on social democracy. He has travelled widely, in England, Italy, France, Spain, and the Federal Republic, and knows Western Europe well. In contrast to Zagladin, little is known about Chernyayev's background, since he has published little and received little public attention. Among Soviet and PCI insiders he is considered a realistic, principled, and openminded political expert.

There are a number of reasons for the change in Moscow's approach to the movements of the "Euroleft," of which only two will be discussed here. The attempt to win the Western European Left's support for Moscow's ideas on arms control and disarmament stands in the foreground. The Socialist International and the Socialists of NATO countries have criticized the Strategic Defense Initiative in common documents and actions, speaking out for a serious examination of Gorbachev's new proposals on security policy.

It has not escaped the Soviets that Socialist and Social Democratic politicians in France, Italy, Spain, Portugal, Greece, Norway, Austria, and Sweden exercise considerable and often determinant influence as presidents or chiefs of government. But Moscow also sees another important factor--in parties like the SPD, the British Labor party and the PCI which affect affairs from the opposition, standing ready to take the reins of government. Both PCI leader Alessandro Natta, who met with Gorbachev in

January 1986, and PCI "foreign minister" Giorgio Napolitano, who met with Dobrynin in July, 1986, have emphasized that their Moscow talks concentrated on political problems and especially security questions; their well-known ideological divergences had played no role-- quite in contrast to previous occasions.[16]

A second important motive for the Soviet reevaluation of the "Euroleft" can be found in new Soviet attitudes toward the European Community. In its more differentiated foreign policy, Moscow is stressing the idea that both superpowers, while maintaining their military-strategic bipolarism, are creating additional centers of power (tsentry sily) on other levels. Among these developments toward a "multipolar" and "multidimensional" world, the Soviets accord great importance to the European Community, which recent Soviet analyses see as gradually becoming more cohesive, not only economically but also politically and even militarily.[17]

At a PCI meeting in Milan in late 1986, Zagladin noted that in future the Soviets would actively pursue a "Westpolitik" analogous to Willy Brandt's "Ostpolitik" of the 1970s.[18] Earlier, in a radical turn from former Soviet positions, Gorbachev had declared (first in talks with PCI European deputy Cervetti, then with PSI leader Bettino Craxi and SPD chairman Brandt) that he was ready to recognize the EC not just as an economic but also as a political unity, and to "seek a common language on concrete international problems."[19] As a sign of this position, in December 1985 the Supreme Soviet played host to representatives of the Socialist fraction in the European parliament, who sounded out the possibilities for closer relations between the EC and the Soviet Union.

This re-evaluation of the EC is an important part of Moscow's overall foreign policy offensive against the West. It has led the Soviets to make a positive evaluation of PCI engagement in the EC. Where the Soviets earlier found cause for criticism, they no longer see an ideological danger to the cohesion of the Communist party system in the increasingly close cooperation between the SPD and the PCI, both pro-EC forces in the "Euroleft." Looking toward possible political advantages for Soviet foreign policy, Moscow is instead rather pleased.

The Soviet leaders may be indulging themselves in the illusion that with the help of the "Euroleft" they can uncouple Western Europe from the U.S. However, the new ideas seem linked to the expectation that the

"Euroleft" will push the West Europeans toward a more energetic defense of specific regional interests against Washington. Moscow has an eye here on security policy, but hopes also that the economic power and technology of Western Europe can increasingly be used to aid the planned modernization of the Soviet economy. Moscow finds it significant that the Left argues for "Western Europe's self-assertion" inside the Atlantic alliance, a slogan coined by the SPD in 1984 and then picked up by the PCI.

Summary and Prognosis

When one compares the documents and materials of the Twenty-seventh CPSU Congress with the estimates of preceding congresses, it is striking that there are no direct references to the Soviet claim to be the model for and leader of the Communist party system. Gorbachev seems in fact to care less about strengthening the worldwide image of the Soviet Communist model of society than about preserving the USSR's hard-won status as a power possessing equal rights and weight in the world with the United States. International party relations have now clearly and consciously been subordinated to this goal. The replacement of the ideologue Ponomarev by the pragmatist Dobrynin underlines this, as does the nomination of Gorbachev's confidant Aleksandr Yakovlev as a Central Committee secretary. A North American expert like Dobrynin, Yakovlev has played a major role in rethinking Soviet foreign policy and is supposed to have drafted the foreign policy section of Gorbachev's political report to the congress.

This new view of the international Communist party system does not much concern itself with the inner circle of state parties in the socialist community. The CPSU will presumably, as in the past, grant them scope for action only insofar as they are ready to contribute to the modernization of the Soviet economy and back the general line of Soviet foreign and security policy. Moscow's flexible and pragmatic approach is instead directed to the wider circle of the other parties in the socialist system and in the capitalist West. The new CPSU leaders evidently hope that by renouncing an obligation to ideological conformity (largely counter-productive) in the Communist movement they can exert influence on these parties to support Soviet foreign policy.

Earlier Soviet leaders tended to keep a specially tight rein on the Communist parties during phases of East-

West detente. Ideological and programmatic solidarity within the movement seemed to them the most important presupposition for a strong bargaining position with the class enemy without. Gorbachev, the efficiency and success-oriented "wheeler-dealer," appears here as in foreign policy to be rethinking old ideas, and to envisage leading a Communist campaign for common goals which employs flexible tactics fitting national and regional conditions. This particularly concerns the Western European Communists, whom he is actually encouraging to enlist in the ranks of the "Euroleft."

With this change of language, Gorbachev has no doubt found greater readiness for dialogue and understanding in the various parts of the "Euroleft," and especially the PCI. The representatives of this current of opinion in Western Europe are in fact among those who argue that the readiness of the new Soviet leaders for compromise and comprehensive cooperation should be put to the test, without illusions, but with a serious desire to seek settlements.

All this presents not only new opportunities, but also fresh problems for Moscow. The new attitudes of the Soviet leaders have seriously upset the traditionalists among Western Communists, such as the comrades in France, Portugal, and Greece. Symptomatic of this insecurity were questions put to Zagladin at the Milan Unità festival in 1986 by members of Armando Cossutta's dogmatic minority in the PCI; they wanted to know if the CPSU was about to liquidate socialism, or turn soft on the United States in security policy. [20]

Representatives of the "Euroleft," for their part, insist that the policy of rethinking in the Soviet Union be carried farther and produce consequences. The PCI, for example, is encouraging the Soviets toward institutional reform and argues for greater autonomy of the individual states in the "socialist community." The SPD thinks that the European Community can only play the more active role the Soviets desire if the latter pay more attention to specific Western European security interests, and therefore demands, for instance, a revision of Soviet offensive military doctrine. The new social movements, in their political manifestation as "Greens," do not see themselves as clearly "left" in the traditional sense as Moscow seems to think. Fundamentally anti-NATO, they also plead just as strongly for human rights in the East and oppose Eastern industrialization that destroys the environment.

The complex relations of the "Euroleft" with the Soviet Union are summed up by a cartoon which appeared in the PCI daily l'Unità after Zagladin had included the USSR in the "integrating part of the European Left." The cartoon Zagladin, asked how the persecution of dissidents fit this policy, replied "they're in Siberia, and Siberia is not part of Europe."[21] The scepticism here, shared by the "Euroleft" in general, throws a floodlight on the limitations of Soviet policy: East-West partnership to secure peace, which the gradualist Left desires, does not mean a partnership of basic values. It even presupposes a competition of ideas and conceptions concerning a society fit for men to live in.

Thus Gorbachev's new orientation away from "ideologizing," and toward "politicizing" relations with the Western European Left has indeed enlarged Moscow's room for maneuver in foreign policy. But at the same time ideological challenges will probably increase (in connection with reform developments in China also) and especially if the Soviets do not succeed in bringing about drastic reforms at home and creating a more "organic" system of alliances. But there is no turning back to that impressive "world Communist movement" which existed in the time of the Comintern, the Cominform and even in the era of world conferences. With the exhaustion of the propulsive force of the Soviet system, as Enrico Berlinguer noted in 1981, the myth of the world Communist movement has finally evaporated.

NOTES

1. Cf. part I, chapter 6 on the Chinese party.
2. Pravda, March 7, 1986 and February 26, 1986. Other references to remarks at the congress refer to this source. Cf. also Wolfgang Berner, "Sowjetische Aussenpolitik und Aussenbeziehungen der Partei auf dem XXVII. KPdSU-Kongress," Beitrage zur Konfliktforschung 16, no. 2 (1986): 121-145.
3. Pravda, March 6, 1986. It is interesting that Gorbachev repeated the central elements of this position in his meeting with Milanko Renovica, chairman of the presidium of the Central Committee of the LCY on December 13, 1986.
4. Cf. my analysis "Moskaus Projekt einer neuen Welt-

konferenz," Deutschland Archiv 18, no. 2 (1985): 121-123.

5. See l'Unità, May 22, 1985, for the interview with Cervetti. Although eighty parties had agreed to a new world conference by late 1986, Gorbachev has not called for a conference, according to Czech presidium member Vasil Bilak, "because of the present situation in our movement." See Rude Pravo, December 6, 1986.

6. Pravda, October 26, 1986.

7. L'Unità, March 12, 1985 reports these remarks, made when Gorbachev attended the funeral of Enrico Berlinguer in June 1984.

8. Soviet representative Yuri Krasin, in a roundtable discussion on "Unity in the Conditions of Multiplicity," Probleme des Friedens und des Sozialismus 29, no. 10 (1986): 1365. Krasin is prorector and professorial chairman of the CPSU Central Committee Academy for Social Sciences.

9. Cf. my contribution "The Fundamentals of Proletarian Internationalism," in Lawrence L. Whetten, ed., The Present State of Communist Internationalism (Lexington, Mass.: D.C. Heath and Company, 1983) pp. 3-17.

10. Pravda, November 2, 1961.

11. See Pravda, March 7, 1986.

12. Pravda, February 8, 1986. Gorbachev was replying to questions raised in the PCF newspaper l'Humanité.

13. Cf. Jerry Hough, "Gorbachev's Strategy," Foreign Affairs 64, no. 1 (1985): 33-55; Seweryn Bialer and Joan Afferica, "The Genesis of Gorbachev's World," Foreign Affairs 64, no. 3 (1985): 605-644; Charles Glickham, "New Directions for Soviet Foreign Policy," Radio Liberty Research Bulletin, RL Supplement 2, September 6, 1986; Archie Brown, "Change in the Soviet Union," Foreign Affairs 64, no. 5 (1986): 1048-1065.

14. Interview with la Repubblica, April 12, 1986.

15. Petr N. Fedosseyev et al., Chto takoye "demokraticheskiy sotsializm"? (Moscow: Politizdat, 1978), p. 113.

16. Cf. l'Unità, February 9, 1986 for the interview with Natta; ibid. June 13, 1986 for the interview with Napolitano.

17. Cf. my article "Gorbatschow zeigt aussenpolitisches Profil. Kurskorrekturen oder Konzeptionswandel?," Osteuropa 36, no. 1 (1986): 3-21.

18. L'Unità, September 14, 1986.

19. In discussion with Craxi, Pravda, May 30, 1986.

20. La Repubblica, September 15, 1986.
21. L'Unità, April 14, 1986.

5

Modifications to Democratic Centralism

Attempts at reform in a number of Communist parties have provoked discussion and controversy within the Communist party system over the character of democratic centralism as the internal organizational principle of Communist parties. In Poland, before and during the Ninth PZPR Party Congress in July 1981, discussions between the party leadership and the fractious party base on the principle of democratic centralism led to temporary concessions in the direction of real democracy. In Hungary dispositions favoring freer expression of opinion and interests are visible even in leadership circles, though proposals for measures to implement such ideas are discussed only among experts and in social science publications.

In Italy, the PCI liquidated democratic centralism in practice at its Sixteenth Party Congress in March 1983, accepting the existence of diverse currents of opinion as well as the principle of free formation of majorities inside the party. Finally, in France the serious defeat of the PCF in the European elections of June 1984 (11.3 percent of votes cast) renewed discussion about relaxing a democratic centralism whose rigid practice had contributed heavily to the paralysis of the party. The then Politbureau member Pierre Juquin, for example, advocated "modification" of the principle, with the notable justification that it had been "developed sixty years ago in another society and under other conditions."[1]

This disavowal within important CP's of a central principle of Marxism-Leninism called the CPSU's ideologists to war. They glimpsed the danger of slippage toward right-revisionist and opportunist positions, with the unavoidable result of an erosion of the Soviet Communist model of society. Among the many explicit Soviet warnings, one came from the future state and party chief Konstantin Chernenko in 1982. Referring to the critics of traditional democratic centralism, he said:

> It is no accident that anti-Communists of all varieties, together with opportunists and revisionists of various tendencies and shades, angrily attack the Leninist principle of democratic centralism and attempt to distort and discredit its true nature. The history of the CPSU and of the other Marxist-Leninist parties shows that elements of various sorts hostile to the party as well as traitors to Marxism-Leninism and proletarian internationalism have continually carried out such attacks. Yes, even in our times opportunist and revisionist elements cultivate malicious falsification in every way: they attempt to undermine the Leninist norms and fundamentals of party life, especially the principle of democratic centralism; they move toward forming factions and groups, on the road to becoming enemies of the party. The experience of history teaches that all attempts to weaken the leading role of the party in building the new society have as a consequence a weakening of its ties with the masses; they unchain forces hostile to socialism, so that all such attempts give rise to the danger of the restoration of capitalism.[2]

In this chapter I will discuss the origins and basic elements of democratic centralism and its interpretation by Soviet traditionalists and their supporters. Then I will investigate the initial attempts to surmount it, listing the arguments with which the CPSU seeks to check the erosion of this traditional organizational principle of Communist parties.

Basic Elements and Ideological Foundations

Democratic centralism, as an integral component of Marxism-Leninism, its "vital law," constitutes an obligatory principle of organization and rule both for Communist parties and for the political-societal system of Communist-ruled states.[3] In party structure it postulates:

Direction of the party by an elected central body; periodic election of all leading party organs from the bottom up; collective leadership; periodic accountability of elected organs to the organizations which elected them; strict party discipline and subordination of the minority to the majority; unconditional obedience to the decisions of higher organs by lower organs and by party members, whose manifold experience is infused into the decisions of higher organs.[4]

In the political system of the Communist-ruled lands democratic centralism links the "unity of central direction and planning" in the state, economy, and society to the democratic initiative of the workers. It thereby sets up a hierarchy of all elements of the whole system, with the Communist party at the top. As the leading power in state and society, the Communist party is called upon to organize the unity of all forces in society, so that it may consciously enforce the objective laws of societal development. In consequence, the CPSU is defined in the Soviet constitution of 1977 as "the leading and directing power of Soviet society," as the "nucleus of its political system, of its state and societal organizations."[5]

Drastic consequences resulted from this claim by Communist parties to represent a prototype for the entire future Communist society, and from their practice of transferring this principle of internal organization as completely as possible to the whole political system. This was a postulate which, for Zdenek Mlynar, a member of the Czech Communist leadership during the Prague spring:

in and of itself--that is, even when carried out in an ideal manner--necessarily leads to the creation of an authoritarian, totalitarian, and undemocratic system, and fundamentally negates the possibility of pluralist democracy. For it inevitably means that there is no legal possibility for the individual in society to express himself on his own account independently of the power center, to combine with others in communities of interest and exert influence on political intent and decision. If the power center at all times has the possibility of permitting or forbidding the expression of alternative political tendencies, a system of pluralist political democracy can never arise, but only a more or less centralized system of totalitarian political dictatorship.[6]

Communist parties see democratic centralism as an integral part of their character as Marxist-Leninist parties militating for revolutionary change in society. Thus it can be dropped only at the price of giving up the revolutionary goal. Communists think they alone have in Marxism-Leninism a scientific theory that demonstrates the objective laws of societal development leading to the attainment of the final Communist goal. As the "conscious vanguard" of the working class--the best organized and most progressive class--they are thus granted legitimacy vis-a-vis all other forces to take the lead in determining the dynamics and direction of the revolutionary process, and through methodical action aiding the objective laws of history to achieve their fulfillment.

The presupposition for the success of this scientifically based political strategy and tactics is the monolithic unity of the Communist party, which is tied to a high degree of discipline. It is just the "unity of revolutionary theory and revolutionary practice" that guarantees that the laws of historical design will prevail, so that the virtues and propulsive forces of socialism can reach their full development.

The Communist parties believe they possess in Marxism-Leninism a reliable scientific compass to guide their political action. Because possible mistaken developments are obviated by collective leadership, criticism and self-criticism, and by extensive discussion within the party in the spirit of the "Leninist norms of party life," in the Communist view no objective possibility exists for ideological-political conflicts in their ranks. The same can be said for the socialist state: the leading role of the working class, based on socialist ownership of the means of production and exchange, guarantees the objective conformity of individual and general social interests. If democratic centralism demands strict unitary planning and direction of all parts of the societal organism, it also concedes to the citizens numerous possibilities for individual initiative and cooperation in the organs of state representation, enterprises, and social organizations. The East German definition puts it thus:

Democratic centralism is the guarantee of a friction-free and unitary functioning of societal life in all areas and in all parts of the country. It makes it possible for central direction and planning, a necessary condition for the maintenance of the political power of the working class, to be tied to a variety of ways, methods, and means to arrive at the common goal. It prevents any limitation on the unfolding of mass initiative by local or corporate egoism or by bureaucratic regimentation from above.[7]

If conflicts nevertheless arise in the party and end in deviation from the Marxist-Leninist line, such as left-sectarian "dogmatism" or right-opportunist "revisionism," the traditionalists maintain that they can be traced back to subjective mistakes by individuals and can in no way be blamed on the party as a whole, for "the party is always right." Special vigilance is supposedly prescribed for the right-revisionist variant, since these deviationists frequently succumb to the pressures of the ideologists of democratic socialism, and take positions characterized by anti-Sovietism and anti-Communism which are helpful to the class enemy. In any case it is the task of every party member "to defend the unity and purity of the party on the basis of Marxism-Leninism."[8] Advocates of deviating views are to be purged on the basis of the principles of Marxism-Leninism, at the latest when they undermine the unity of the party by forming factions and pursuing schismatic activities.

The Historic Demarcation from Social Democracy

Democratic centralism serves among other things in Communist parties as a rampart against anarchist tendencies and spontaneous democracy at the party base (Luxemburgism). For "anarchism as an ideological expression of rootless, radicalized elements of the petty bourgeoisie, which see themselves as helpless in the grasp of historical forces, denies in general the necessity for a unitary organization of revolutionary forces, directed from its center, and in particular denies the necessity of the working class."[9] Furthermore, the bourgeoisie in its battle against socialism relies on anarchist, petty bourgeois, and spontaneist elements—in 1921 in Kronstadt, as in 1953 in the GDR, 1956 in Hungary, and 1968 in Czechoslovakia—to confuse the workers and upset the planned development of the new society.[10]

Sometimes the concept of "democratic centralism" is put forward as a counter-model to "bureaucratic centralism," the ruling principle of the bourgeoisie. Whereas under socialism the people itself decides its fate, so runs this dictum, in state monopoly capitalism a small group of the bourgeoisie uses the state apparatus to exercise real and uncontrolled power. This is expressed, according to an East German author, in "the continuous perfection of bureaucracy as a system for regimentation and oppression of the workers, hindering progressive forces from exerting influence on state policies and on the development of the state apparatus."[11]

Grave consequences ensued from a very different aspect of democratic centralism. Historically, Lenin thought this instrument for decision-making in the party one of the most important principles that characterized the distinction between the Bolsheviks and the national sections of the Comintern, "parties of a new type," and the social democracy of the Second International.[12]

Lenin considered that the emergence of various currents in the social democratic parties had not merely weakened their organizational impact and their combative readiness against the class enemy. Worse, these currents had set the stage for the abandonment of the revolutionary character of the socialist parties and for their treason in 1914, as revisionist tendencies became factions and influenced their parties toward a gradual integration of social democracy into the capitalist system.

The bolshevization of the Communist parties that enforced democratic centralism was thus not merely intended to guarantee for all Communists a binding, program-oriented unity of action--the necessity of which has never been disputed by democratic socialists or indeed any political party. It was intended above all to guarantee ideological fidelity to the party line, so that parties of the revolutionary left would no longer be revolutionary in theory and revisionist in practice, but would conduct themselves as revolutionaries in theory and practice. Therefore the Marxist-Leninists drew the ideological frontier line between themselves and social democracy more sharply after World War II when the socialists and social democrats adopted a reformist policy, oriented to basic democratic values. Taking pluralism as their guiding principle, they no longer considered socialism to be a final goal but instead an "ongoing task."

The use of democratic centralism to demarcate the border with social democracy simultaneously implied a fundamental renunciation of political democracy. The trend was strengthened by generalizing the value of Bolshevik experience in organization--the experience of a party which traced its success precisely to the strict centralization of internal decision-making. The famous twenty-one conditions of the Second Comintern Congress in 1920 had pledged member parties to the principles of democratic centralism and thus to centralized organization, iron discipline, and the grant of extensive authority to the party leadership.[13]

These principles were extended at the Tenth Congress of the Bolshevik party by prohibiting groups and factions with political platforms in the party (something which had earlier been common and accepted practice). Though tailored to the conditions of civil war in Russia and characterized by Lenin himself as "too Russian," this form of democratic centralism, with the entire emphasis on centralism, was gradually carried over to all Comintern parties. Finally, during the Cominform period it became the organizational principle of the East European states that had come under Soviet hegemony.

In theory--and also in the self-image of the traditionalists--democratic centralism is perfectly reconciliable with freedom of choice in party decision making. To quote again the Czech reformer Zdenek Mlynar:

> In its theoretical conception, democratic centralism in the life of Leninist parties represents the way in which democratic discussion prior to acceptance of a given decision can be joined with the strict discipline of all party members after its acceptance. It is supposed to allow for the expression of various conflicts and opinions during the process of preparing the decision, so that with the principle of the subordination of the minority to the majority, a majority can then make a given decision binding on all, including those who originally opposed it. Thus theoretically the democratic and the authoritative principles remain in balance: the democratic principle comes into play during the preparatory phase before a decision, while the authoritative principle and strict

centralism are asserted in the execution of a decision.[14]

In practice, however, democratic centralism created a party hierarchy with gradations of power, guaranteeing a frictionless processing of orders from the top down, and replacing election to leadership positions with cooptation. Democratic centralism thereby became the chief instrument to defend the positions of any top leadership and its version of party tasks, strategy and tactics. The role of the party member became limited to applause and to lesser organizational chores.

The ideologically conditioned belief in a way to socialism/communism governed by scientific laws, hence objectively free from any conflict, has shown itself to be a fiction. The suppression of divergent opinion in Communist parties and of pluralistic development in Communist societies, which grew from this belief and was enforced by the weapon of democratic centralism, has hindered any timely correction of errors and has repeatedly led to outbreaks in Eastern Europe--sometimes accompanied by violence. Mlynar finds that the problem was "whether the political parties which came into being as instruments for the installation of a political dictatorship of the Soviet type could restructure themselves into political organizations capable of solving political and social tasks that often contrasted with their original ones. The experience of the Prague reforms showed, he wrote, that "the transformation of a totalitarian system into a democratic one is impossible without the transformation of the ruling Communist party into a democratic organization."[15]

Attempts to Overcome Democratic Centralism

It was scarcely an accident that democratic centralism in its Marxist-Leninist version became the central point of attack for those forces in Eastern Europe which urged reforms in party, state, and society that would recognize objectively existent conflicts of interest as such, and seek to solve them constructively with a broad association of participants. This demand did not merely imply a redefinition of the "leading role of the party," but reduced its complex directing function throughout the political system to one of providing inspiration and ideals. The reformers were thinking especially of greater autonomy for the parliament, the other political parties, the trade unions and, not least, the press--measures envisaged in the reform process in Czechoslovakia in 1968, and in Poland in 1956, in 1980 and thereafter.

As experience in Eastern Europe had shown that democratization of the political system could not be realized without a democratization of the ruling Communist party, pressure for reform boiled down to a demand for radical change in the functional mechanisms of the party itself. The reformers thought that if conflicts of interest were to be settled and representatives of alternative ideas given a chance to create new majorities, alternative candidacies must be permitted in party elections, with the minority then allowed to solicit support for its opinions and continue to present them for discussion at the relevant levels of the party.

Certain concessions in this spirit by the Polish party leadership were tentatively sketched out during the preparations for the Ninth PZPR Congress in July 1981. Responding to demands from the party base for more democracy, free and secret elections were permitted to elect congress delegates and members of the leadership at the various levels. The real novelty here was not in the secret character of the elections, already prescribed in the old party statutes but carefully structured by electoral commissions appointed from above. It rather consisted in the tie between electoral secrecy and the right--cited in the modified party statute--"to present an unlimited number of candidates." The number of candidates was to be "higher than the number of persons to be chosen."[16]

The explosive effect of this modification of democratic centralism is shown by the fact that the Ninth PZPR Congress witnessed a massive replacement of previous cadres in electoral and appointive positions.[17] These innovations were abruptly suspended by the PZPR leadership with the proclamation of martial law on December 13, 1981, and the simultaneous strengthening of the powers of the party executive.[18]

Earlier, the Czechoslovak party of the Prague spring had taken even more drastic measures to overcome democratic centralism. Beyond existing party stipulations for free internal discussion and freedom of choice, each party member was statutorily guaranteed the right to maintain his dissident opinion and--while obeying the decisions of the majority--could continue to present it, associating himself for this purpose with other members of the party.

Minorities could thus have a democratic means of gaining a majority for their arguments. On this point the draft for a new party statute of August 1968 ran as follows:

> Democratic centralism means: the democratic formation of the program and the political line of the party as the result of a creative Marxist-Leninist activity based on the most recent scientific findings, on confrontation of opinions with respect for the various considerations of Communists and non-Communists;
> --participation of party members and representatives of subsidiary party organs in the formation and execution of party policy, and uninterrupted checking of its correctness in practice;
> --equal opportunity for all members of the party to express their views on party policy, to present suggestions, and to criticize any member, any organization, and any party organ.

> The whole system of party organs for leadership and control will be structured from the bottom to the top by election, evaluation, and control of the functionaries....Prior to the acceptance of important decisions, the Central Committee of the Communist Party of Czechoslovakia or the central committees of the national territorial organizations shall organize an internal party discussion or consultation. They will inform the party at large of the results.

The draft statutes proposed the following rules to govern the relations of majority and minority:

> In the spirit of democratic centralism the minority subjugates itself to the majority and carries out decisions that have been taken. The minority has the right: a) to formulate its positions and to desire them to be included in the final protocol; b) to maintain its opinions, and on the basis of new knowledge, once decisions have been tested in practice, to demand a new decision on its views by the relevant party organ or organization....

> No measures other than argument may be used against representatives of a minority opinion, as long as they

do not enter into fundamental contradiction to the program and statutes of the party. Formations by members of a minority outside the framework of the statute, formation of groups of party members with their own fractional discipline are not admissible.[19]

The upper levels of the CPSU reacted with alarm to these proposals, which would effectively have done away with the myth whereby the party (or rather its leadership) is always right. The new ideas were borne by a dynamic of greater independence in the affairs of state and society (strengthening of the parliament in Prague and the Sejm in Warsaw; independence for Solidarnosc etc.) The CPSU characterized them as an "attack on the unity of the ranks of the party," especially condemning the "embodiment in the statutes of the 'rights of minorities and group opinions.'" The threat of a victory by the reformers over the traditional concept of democratic centralism was a major factor in the decision by CPSU leaders to suppress the Dubcek leadership and to pressure the PZPR leaders "to make a change in the course of things."[20]

The PCI has made the clearest departure from democratic centralism of all the Eurocommunist parties. It drew the logical consequence of accepting political democracy of a Western type, i.e. a strategy of maintaining a presence everywhere in a complex society in order to win the broadest possible electoral support. In the new version of its statutes in 1979 the PCI specifically rejected a "sectarian" and "clerical" concept of the party, as expressed in the principles of democratic centralism that place ideological purity and fidelity to the party line above political effectiveness. It revised the earlier version of a primary ideological bond of party members to "Marxism-Leninism," referred to the "secular and rational character" of the party, reduced the requirements for membership to agreement with its "political program," and underlined its intention to "measure itself in working out this program against all currents of modern thought."[21]

This new orientation reached its culmination in the Sixteenth PCI Congress of March 1983.[22] It was symbolized in the decision to take from democratic centralism its rank as a "principle" for the internal functioning of the party, and to make of it only a "method" for internal decision-making. The most drastic change in the statutes was undoubtedly this phrasing:

When divergences occur on important questions of the direction of political action in the party leadership or in regional or federation executives, and no unitary formulations can be found, they must be submitted without delay to the elected organs for discussion and decision....Beyond this, it is necessary and useful for the executive organs to make it clear, when setting forth party lines and decisions, what divergent hypotheses it discarded in arriving at the formulation of its proposals.[23]

Before this innovation, a minority in any party organ was not only obliged to respect the opinion of the majority, but also to keep its opinions to itself during further discussions and support the decisions taken. The process and the contents of discussion at the top remained hidden from the party as a whole (including the Central Committee). The openness in decision-making now fixed in the statutes, and the protection and legitimation of internal dissent now give a minority the chance to plead openly for its positions, for example by publication of its opinions in the party press or by horizontal communication with party organizations at the same level, with the hope of some day possibly becoming a majority. In any case, the long existent currents in the PCI, which resembled party factions, were formally legitimized in their right to exert influence. Over and above these far-reaching changes, the Seventeenth PCI Congress in April 1986 sanctioned the right of any party member to express dissent not only within the party but also in public without fear of exclusion from positions of leadership.

Criticism from Moscow

The Soviets strongly condemned such concessions to democracy in party affairs and in society, for they called into question the rights of party leaders that Moscow has rigidly maintained. The CPSU claims to admit the possibility of varying positions in the Communist parties, insofar as they do not lead to the formation of groups and factions. Such divergences are usually overcome in the course of regular party activity. As the history of Russian social democracy shows, there can even be majorities and minorities in a Communist party. And in all this the demand for subordination of the minority to the majority must not be interpreted as forbidding "the principled battle against opportunism and opportunists."[24]

Here it becomes plain that the traditionalists with all their emphasis on discipline and subordination mean to keep open a way to support "revolutionary" groups inside Communist parties. Where factions loyal to Moscow are under pressure from "revisionist" majorities, as in Finland after 1966, in Czechoslovakia in 1968, among Eurocommunist parties since the beginning of the 1970s and in certain trends in Poland, Moscow returns to the patterns of behavior developed in the Comintern and Cominform years. These were exemplified in the overthrow of disobedient CP leaderships in the 1920s or the call to the Yugoslav Communist base in 1948 to overthrow the "Tito clique."

These are special cases, however. As the quotation from Chernenko cited above emphasizes, the CPSU leaders normally have no reservations on the principle that "revolutionary Weltanschauung" and "proletarian organization" are unbreakably linked, since "a basic idea in Lenin's teaching on the revolutionary party is the organic unity among ideological, political, and organizational principles."[25] In this spirit the CPSU conducts bitter polemics against attempts to transform the "party of a new type" of the Leninist mold into a "new party with a broad opening to the masses."[26] This attack is clearly directed against the PCI, which under Togliatti after 1944 consciously replaced the model of a cadre party with the concept of a mass party with a broad social base. Under Berlinguer, the PCI developed further in the direction of a pluralist, left-reformist peoples' party.

In the Soviet view, such appeals for "a catch-all party" in the last analysis reflect "liquidating tendencies, whose goal it is to loosen the organizational structure of the Communist parties by changing their proletarian social base, to undermine their influence on the masses, and in the end to lure them into a 'social partnership' with capitalism, i.e. to give them a social democratic imprint."[27] Such transformations of Communist parties into parties of "the old, social democratic type" are, according to the Soviets, attempts to cancel out Lenin's historical achievement of 1903--the creation of a "truly new proletarian and revolutionary party," which distinguishes itself "fundamentally from parties of a social democratic type." For the Soviets, all real successes of the workers' movement have been won by parties of this Leninist stamp, while social democracy has led "neither to revolution nor to socialism."[28]

Seen thus, any loosening up of democratic centralism must in CPSU eyes unavoidably end with a loss of identity by a given party, and consequently of its capacity to initiate a socialist revolution or play the leading role in state and society. On the other hand, abiding by democratic centralism "prevents the spread of opportunism, sectarianism, and deviations from revolutionary Marxist-Leninist theory."[29] This stricture is directed not least at the ruling Communist parties of Eastern Europe, for in the Polish reform process one of the chief concerns of the CPSU leaders was the danger that the PZPR might, in ideological softening and factionalization, lose what Brezhnev called its "militant capacity," and thus its leading role.

Future Prospects

In their hegemonic domains the Soviets are able to halt and reverse such developments by the exertion of pressure, and where necessary by military power. The Czechoslovak Communist party has reverted since the purges conducted by the Husak leadership in 1969 to a reliable party of the Marxist-Leninist type, and the PZPR leadership under Jaruzelski is trying to conform to Moscow's demand of March 1981 "to make a turn in the course of things"[30] and stabilize the party along traditional organizational lines. But it remains questionable whether in the long run the leadership elites of Eastern Europe can succeed in enhancing the governability of increasingly complex industrial societies, which rests on efficiency and consensus--unless they introduce articulated decision-making in the party and institutionally guaranteed feedback. Only the future can show whether developments in Hungary can offer a solution--but they are in any case not automatically transferable to other Warsaw Pact states.[31]

It is also an open question whether the internal structural reforms to which Gorbachev aspires will in the long run also be applied to the principles of democratic centralism. His intentions to increase openness (glasnost') in decision-making and to strengthen "socialist self-administration" in all areas of society must, should they be successful, unavoidably bring with them modifications to the principles of democratic centralism in their traditional form. Gorbachev's proposal of January 1987 may possibly begin this process. He proposed that party committees from the local level up to union republics be given the right to the secret ballot in electing party secretaries, "placing any number of candidates on the ballot."[32] Certainly manipulation and interference from above would in no way be excluded here. Thus Gorbachev emphasized in the same breath that he had no intention of touching the centralist principle, and that "decisions by higher organs, including those on personnel matters, are binding on all lower organs." Nevertheless, the general secretary's proposals are a nearly revolutionary initiative, compared to previous mechanisms for decision-making in the CPSU. If put into practice, they could have striking consequences in revivifying party and society, not only in the Soviet Union, but also in their effect on Eastern Europe.

In any case, the CPSU will not be able to halt a process of programatic westernization in important parties like the PCI that will affect their internal functional mechanisms. With the liquidation of democratic centralism an important boundary line on the historical frontier between Communism and social democracy will gradually disappear. The new orientation leads in fact to what Moscow feared in Brezhnev's time—to moving away from Lenin's theory of the party and its ideological-political implications. This is both logical and consequent if one agrees with the PCI that real socialism of the Soviet Communist variety has "lost its propulsive force."[33] As the PCI leaders see it, overcoming traditional democratic centralism is in fact the prerequisite for the ability of Communism to absorb the new impulses arising from society, drawing from them new impetus for a consensus-oriented democratic and socialist transformation.

NOTES

1. "M. Juquin envisage des 'modifications' du centralisme démocratique," Le Monde, June 26, 1984.
2. "Vopros, vazhniy dlya vsei partii," Voprosy istorii KPSS 26, no. 2 (February 1982): 15.
3. Cf. Georg Brunner, Das Parteistatut der KPdSU

1903-1961, (Cologne: Wissenschaft und Politik, 1965); Karl Wilhelm Fricke, ed., Programm und Statut der SED (Cologne: Wissenschaft und Politik, 1976); Zdenek Mlynar, "Leninistische Partei und pluralistische politische Demokratie," Forum ds 4, no. 7 (1979); Georg Schüssler et al., Der demokratische Zentralismus: Theorie und Praxis, (East Berlin: Staatsverlag, 1981); Ronald Tiersky, "Das Problem des demokratischen Zentralismus," in Heinz Timmermann, ed., Die kommunistischen Parteien Südeuropas (Baden-Baden: Nomos, 1979); Heinz Timmermann, "Aspekte der innerparteilichen Struktur und Willensbildung bei den 'Eurokommunisten,'" in Sozialismus in Theorie und Praxis, Festschrift für Richard Löwenthal (Berlin and New York: de Gruyter, 1978); Michael Waller, Democratic Centralism: An Historical Commentary (Manchester: University Press, 1981).

4. "Demokratischer Zentralismus," rubric in Kleines Politisches Wörterbuch (East Berlin: Dietz, 1983), p. 172.

5. Cited from the text of the Soviet constitution in Neue Zeit 39, no. 41 (1977): 16.

6. Mlynar, "Leninistische Partei," p. 112.

7. Kleines Politisches Wörterbuch, p. 172. Emphasis added.

8. Fricke, Statut der SED, p. 121.

9. Schüssler, Der demokratische Zentralismus, p. 17.

10. Ibid., p. 31.

11. Ibid., p. 18.

12. Cf. my analysis "The Fundamentals of Proletarian Internationalism," in Lawrence L. Whetten, ed., The Present State of Communist Internationalism (Lexington, Mass.: D.C. Heath, 1983) p. 4ff.

13. Point 12 in "Leitsätze über die Bedingungen der Aufnahme in die Kommunistische Internationale," in Claus D. Kernig, Die Kommunistischen Parteien der Welt (Freiburg: Herder, 1969), column 30.

14. Mlynar, "Leninistische Partei," p. 109.

15. Ibid., p. 108 ff.

16. For the reworked PZPR party statute, see IX. Ausserordentlicher Parteitag der Polnischen Vereinigten Arbeiterpartei 14.-20. Juli 1981: Dokumente und Materialien (Warsaw: Interpress, 1981), p. 371. Cf. also the written report and the speech by party chief Stanislaw Kania, ibid., p. 58ff. and p. 151ff.

17. A good overview of the entire subject can be found in David S. Mason, "The Polish Party in Crisis, 1980-1982," Slavic Review 43, no. 1 (1984): 30-45. Cf. Werner Hahn, Democracy in a Communist Party: Poland's

Experience Since 1980 (forthcoming).

18. On this point a lead article in Polityka in March 1982 stated: "In a party under martial law the institution of elections is suspended. Any changes in the composition of the party organs at all levels are made by cooptation, nomination, or deposition. In this framework, decisions can be made by party instances (plenary sessions) or by the executive organs of the PZPR committees." The PZPR secretariats in the voivoda committees received the right to dissolve party organizations at the base and in enterprises. See Jozef Cegla, "Grudzien, Luty i dalej," Polityka 26, no. 3 (March 6, 1982): 1.

19. The statute appears in Wolf Oschlies, "Zum Entwurf des neuen Parteistatuts der KPC," Berichte des Bundesinstitut für ostwissenschaftliche und internationale Studien (hereafter BIOst) no. 12 (1969): 69 ff.

20. As cited in the communique of a meeting between the leaders of the CPSU and the PZPR on March 4, 1981, in Pravda, March 5, 1981.

21. The 1979 statute can be found in La politica e l'organizzazione dei comunisti italiani (Rome: Editori Riuniti, 1979), pp. 149-193.

22. Cf. my article "Die genetischen Mutationen der KPI," Die Neue Gesellschaft 30, no. 5 (1983): 449-455.

23. L'Unità (Milan edition), March 6, 1983.

24. Boris Leibson, contribution to a roundtable discussion organized by Problems of Peace and Socialism on the theme "An Organized, An Organizing Force," Probleme des Friedens und des Sozialismus, 26, no. 12 (1983): 1628. Leibson is a member of the Academy of Social Sciences of the CPSU Central Committee.

25. Nikolai Owtscharenko, "Partei der revolutionären Erneuerung," Neue Zeit 44, no. 22 (1984): 20.

26. Vadim Zagladin, "Vazhneyshiy faktor sotsial'nogo progressa," Pravda, June 5, 1984. Zagladin, a Central Committee member, is first deputy chief of the International Department of the CPSU Central Committee secretariat.

27. Owtscharenko, "Partei," p. 19.

28. Zagladin, "Vazhneyshiy faktor," and Owtscharenko, "Partei," p. 19.

29. Owtscharenko, "Partei," p. 19.

30. Communique of CPSU-PZPR meeting, March 4, 1981, Pravda, March 5, 1981.

31. Cf. Josef Schmidt, "Interessen in der ungarischen

Gesellschaft. Theoretische und politische Aspekte," <u>Berichte des BIOst</u> no. 29 (1979), and Maria Huber, "Die Ungarische Sozialistische Arbeiterpartei. Binnenstruktur und Funktionsprobleme," <u>Berichte des BIOst</u> nos. 23-24, (1984).

32. See <u>Pravda</u>, January 28, 1987 for Gorbachev's speech "On Restructuring and the Personnel Policy of the Party." Emphasis supplied.

33. "Riflessione sui drammatici fatti di Polonia: Aprire una nuova fase della lotta per il socialismo," PCI party resolution, <u>l'Unità</u>, December 30, 1981.

6

The Chinese Communist Party

In 1977 the Chinese Communist party (CPC) began to emerge from a long period of self-imposed isolation and to reinsert itself into the international Communist party system. After Tito's August 1977 visit to Beijing, the Chinese party reestablished official ties with the League of Yugoslav Communists in 1978--with a party which the Chinese had previously considered a paradigm of revisionist degeneration, a clique of renegades worthy only of bitter opposition.

This move represented Chinese willingness to put ideological divergences among Communists into perspective. If such differences were no longer to stand in the way of interparty cooperation, the Chinese party could make a gradual return to the international party system. In fact, in a series of remarkable initiatives the Chinese have recently renewed ties with a number of other parties. The new intimacy with the Yugoslavs was followed by successful approaches to the Italian, Spanish, Greek (Interior) and San Marino Communist parties in 1980; the Dutch and French parties were next in 1982, and 1983 saw new friendship with Mexico's leftist Socialist Unity party, then the Communist parties of Sweden, India (Marxists), and Belgium, followed by the parties of Australia, Norway, Portugal, Austria and Finland. So far the Chinese party has established "good relations with, or contacted, more than eighty Communist parties and organizations the world over."[1] However, one must note that that number includes political groups with long-standing sympathies towards and official ties to Beijing, some of them organizations that had split away from their national parties in the 1960s--old friends which the Chinese did not wish to desert.

With these approaches to fraternal parties, the Chinese party's period of isolation has ended--an isolation the Chinese brought on themselves after the rupture of their relations with Moscow in the early 1960s, with the confusion and disruption of the Cultural Revolution that followed. During this period, the Chinese became strangers in the Communist camp. Official links to most Communist parties were severed, and formal ties were retained only with the ruling parties in Albania, North Korea, North Vietnam, and Romania, and with nonruling parties in Burma, Indonesia, Kampuchea, Malaysia, New Zealand, and Thailand.

In contrast, the Chinese party is now successfully attempting to make its presence felt on all five continents, and it is particularly interested in demonstrating to the international Communist party system the extensive reach of its influence. In the spring of 1983, the Chinese party even began to put out feelers to some of the governing Communist parties in Eastern Europe, sounding out possibilities for renewing official ties.

Success came in 1986, when Poland's president Jaruzelski and his East German colleague Honecker both traveled to Beijing. Now it seems to be only a question of time until official links to other parties in Eastern Europe are reestablished.

The Chinese party's obvious efforts to play a more active role in international Communism fit logically into the framework of Beijing's new foreign policy and reflect changes in emphasis that have been taking shape since 1981/1982. These changes signify a divergence from the policy that had been in effect since 1977. That policy was designed to present China, the United States, Japan, and Western Europe as a unified front to block the expansionist urges of the Soviet hegemonists. Apparently Beijing was worried that this policy made China much too dependent on Washington. As the United States' partner, China might eventually be forced to sacrifice some of its hard-won independence.

In a way, China's new political line amounts to a revival of the Three Worlds theory, which is still formally valid. China uses this theory to justify its call to the Third World (and China considers itself a Third World nation) to form an alliance to resist the imperialist and hegemonic tendencies of both superpowers (the First World) and Western Europe and Japan (the Second World).

This framework allows the Chinese leaders to keep their distance from the United States--a country perceived as violating Beijing's interests on the issue of Taiwan and as pursuing imperialist goals in the Third World. The Chinese also seem interested in heading off confrontation with the Soviet Union so that they can devote themselves to their main objective: rapid development and modernization of the Chinese economy. For the long run, this policy emphasizes Beijing's determination to demonstrate its distance from both superpowers, to gain more room for maneuvering in foreign policy, and above all to secure China's independence. Indeed, there are signs that China can imagine its long-term relationship with the Soviet Union and the United States "only as that of an equal among equals, if not even the first among equals."[2]

In reinserting itself in the international Communist party system the Chinese party is clearly not trying to recreate a structured, or even a centrally controlled world Communist movement, that would elaborate an obligatory general strategy for all parties. The three world Communist conferences in 1957, 1960, and 1969 aimed at this goal, which Beijing now rules out, if only because it fears that the CPSU would force the Chinese into a minority position, subjugating them to Soviet will. Past experience justifies such a fear. China instead expects its change in course to create more leverage for carrying out the general line of its foreign policy, which is designed to shore up China's independence and broaden its elbow room.

This perspective shows that the Chinese party's interest in wide-ranging relations within the Communist party system are comparable to Soviet interests. Though their methods differ, both parties are less concerned with supporting independent revolutionary movements than they are with lining up Communist parties in support of their own foreign policy goals. In contrast to the 1950s and 1960s, both Moscow and Beijing consider their activities in world Communism today as secondary. However, both parties will continue to consider successes or failures in this arena as more (Moscow) or less (Beijing) important factors in their foreign relations as a whole.

Historical developments form the background for the following examination of key aspects of the Chinese Communist party's return to the Communist party system and for an analysis of the consequences of that return for the world Communist movement. What are the premises of and motives for Beijing's new activities? What expectations do other parties attach to renewed connections with the Chinese party? What is Moscow's reaction to the new developments? What makes up the "new unity," and what are its prospects? This last question is important in the light of the fact that this "new unity" represents a key point in Beijing's discussions with other parties. The "new unity" is considered a necessary feature of future relations within the Communist party system. It appears to represent a consensus of views in the Chinese leadership concerning international relations and there are no indications that the fall of Secretary General Hu Yaobang will bring changes in this policy.

A New Tack in World Communism

In order to make meaningful statements about China's new orientation, to understand the character of the change, and to analyze its future prospects, it is essential to examine Beijing's attitude to the world Communist movement during the entire postwar period.[3] Since World War II the Chinese party has repeatedly changed its policies, and the changes have been exceptionally radical. However, a closer look shows that the frequent policy shifts can be traced back to a basic constant in the policies of China's leaders: their effort to ensure China's security and independence and to secure a place in the world that is worthy of China's history, significance, and national pride. The positions that the Chinese party has taken towards the international Communist party system have thus always expressed Beijing's specific national interests, important as they have been for the processes of diversification and change in world Communism. Ideological affinities or demarcations have tended to hide this important fact, and continue to do so. Beijing says that all party work and connections abroad should be subordinated to "the central task for the new historical stage...to carry out the socialist modernization drive." For only then will China be able to make its "greatest contribution to world peace, international economic prosperity, and human progress....This would also be the CPC's greatest contribution to the working classes and to the peoples of the world."[4]

After the proclamation of the People's Republic in 1949, China's active role in the Soviet-led Communist party system stemmed in large part from China's need for

Soviet support. In the circumstances of the time, the USSR was the partner best suited to help China develop an industrial base and fend off possible American efforts to weaken or even overthrow the Communist regime. It was no accident that at the first world Communist conference in Moscow in 1957 Mao Zedong emphasized the special position of the Soviet Union. He insisted on including a phrase in the final twelve-party declaration that spoke of the USSR's leadership of the socialist camp. This statement ran contrary to a growing desire for autonomy that had surfaced among Communist parties after the Twentieth Congress of the CPSU in 1956, and participants in the world conference later reported how irritated parties like the Poles and Italians had been by Mao's presumptuous statement.[5] However, given China's particular situation at the time, Beijing's maneuver made perfect sense. China's move was designed to oblige Moscow, as the leader and strongest power in the socialist camp, to aid the economic development of weaker partners, especially the People's Republic of China, and to give substantive aid to their economic development and in their struggle against imperialism.

As the Chinese gained the impression that the Soviets were not fully living up to their obligations, and worse, were trying to strike a balance with the United States at the expense of fraternal parties, they changed their tactics. In an attempt to pressure the Soviet leadership into reversing its political course, the Chinese tried to mobilize the Communist parties against the CPSU's policy of coexistence. The result was a painful defeat for the Chinese. It is true that at the second world Communist conference in 1960, held at Beijing's urging, the Chinese party managed to put some of its theses into the final declaration, thus modifying the CPSU's influence. Each party was explicitly guaranteed independence and equality in interparty relations, a passage of great significance for the future structure of world Communism. Henceforth, parties could refer to this guarantee as justification for the development of their own domestic policies in the name of "national particularity." Nevertheless, the Chinese party remained totally isolated in its original plan to mobilize world Communism against the CPSU. With the exception of the Albanians and the few Southeast Asian parties mentioned above, no party was willing to align itself with China.

In the end, Beijing's last attempt to use the world Communist movement to promote its own goals resulted in a fiasco. In their June 1963 "Proposal for a General Line for the World Communist Movement," the Chinese developed their own program in twenty-five points.[6] Soviet concepts like peaceful coexistence and peaceful transition to socialism were branded as an abandonment of the mission of the world revolution. The proposal also summoned Communists worldwide to overthrow leaders who steered their parties toward reformism. The program amounted to a declaration of independence from Moscow, with far-reaching consequences for the Communist movement. It "legitimized in principle all future special path concepts or claims to autonomy by other members of the Communist state and party system."[7]

For the Chinese this was small consolation. A few years later, they were forced to recognize the failure of their efforts to split the movement horizontally and move the command post of world revolution from Moscow to Beijing. Pro-Chinese splinter parties throughout the world never advanced beyond the role of sects. After Beijing's opening to the West in the 1970s and in the course of de-Maoization the Chinese gradually dropped these groups, which began to look elsewhere for guidance. Many of them turned to the Albanians, or simply dissolved themselves.

It was only toward the end of the 1970s that the Chinese showed some renewed interest in the development of those Communist parties with which they had severed ties. (The Spanish Communist leader Carrillo's visit to Beijing in 1971 was an episode without political consequences.) This interest indeed manifested itself at first in rather negative assessments. In its 1977 statement on Eurocommunism, Beijing dismissed the "peaceful, parliamentary" path to socialism to which some parties subscribed as inevitably leading the revolution to a dead end. The Chinese insisted that a Communist party is defined by the exaltation of the dictatorship of the proletariat and the pursuit of revolutionary overthrow. It claimed that "old and new revisionists" had turned away from these two essential principles.[8]

Statements like these, however, should probably be considered as ideological rearguard actions. They seem to have been designed to facilitate China's change of course during the transitional phase from de-Maoization toward a more pragmatic approach. In spite of his pronounced scepticism toward Western Communists, Deng Xiaoping was simultaneously admitting that these Western parties were moving toward greater independence from Moscow.[9] This was an obvious signal that Chinese leaders were willing to reflect on their relation with the Communist party system and to consider the reintegration of the Chinese party into the network of party relations.[10]

The New Chinese Internationalism

Having reestablished relations with the League of Yugoslav Communists in 1978, Beijing actually began in 1980 to renew relations with a number of Communist parties, showing a willingness to put various interpretations of Marxist doctrine into perspective and accept pluralization within the system. A Chinese source puts it as follows:

> The CPC considers Marxism its theoretical foundation. It holds that Marxism is a guide to action, not a rigid dogma. The fundamental principles of Marxism are not only to be adhered to, but also to be developed. It adheres to dialectical materialism and historical materialism, trying to analyze and solve problems according to the Marxist stand, viewpoints and methods. However, Marxism is a developing science. The CPC should not rely on those principles and conclusions that are outdated and not appropriate today. Nor should the CPC rigidly adhere to principles that have not been well-developed or are applicable to only one particular situation. It should integrate Marxism with reality. Practice shows that not only some of Marxism's isolated conclusions are in need of changes but also its fundamental principles need constant testing, additions, enrichment, and development. This principle has been repeatedly expounded by classic Marxist writers. In fact, Marxism has great vitality precisely because of its flawless integration with practice--it has provided approaches for answering new questions and solving new problems. Both the success of the October Revolution led by Lenin and the victory of the Chinese revolution led by Mao Zedong proved this. It has also been proved by the revolutionary practices of other Communist parties.[11]

In addition, the reestablishment of party relations was characterized by a new concept of unity that was of specifically Chinese coinage. This new view of unity was firmly embedded in a global foreign policy intended to obtain more independence, and reflected China's growing national self-confidence. By determining the date for the reestablishment of relations and setting Beijing as the site for negotiations and agreements, the Chinese party clearly demonstrated this new self-esteem. Certainly, one should not overlook the fact that in the late 1970s, when turning to the Communist parties of Yugoslavia, Italy, and Spain, the Chinese were looking first to parties critical of the CPSU. The Chinese went to these parties hoping to line them up in an united front against the Soviet hegemonists. Interestingly, even in today's climate of normalization, in countries like Greece, Sweden, and India, where the Communist movement has split into pro-Soviet and autonomist branches, the Chinese still show a preference for the party that has emancipated itself from Moscow.

Nevertheless, the change in foreign policy emphasis, which began in 1981 and stressed independence and separation from both superpowers, resulted in an important reorientation of the Chinese relation with the Communist party system.[12] Chinese readiness to reestablish relations with a particular party was no longer based on the extent of that party's aloofness toward the CPSU. Instead, Beijing began to stress the importance of a party's desire to cultivate friendship and cooperation with the Chinese party. A prime example of China's new attitude was the normalization of relations with the French Communist party (PCF), which took place despite the PCF's strong ties to Moscow. Asked if a party could simultaneously retain good relations with the CPSU and the CPC, former Secretary General Hu Yaobang replied that a decision of that sort was an internal decision for that party, in which Beijing did not wish to interfere.[13] This new attitude eases the process of normalization with the state parties within the Soviet alliance, which has been moving at full speed since the reestablishment of relations with the Polish and East German Communists.

Conditions for Normalization of Party Relations

There is, then, some logic behind the Chinese call for a "new unity" among Communist parties and for a "new type of relations" without the traditional "rigidity of dogmas and harmful models."[14] In this context, the Chinese are even talking again about "the international Communist movement," although China had for a time questioned the need for the movement's existence. Beijing now says that since Communists "have great ideals and great goals in common" they should unite and work together for the future.[15] If they allow themselves to be led by "principles of independence, complete equality, mutual respect, and non-interference in each other's internal affairs," it is even possible for the international Communist movement to "grow and blossom."

This last formulation took a central place in the section devoted to international party relations of Hu Yaobang's report to the Twelfth Party Congress in September 1982.[16] Placed in the new statutes of the Chinese party,[17] it is at the heart of the new internationalism of the Chinese party. The consequences of this new internationalism were first discussed extensively in 1983 in a position paper entitled "Principles Governing Relations with Foreign Communist Parties."[18] Because this paper offers a sketch of current Chinese positions as they have emerged in Chinese normalization talks with the parties mentioned above, it must serve as a basis for the following explanation of Beijing's new internationalism.

The starting point for the Chinese position is the perception that Communist parties have been leaning more and more towards the ideas of independence and self-reliance, and that these ideas have become the "main tide" within the international Communist movement. The Chinese note that even Marx and Lenin spoke out against attempts by the German Social Democrats and the French Socialists to make rules for the parties of other countries. As heavily as Marx and Engels stressed the orientation of the workers' movement toward the same final goals, so did they point out just as clearly that "each people or nation carries out its own proletarian struggle."[19] Accordingly, there should today be no "center of leadership," no "leading party," "patriarchal party" or "ready-made model" of socialism that other parties must follow. Practice has shown, according to the "Principles:"

> that any attempt to forbid another party to become independent, to impose one's views on another party or to interfere in another party's internal affairs can only lead to setbacks and failures in the revolutionary

cause of the countries concerned, and will only undermine the international Communist movement.[20]

Therefore, the "Principles" goes on to say, no party has the right to put itself above other parties, "no matter how long its history, how early its revolutionary success, or how rich its experience." Only a party that "maintains its independence and self-reliance" can be successful. With this in mind, Communist parties of all countries should "respect each other" and "learn from each other and emulate the strengths of others to overcome their weaknesses." Basically, it should be normal, unavoidable, and in a certain sense even useful if differences of opinion and disagreements arise. It is only important that no party allow itself to "lightly criticize openly another party, much less gather together one group of parties to criticize or repudiate another party or parties." Instead, differences of opinion" should be reconciled in the spirit of seeking truth from facts, by exchanging ideas, promoting mutual understanding and friendly consultations." Should problems arise that cannot be solved in this way, those involved must simply wait until practice has furnished an answer.[21]

This concept of a "new unity" in the Communist party system actually converges with the views on "new internationalism" propagated by parties like the Yugoslavs and Italians that have emancipated themselves from Moscow, or (like the French party) have developed at least some ideas of their own. The same holds true for the substance of the argumentation developed by Beijing in its demand for independence and self-reliance for any and all parties--in sharp contrast to Soviet ideas. Beijing argues on two levels: objective developments and subjective experiences.

On the first point, objective processes, the Chinese party posits that "countries differ from each other in socio-economic conditions and development," and that "class relations ⟨and⟩ the balance of class forces," as well as the "consciousness and organization of their peoples" have developed in different directions. Today, therefore, "revolution and construction cannot follow a fixed model or formula." The "Principles" goes on to say that the historical experience of the international Communist movement shows that the success of revolution and of socialist construction can only be achieved if strategies and tactics fit the respective country and can only be determined by the

Communist party of that country.[22] As an example of such flexible adjustments of Marxism to concrete conditions Hu noted the revolutions in Russia and China. In his speech on the one hundredth anniversary of Karl Marx's death Hu remarked:

> If Lenin and the Russian Bolshevik Party had failed to act in the light of the actual conditions in Russia but had held rigidly to the specific conclusion of Marxism that the proletarian revolution must win victory simultaneously in the major capitalist countries, what would have been the result? There would have been no victory of the October Revolution. The triumph of the Chinese revolution is the most significant event in the history of Marxism's development after the October Revolution. Under the conditions then prevailing in the world's East, Comrade Mao Zedong and our Party integrated the universal truth of Marxism-Leninism with the concrete realities in China, relied closely on the peasants--the powerful ally of the working class in the rural areas and the main revolutionary force against feudalism--and found the correct path of encircling the cities from the countryside. From this flowed the birth of Mao Zedong Thought and the triumph of the Chinese revolution. If we had not taken this path, but had held rigidly to the traditional mode of revolution in modern Europe, that is the seizure of state power through armed urban uprisings, what would have been the result? There would have been no triumph of the Chinese revolution.[23]

This passage is indirectly but clearly aimed at the traditional Soviet concept of international Communist relations, still advocated until recently by Brezhnev's chief ideologist Mikhail Suslov. The concept admits that there can be a variety of _forms_ of socialist revolution and building socialism. At the same time, however, it makes the claim that in effect the October Revolution and the creation of a Soviet Communist societal system formed the basic model for later socialist transformations in other countries. Hu Yaobang, however, has explicitly taken his distance from such interpretations. During his visit to Italy in the summer of 1986, taking up the position expressed by the late PCI leader Berlinguer, Hu stated:

Marx tells us that the actual historical and social process is undoubtedly influenced by ideas and ideologies. In this process, ideas and ideologies (including Marx's ideology and other revolutionary ideology) are in turn restricted by the actual movement, and even undergo real changes and gradually acquire new meanings, new forms, and new content. I appreciate this scientific approach of Comrade Berlinguer toward Marxism. Facts prove that there is no fixed formula as to how different countries should go socialist and how they should build socialism, nor is it possible to find a set of ready answers in books. In the final analysis, socialism is still being tried out in practice. In the West, you have been trying to explore a way to socialism in the new and complicated situation in the post-war years. In the East we are carrying out reforms with a view to perfecting the socialist system and exploring ways as to how to build socialism with Chinese characteristics. We do not deny that we face most complex and strenuous tasks, nor do we have any doubt that it is in the complex and arduous human endeavor to change society as well as nature that Marxism has developed considerably. We are convinced that so long as we dare to practice and be good at summing up experience, we will succeed in our exploratory efforts and thus make due contributions to the progress of human society and the development of Marxism.[24]

In the second justification of their demand for the independence of individual parties, the Chinese pointed to their subjective experiences with the leadership claims of the CPSU in world Communism. The "Principles" states that it cannot be denied that because of the irregularity of the historical process worker consciousness develops unevenly, that "the proletariat and its political party of this or that country will, at different historical temporarily (sic) stand at the forefront of the international movement and find itself in a pioneer position."[25] This is an undisguised reference to the core sentence in the final document of the 1960 world conference, which runs: "recognized by all, the Communist Party of the Soviet Union is and remains the vanguard of the world Communist movement as the most experienced and tempered pillar of the international

Communist movement."[26] This prominence was in the Chinese view more an obligation than a privilege, and the unspoken Chinese reproach was that the Soviets had not lived up to it but instead interpreted it as a claim to leadership. The "Principles" says on this question:

> This position, however, should not become a means by which the proletariat and its party, particularly a victorious party, styles itself the "centre of leadership," or dominates or commands the proletariat and political parties of other countries, or interfere (sic) in others' international affairs. Nor can that party, because of its early revolutionary success, claim any right to monopolize or be the sole interpreter of Marxism-Leninism, and describe its own practice as the "universal truth" or "common law" or accuse anyone, who refuses to copy its way, of "departing from the classics and rebelling against orthodoxy."[27]

From the Chinese point of view, it is essential to reject such claims. If a country's Communist party has come under the control of the CPSU, foreign policy decisions will be affected as well. Hu Yaobang's report to the Twelfth Party Congress claims that China's independent foreign policy only survived by "resisting such control."[28] The Chinese party "opposes a so-called 'common strategy' and 'coordinated action,' which restrict the decision-making powers of parties.... All parties should have the right to decide their own positions on world affairs, and should not serve the interests of a larger party or any country's foreign policy."[29] Given the great importance Beijing attaches to an independent Chinese foreign policy, it is clear that the normalization of relations with a series of Communist parties in no way indicates any Chinese intent of even indirectly risking dependence on the CPSU by participation in a Communist party system led by Moscow.

Motives for Rejoining the Party System

After its negative experiences with the Soviet-run party system, it is extremely unlikely that the Chinese party aims even in the long run at reestablishing a relatively closed "world Communist movement," as Moscow desired to do under Brezhnev (for example with the

projected fourth world Communist conference).
Significantly, world conferences were not mentioned in
Chinese party documents or in discussions on normalization
with Communist party leaders. Party cooperation had
manifested itself in these conferences after the dissolutions
of the Comintern in 1943 and the Cominform in 1956. The
Chinese did not explicitly take a stand on the problem of a
world conference until early 1985, when a spokesman for
the Central Committee emphasized that such a conference
would be "harmful" to the struggle to preserve world peace.
Under current conditions, it would only "aggravate
differences and widen the gaps within the international
Communist movement."[30] The Chinese party's references to
past disagreements within the Communist party system are
conspicuously rare, and when they occur they are made
only in general terms. One of the few references occurred
in a remark Santiago Carrillo made to journalists in
Beijing. According to Carrillo, Hua Guofeng and Hu Yaobang
had criticized past Chinese support for the exclusion of the
Yugoslav Communists from the Cominform and praised Tito's
resistance to the Cominform.[31] Nor did the documents of
the Twelfth Party Congress and Chinese accounts of
normalization discussions with Western Communist leaders
make any mention of the Maoist splinter parties.[32] The
documents on these discussions commonly noted that all
parties had made mistakes.[33] All of this belonged to the
past, and it was now important for all parties to "join
hands again in a forward-looking spirit."[34]

There are two main reasons for the Chinese refusal to
deal with the specific facts of the aberrant development of
the world Communist movement. First, the party wishes to
avoid a clear and precise admission of its own mistakes.
After all, in the 1960s the Chinese party had attempted to
align the Communist movement with Beijing and make
Sinocommunism the model for Communists everywhere.
Obviously, Chinese self-esteem does not allow comprehensive or well-founded criticism of its own behavior during
that period. (To this day, Chinese refusal to condemn the
schismatic activities they provoked in the Japanese
Communist party forms an obstacle to normalization with
the JCP, which also places great value on self-respect).
One passage in the normalization talks vaguely suggests
that the Chinese had formerly misjudged the conditions
under which the Communist parties had to struggle.[35] At
the climax of the Cultural Revolution, the Chinese party's
"views on many things were in a muddle."[36] The party's

past erroneous practices" were a result of "the Lin Biao and Jiang Qing counterrevolutionary cliques," and the CPC has now "thoroughly exposed and criticized" them.[37]

This assessment fits with the Chinese judgment of the Cultural Revolution as a passing crisis arising from subjective goals--but it is only a single crisis in a line development that has otherwise been generally positive. This judgment conforms completely with the Comintern tradition of blaming mistakes on certain factions in the party. The party as a whole is thus kept free from any spot, and no doubts may be raised on the legitimacy of its claims to authority. On the other hand, Beijing now ranks the international Communist movement relatively low on its list of priorities for foreign relations. This is a new development, in contrast to the importance the Chinese gave to the Communist movement in the 1950s and 1960s-- and is the other reason why Beijing has no great interest in dealing with its past record in world Communism.

The reestablishment of relations with the Communist party system offers the Chinese additional leverage for the conduct of a foreign policy designed to assure China's independence and expand its elbow room. Thus the Chinese expect normalization of _party_ relations to lead to the improvement of _state_ relations. After all, in their visits to Beijing the secretaries general of the PCI and the PCE, Berlinguer and Carrillo, spoke out in favor of a strong and modern China and supported China's efforts to gain a worthy place in the community of nations.[38] In turn, PCF Secretary General Marchais spoke in Beijing of the necessity of improving relations between the "two great nations," China and France.[39]

In addition, by rejoining the Communist party system, the Chinese party is reinforcing China's prestige as an antiimperialist and antihegemonist power. It hopes to increase its chances of influencing those forces that are fighting for independence from the superpowers (like the members of the non-aligned movement) or those working for greater autonomy within the blocs (like leftists in Western Europe and--as Beijing hopes--some of the state parties in Eastern Europe). In any case, normalization of party relations fits Beijing's political line; the Chinese no longer want to give Moscow a clear field. Instead, from an independent position of their own, the Chinese want to make contacts around the world and strengthen the forces which China considers national and progressive in their aspirations to autonomy and independence.

The Chinese party's understanding of internationalism thus differs radically from traditional Soviet interpretations of "proletarian internationalism," and agrees on many points with the ideas of the Yugoslav and Italian Communists, the most determined champions of independence in interparty relations. Like them, the Chinese support ideological pluralism within the ranks of the Communist parties and reject the creation of a common political strategy. This stand implies that differences are natural and in some ways stimulating. By promoting "overall analysis and understanding of the very complex international events," such differences offer Communist parties an opportunity to learn from and support each other. In contrast, open criticism of other parties can only have a negative effect-- even if the criticism is justified.[40] For Beijing it is quite another matter "if a party and the country it rules practice hegemonism, dictate to, manipulate, and control other parties, interfere in the internal affairs of other countries, subvert and invade other countries."[41] Such acts must be vehemently condemned because such behavior by a Communist party in power "will damage the image of socialism if it practices hegemonism and this will make it difficult for those parties not yet in power to speak to the people."[42]

This concept of a "new unity" is a sign that Beijing is trying to show a new low profile. By working to solidify relations with all powers that--in the Chinese view--are fighting for national independence and progressive changes in society, the Chinese party is overcoming the traditional character of Leninist proletarian internationalism, which gave priority to solidarity and cooperation among Communist parties.

In fact, the Chinese want to develop relations with other Communist parties, but at the same time they accord equal importance to relations with other "working class parties."[43] Like the Yugoslav and Italian parties, the CPC is reordering the old hierarchical system of progressive forces under the self-proclaimed leadership of Communist parties. It is exchanging this system for a richly articulated movement made up of formations with different ideological and political orientations, conducting relations in a spirit of complete equality and balance. The PCI leader Giancarlo Pajetta already called attention to this specific aspect of China's new policy during a visit to Beijing in 1980, when he referred to Chinese interest in a concept of internationalism "which includes relations with socialists, social democrats, and Third World countries."[44]

In this spirit, the Chinese have since intensified their relations with non-Communist "progressive forces" the world over. At the end of 1984, they maintained ties with 150 parties and organizations abroad.[45] By mid-1986, the number had risen to more than two hundred,[46] and the most important of these for the Chinese were "other progressive and friendly political parties and organizations in the Third World." In Beijing's view, the most important consideration is to "seek exchanges of views...on major issues such as the maintenance of world peace, safeguarding the rights and interests of the Third World and the establishment of a new international economic order. They also hope to promote mutual understanding and exchange experiences in party construction, the training of cadres, mass and economic construction."[47]

However, Beijing's attempts to improve contacts with various parties within the Socialist International (SI) should also be noted. These parties include the French Socialists, (with whom the Chinese had already established official relations on the occasion of Mitterrand's visit to Beijing in February 1981),[48] the British Labor Party and the Italian Socialists. The CPC's most active relations are indeed with the German Social Democrats--to whom Chinese representatives have expressed the wish to participate in some form in the work of the Socialist International. After the visit of SPD chairman (and SI president) Willy Brandt to Beijing in 1984, Hu Yaobang accepted the SPD's invitation to visit West Germany to discuss problems of disarmament, detente, and North-South issues. Over and above all ideological differences, the Chinese party is seeking to intensify its contacts with international social democracy:

> All these political parties, however, have considerable influence on their nations' workers as well as on the middle-class and petty bourgeoisie. Many of them are in power, take part in the government, or constitute the chief opposition parties with both domestic and international influence. Now they advocate improved relations throughout the world, an end to the arms race, North-South dialogue, and the development of the Third World. Many of their viewpoints on international affairs coincide with those of the CPC. They are also friendly to China, and are willing to set

up and develop cooperative relations beneficial to both sides.[49]

Beijing and Moscow

Up to now, the Chinese have left open the question of whether they will reestablish relations with the CPSU. However, when Gorbachev took office the CPC leadership did signal a change of course, calling the new general secretary "comrade,"[50] and once again explicitly referring to the Soviet Union as a "socialist state."[51] In doing so the Chinese leaders were giving up their earlier position that the Soviet Union had lost the characteristics of a socialist country. By the Soviet intervention in Czechoslovakia in 1968 at the latest, Beijing had decided to discredit the foreign policy conduct of "the Soviet revisionist clique of renegades," citing Lenin's phrase "socialism in words, imperialism in deeds," and distinguishing between "authentic socialism" and Soviet revisionist "pseudo-socialism."

Nevertheless, the Chinese still decidedly reject any reestablishment of party relations. They refused to respond to an invitation to participate in the Twenty-seventh Party Congress of the CPSU in February-March 1986. Party relations might be reestablished, Beijing says, only if Moscow eliminates the familiar "three obstacles to normalization."[52] The reference here is to Chinese demands that the Soviet Union pull its troops both out of the People's Republic of Mongolia and Afghanistan, and that it halt its support of Vietnamese expansionism in Indochina. However, Wu Xingtang, spokesman of the International Department of the Central Committee, has stressed that even if these obstacles are removed and party contacts are reestablished "the situation will never be reversed to the state it was in the 1950s."[53]

For its part, the CPSU first attempted to hinder Chinese reentry into the Communist party system by pressuring the autonomists, and then tried to limit the damage caused by the Beijing visits of PCI leader Berlinguer in April 1980 and PCE chief Carrillo in November of that year. According to Moscow, the Chinese policy of "selective normalization" was tantamount to harnessing the Communist parties to "its own hegemonist great power policies," and represented China's attempt to regain "its own lost prestige with the democratic forces in the world." Moscow charged that with these goals in mind the Chinese Communist party has been trying for almost twenty years "to force Beijing's hegemony of the world Communist movement and to replace the vital principles of Marxism-Leninism with Maoist concepts." China's plan was for Communist parties to become enemies, thus splitting and weakening the world Communist movement in order to better isolate the CPSU and the USSR.[54]

In fact, the Soviets were not able to defend this interpretation for very long. In early 1982, in the context of CPSU sensitivity to PCI reproval of the December 1981 coup in Poland, the CPSU openly criticized PCI-CPC relations. At the same time, the Moscow-oriented French Communist Party was already in close contact with the Chinese, working out the conditions for a visit by party leader Marchais to Beijing. The fact that the CPSU has now fallen silent on Chinese activities in the world Communist movement is certainly in part a result of Chinese abandonment of the idea of an united anti-Soviet front, with a display of interest in diminishing confrontation with the USSR. CPSU silence also clearly indicates a certain perplexity in Moscow on the best way to handle Beijing's new strategy in world Communism.

New life was breathed into Soviet-Chinese relations only when Gorbachev took office. This has not meant any great breakthrough; the "three obstacles to normalization" still stand in the way. Clearly, Moscow is counting on an improvement in bilateral relations on the state level to create the basis for reestablishing relations at a later time on the party level. This hope would explain why the Soviet leadership gave Jaruzelski and Honecker the green light for their trips to Beijing. Both men went to China in their capacities of both state and party leaders, and so paved the way for Soviet leaders to do the same sometime in the future.

In fact, China presents formidable problems to the Soviet leaders. By standing up for the independence of individual parties and treating the existence of divergent views among Communists as unavoidable and sometimes even useful, the Chinese provide an alternative model for cooperation within the Communist party system.[55] It was scarcely an accident that during his trip to China Enrico Berlinguer repeatedly emphasized just that idea in connection with CPSU claims to the right of leadership. The PCI leader maintained that the normalization talks were proof that divergences were no obstacle to dialogue and cooperation and that autonomy and equality could certainly be made compatible with "friendship, understanding, and

-111-

agreement."[56] Such an approach, he said, would be very significant, not only for relations between the PCI and the CPC, but "also for overall relations among Communist parties, and beyond these, among the forces striving for liberation, progress, and peace."[57] The success of these methods, said Berlinguer, would mean a "real leap forward in the international workers' movement."[58] In a speech in Bucharest in 1983, Hu Yaobang stressed that if more and more Communist and workers' parties moved in this same direction the result would be "a new situation in the relations among parties in various countries, and a new chapter in the international Communist movement would be written."[59]

Beijing and the Autonomists

All this doubtless leads objectively to a further weakening of the CPSU role in international party relations, and undermines Soviet efforts to structure the Communist party system and align it with Moscow. In the 1960s, the Chinese policies of polemics and splitting pushed autonomist parties, including the PCI, closer to Moscow. (An example is the organizing of the third world Communist conference in 1969.) Today the open and flexible positions of the Chinese party offer the autonomists stronger support and better opportunities to make the case for their own concepts of new internationalism. In this context, it is logical that it was the autonomists (and not the Chinese themselves) who declared their desire to renew relations with the CPC. Not least among their motives was the desire to change completely the character of the world Communist movement. The autonomists are drawn to the new Chinese internationalism because it is based on total independence and equality for each party. This concept makes it legitimate and even desirable for each party to determine its own emphases when working with others.

The Chinese and Romania share a desire to defend the national independence of socialist states regardless of all class ties. In addition, both countries believe that the various historical, political, and socio-economic conditions of any nation are the main reference points in the struggle for Socialism/Communism. During a trip to Bucharest, Hu Yaobang stated that "in the common struggle to defend the correct Marxist principles guiding international relations and relations among Communist parties of various countries, Comrade Ceausescu and the Romanian Communist party have more than once come out boldly at critical moments to give us their most precious trust and support."[60] In view of intense Romanian disagreements with the Soviets over the meaning of class and nation, this moral support by the Chinese is important and very timely. For the Yugoslavs, China's new internationalism is interesting because it includes the intent to widen maneuvering room for independent forces between the superpowers and supports the goals of Third World states and the non-aligned movement. It was no coincidence that Hu Yaobang placed great stress on this in a speech given in Belgrade when he honored "Yugoslavia's consistent policy of non-alignment,"[61] and "reaffirmed China's consistent position of supporting the non-aligned movement's aims... as well as its stand of opposing imperialism, colonialism, racism, and all forms of foreign domination and hegemonism."[62] This policy is tightly bound to the common desire of both parties to overcome the limitations of the Communist party system and to establish relations with a variety of parties and movements that work for national independence and socialist transformation. Indeed, according to Belgrade, it is not necessarily always Communist parties that lead the way in such processes of change. The essential factor in this broad global process is rather the disappearance of the "Communist monopoly" in socialist initiative.[63]

This downgrading of the unique mission of the Communist parties is one of the most important ideas shared by the Chinese and Italian Communists (as well as several other Western European Communist parties, including the Spaniards). It was underscored when the PCI formally renounced its preferential relations with the Moscow-oriented party system after the events in Poland. Berlinguer made a point during his trip to China of referring to "the international workers' movement" (and not, as previously, to the "international Communist movement") when he wished to describe the PCI's overall frame of reference. The Chinese had already honored an earlier PCI leader, Togliatti, as "the first Communist leader to defend polycentrism."[64] Thereafter the Chinese supported the Italians in their disagreements with the Soviets, praising the PCI's refusal to "dance to Moscow's tune" and its insistence on deciding "things for itself in the international arena."[65] Ties between the two parties were further strengthened when Berlinguer's successor Alessandro Natta visited Beijing in October 1985 and Hu Yaobang went to Rome in June 1986. According to Hu Yaobang, in their drives for independence and equality, the CPC and PCI represent a "model of party-to-party relations."[66]

It is more difficult for the Chinese to reconcile their new concept of internationalism with the resumption of party relations with the French and Indian Communist parties. These two parties are strongly Moscow-oriented in foreign relations and support the basic tenets of Soviet foreign policy in Afghanistan and Kampuchea. The French party even tried to give the impression that China was a part of an anti-imperialist front directed against the United States. Politburo member Maxime Gremetz claimed that it had become clear in talks in Beijing that the Chinese considered "American hegemony" a greater danger than the Soviet variety because U.S. hegemonic tendencies were rooted in the very nature of capitalism.[67] The Indian Communist party (Marxists) and the PCF have however rejected any claims that a particular socialist model is to be considered exemplary. The PCF has declared its solidarity with all ruling Communist parties and advocates a "new internationalism" based on self-reliant national parties.[68] In this spirit party chief Marchais, speaking in Beijing, expressed an implicit criticism of Moscow in his explicit disapproval of the idea of a "center" and a "paternal party" in world Communism. He stressed that there is "no structured Communist movement which would work out a strategy and policy to which the various parties would have to adhere."[69] There is here a clear convergence with the Chinese position, which gives the Chinese grounds for hope that they will sooner or later be able to loosen the PCF's fixation on the Soviet foreign policy line.

Despite a profusion of predictions to the contrary, it is unlikely that relations between the Chinese and the Japanese Communists will be normalized in the near future. However, preliminary talks were held in 1985 at the request of the Chinese.[70] It is true that opinions about the character of a new internationalism hardly differ between the two parties, as shown by the close JCP relations with the Yugoslav, Romanian, and Italian Communists.[71] However, the real obstacle to normalization is the Japanese demand that the Chinese take the blame for the 1966 breach in party relations and condemn Maoist attempts to split the JCP.[72] As noted above, the Chinese refuse to practice such self-criticism in principle (and in normalization talks with the ten parties mentioned above, no other party asked them to do so).

The conditions laid out by the JCP express the injured pride of a party which, in spite of its historically close ties to the Chinese, was classified in 1967 under the theory of the "four enemies" as one of the chief opponents of China (the other three being the U.S., the USSR, and the Japanese government.)[73] In addition, the JCP may be insisting on these conditions because dropping them would devalue one of the main CPSU concessions to the Japanese party. In the course of normalization talks, the Soviets, at Japanese insistence, implicitly criticized their own past behavior in supporting the splinter movement under Yoshio Shiga, and agreed to sever their connections with this group once and for all.[74] The Chinese are for the moment limiting themselves to relations with the Japanese Socialist party, which were resumed in 1983.

The most recent renewal of Chinese contacts came with the Communist parties of Poland and East Germany. Interestingly enough, as Deng Xiaoping told Erich Honecker, the Chinese assumed that after the Soviet-Chinese breakup in the mid-1960s relations between the Chinese and East German parties were frozen but were never formally terminated. "There is no such thing as restoring ties between our two parties. Our relations should continue to develop since they have never been interrupted."[75] This is a formula that could quite possibly one day be applied to the relationship between the CPC and the CPSU; its pragmatic character cleverly excludes the question of the originator and the causes of the disruption.

Given the improvements in climate between Moscow and Beijing, the reestablishment of party relations between the Chinese and East European state parties shows a certain intrinsic logic. At no time were there any fundamental conflicts of interest between the two sides that were comparable to those arising between the two Communist superpowers on such issues as world Communism, border problems, Third World politics, or regional hot spots. On the contrary, Beijing was well aware of the fact that despite an outward show of loyalty and solidarity towards Moscow, East European attitudes toward Soviet involvement in Vietnam and Afghanistan were at best reserved and their efforts in those two countries were basically limited to economic aid.[76]

The Chinese were thus happy to comply with a wish for closer relations. To the Poles, closer relations represent a means of escape from isolation and improved international status. Meanwhile, the East Germans are looking for a way to expand their maneuvering room in foreign policy. For the Chinese, this is simply a continuation of the course they began in 1956, when they took an active stand in European politics for the first time in their history, supporting the Polish reformer Gomulka despite Soviet opposition.[77]

Once again, the Chinese are standing up for the right to independence for every state and every party in East Europe, since "any intervention in, aggression against, or humiliation of another state is an act that runs contrary to the norms of international relations."[78] Above all, however, rapprochement with the East Europeans rounds out China's foreign policy in Europe--a policy intended to encourage both East and West Europeans to acknowledge their common interests in detente and disarmament. Both China's plea for independence and its call for the development of independent initiatives are undoubtedly also attacks on Moscow's hegemonic policies in East Europe.

Summary and Prognosis

In his analysis on "China and the World Communist Movement," Wolfgang Berner concluded in 1975 that the separation of the CPC from the Soviet-led party system was irreversible precisely "because of the unequivocal nature of the ⟨CPC's⟩ defeat and the completeness of the Soviet triumph." However, this did not at all mean that Beijing would be permanently isolated from all of the international Communist movement.[79]

Both predictions have proved correct. The CPC has once again become active in the international network of party affairs, on its own terms, and has pledged to work with like-minded parties "to restore the lofty prestige of the international Communist movement and Marxism in the world."[80] Unquestionably, the turnabout for the Chinese was facilitated by the fact that previously unfavorable basic conditions in the movement began to change in the 1970s. When several other parties had emancipated themselves from Moscow (following the Yugoslavs), the CPC no longer had to fear isolation. On the contrary, central elements of the "new internationalism" propagated by the autonomists converged with the concept of "new unity" in inter-party relations that the Chinese developed in the post-Mao phase.

Of course, this model of a "new unity" has little in common with the idea of internationalism developed by

Marx, Engels, and Lenin (though the CPC still continues to use their names). For these classical thinkers assumed that the revolutionary workers' movements had a common interest in the struggle against the bourgeoisie and imperialism, to which they would subordinate their individual formations as a sign of international solidarity. The new Chinese internationalism, carefully examined, is not strongly concerned with the nature of societal and class structures. Instead, much like the practices of the CPSU, CPC policy is a function of China's foreign policy interests and goals. It is just as free of ideology and as concerned with power as were earlier theories of "buffer zones," the "four enemies," the "three worlds," and the "united front against hegemony." Although its substance may well change in the future, the new Chinese internationalism serves to open new fields of influence without involving Beijing too deeply.

On the one hand, this means that the Chinese party will concentrate more intensively on participation in party relations. However, it will focus on bilateral cooperation, avoiding more general cooperation on a regional or global level. It will seek renewed relations with the other state parties of Eastern Europe. As their renewed relations with the East Germans, Poles, the PCF, and other Soviet-oriented parties demonstrate, the Chinese are no longer much concerned whether a given party is or is not close to Moscow. China is more likely to measure a party according to whether or not it "practices hegemony." From the Chinese viewpoint, the Soviets and Vietnamese are decidedly in the hegemonist category.

On the other hand, however, with China's rapid reinvolvement the erosion of the traditional Moscow-centric Communist party system becomes more and more evident. The Chinese party, with its forty million members, is by far the largest in the world. Beijing's alternative model for interparty relations will further undermine Moscow's claims to leadership, and Beijing is ensuring this erosion of Moscow's authority by expressly renouncing any claim of its own to ideological leadership. All this makes it more and more difficult to speak of a broad "world Communist movement" in the traditional sense. Perhaps this will be one of the conclusions reached by the group of Chinese historians which the Central Committee has commissioned to write the official party history of the international Communist movement.

NOTES

1. Wu Xingtang, spokesman for the CCP Central Committee International Liaison Department, in Beijing Review (hereafter BR) 29, no. 41 (October 13, 1987): 7.
2. Dieter Heinzig, "Entspannung zwischen Moskau und Peking," Europa Archiv 38, no 8 (April 26, 1983): 250. Cf. also William Griffith, "Sino-Soviet Rapprochement?", Problems of Communism 32, no. 2 (1983): 20-29.
3. Cf. Heinz Brahm, "Der chinesisch-sowjetische Konflikt," in Dietrich Geyer, ed., Sowjetunion: Aussenpolitik 1955-1973 (Cologne/Vienna: Böhlau, 1976), pp. 469-536; and Wolfgang Berner, "China in der kommunistischen Weltbewegung," in Franz Ansprenger et al., Die Aussenpolitik Chinas (Munich/Vienna: R. Oldenbourg, 1975), pp. 335-336.
4. Lian Yan, "The CPC's Relations with Other Parties," BR 29, no. 27 (1986): 25.
5. Pietro Ingrao, "Mao a Mosca," Rinascita 33, no. 37. (September 17, 1976): 10ff. Ingrao is a longtime member of the PCI Direzione.
6. Cf. Die Polemik über die Generallinie der internationalen kommunistischen Bewegung (Beijing: Verlag für fremdsprachliche Literatur, 1965), pp. 3-61.
7. Wolfgang Berner, "Die polnischen Reformkommunisten und das internationale kommunistische Staatensystem," Aktuelle Analyse des Bundesinstituts für ostwissenschaftliche und internationale Studien, no. 31 (August 4, 1981): 8.
8. Renmin Ribao, June 9, 1977.
9. Corriere della Sera, October 20, 1977.
10. Interesting details on this process can be found in Alain Jacob, "La Lente réinsertion de la Chine dans le monde communiste," Politique étrangère 3, no. 1 (1983): 63-73. Cf. also Lilly Marcou, "Le Grand virage du communisme chinois," Le Monde diplomatique 33, no. 12 (1986): 12ff.
11. Lian Yan, "CPC's Relations," p. 22.
12. According to Lin Yan, in Beijing Rundschau 23, no. 27 (July 8, 1986): 22.
13. L'Humanité, October 18, 1982.
14. Communique on Hu Yaobang's visit to Romania, Radio Bucharest, May 10, 1983. Repeated by Hu during his stay in Yugoslavia, la Repubblica, May 17, 1983.
15. Hu Yaobang in his farewell address to the Italian Communist party delegation, l'Unità, April 23, 1983.
16. Hu Yaobang's report to the Twelfth CPC Party Congress, BR 25, no. 37 (September 13, 1982): 32.

17. BR 25, no. 38 (September 20, 1982): 10.

18. BR 26, no. 17 (April 25, 1983): 15-19 (hereafter referred to as "Principles"). The authors, Li Ji and Guo Qingshi, are described as members or vice presidents of the Chinese Society for the History of the International Communist Movement. As early as 1980, Deng Xiaoping had made a similar statement in a conversation with leading CPC members. This later was published under the title "An Important Principle for Handling Relations between Fraternal Parties," in BR 26, no. 34 (August 22, 1983). Cf. also "Foreign Contacts of the Communist Party," interview with the chief of the Department for International Liaison, BR 27, no. 42 (October 15, 1984), as well as the contribution of Lin Yan cited in footnote 4 above.

19. "Principles," p. 16.

20. Ibid., p. 16ff.

21. Ibid., pp. 17-18.

22. Ibid., p. 16.

23. "The Radiance of the Great Truth of Marxism Lights Our Way Forward," BR 26, no. 12 (March 21, 1983): IIIff.

24. From the complete English version by the Chinese embassy in Bonn. Excerpts from the speech may be found in l'Unità, June 22, 1986, and BR 29, no. 26 (June 30, 1986): 6.

25. "Principles," p. 17.

26. See Pravda, December 6, 1960 for the explanation.

27. "Principles," p. 17.

28. BR 25, no. 37 (September 9, 1982): 32.

29. Lian Yan, "CPC's Relations," p. 23.

30. Xinhua, January 29, 1985.

31. Le Monde, November 21, 1980.

32. L'Unità, April 23, 1980.

33. Cf. l'Humanité, October 26, 1982, citing Deng Xiaoping.

34. "Principles," p. 16.

35. Central Committee Secretary Deng Liqun in an interview with l'Unità, January 30, 1983.

36. Deng Xiaoping to Secretary General Namboodiripad of the Indian Communist party (Marxists), BR 26, no. 19 (May 9, 1983): 9.

37. "Principles," p. 15.

38. L'Unità, April 15, 1980, and BR 23, no. 47 (November 23, 1980): 18ff.

39. L'Humanité, October 27, 1982.

40. "Principles," p. 17. Cf. also Xavier Luccioni, "Pékin et l'unité dans la diversité," le Monde diplomatique 27, no. 6 (1980): 4.

41. "Principles," p. 18.
42. Hu Yaobang to the Indian Communist party (Marxist) secretary general, Namboodiripad, BR 26, no. 18 (May 2, 1983): 7.
43. Hu Yaobang's report to the Twelfth Party Congress. See footnote 16.
44. L'Unità, April 18, 1980.
45. "Foreign Contacts," p. 19.
46. Lian Yan, "CPC's Relations," p. 23.
47. Ibid., p. 22.
48. Cf. BR 24, no. 8 (February 23, 1981): 5ff.
49. Lian Yan, "CPC's Relations," p. 22ff. For a similar view, see "Foreign Contacts," p. 19ff.
50. Peng Zhen, chairman of the Standing Committee of the National People's Congress, during his condolence visit to the Soviet embassy in Beijing after Chernenko's death, Radio Beijing, March 12, 1985.
51. Deputy prime minister Li Peng to Gorbachev, Xinhua, March 14, 1985.
52. Wu Xingtang, spokesman for the International Liaison Department, le Monde, April 2, 1986.
53. Reuter, October 3, 1986.
54. "Peking wechselt die Taktik: Zur Chinareise einer Delegation der KP Spanien," Neue Zeit 28, no. 51 (1980): 10ff; similar in substance is "Zum Besuch einer IKP-Delegation in Peking," Neue Zeit 28, no. 20 (1980): 10ff. Cf. also B. Pyshkov and B. Starostin, "Spiral' predatel'stva. Pekin i mezhdunarodnoye kommunisticheskoye dvizheniye," Kommunist, no. 12 (1981): 73-81.
55. Hu Yaobang speech to PCI leaders. See footnote 24.
56. L'Unità, April 28, 1980.
57. L'Unità, April 23, 1980.
58. L'Unità, April 27, 1980.
59. Xinhua, May 9, 1983; cf. Renmin Ribao, May 17, 1983.
60. BR 26, no. 20 (May 16, 1983): 14.
61. Xinhua, May 15, 1983.
62. BR 26, no. 21 (May 23, 1983): 14.
63. Cedomir Strabac, "Zeitgenössischer Sozialismus und Internationalismus," Internationaler Politik 34, no. 795 (May 20, 1983): 23-27.
64. Deng Xiaoping to Italian Foreign Trade Minister Vittorio Colombo, la Repubblica, March 16/17, 1978.
65. "Moscow Was More Than Rude," BR 24, no. 12 (March 24, 1981): 13ff.; cf. also "Polemics between the PCI and the CPSU," BR 25, no. 10 (March 9, 1982): 11.
66. See footnote 24.

67. "De retour de Chine," Cahiers du Communisme 58, no. 12 (1982): 72. See also Marchais' press conference in Beijing, l'Humanité, October 18, 1982.

68. Cf. Marchais' report to the Twenty-fourth PCF Party Congress in February 1982, Cahiers du Communisme 58, no.2/3 (1982): 62.

69. L'Humanité, October 26, 1982.

70. Akahata, November 15 and 20, 1985.

71. Peter A. Berton, "Japan: Euro-Nippo-Communism," in Vernon V. Aspaturian, Jiri Valenta, and David P. Burke, eds., Eurocommunism between East and West (Bloomington: Indiana University Press, 1980), pp. 326-362; and Berton, "Japanese Eurocommunists: Running in Place," Problems of Communism 35, no. 4 (1986): 1-30.

72. Cf. Akahata, August 22, 1981; October 15, 1981; September 25, 1982; April 29, 1983.

73. See Margarete Donath, "Die kommunistische Partei Japans zwischen Peking und Moskau," Berichte des Bundesinstituts für ostwissenschaftliche und internationale Studien no. 28 (1975); also Central Committee of the JCP, Sixty-year History of the Japanese Communist Party (Tokyo: Japan Press Service, 1984).

74. Peter A. Berton, "The Japanese Communists' Rapprochement with the Soviet Union," Asian Survey 20, no. 12 (1980): 1216ff.

75. "Honecker in Peking--Inhaltsreiche und fruchtbare Gespräche," Beijing Rundschau 33, no. 43 (October 28, 1986): 7. Abbreviated in "Honecker's China Visit Fruitful," BR 29, no. 44 (November 3, 1986): 5. The Chinese settled resumption of party relations with Hungary in a similarly pragmatic manner. Cf. the remarks by Central Committee secretary Matyas Szürös, MTI, February 12, 1987.

76. Radio Beijing, October 7, 1986, and Wu Xingtang, cited by Reuter, October 3, 1986.

77. Cf. Richard Löwenthal, Chruschtschow und der Weltkommunismus (Stuttgart: Kohlhammer, 1963), p. 59ff.

78. Hu Yaobang to Honecker, in "Erich Honecker's Chinabesuch von vollem Erfolg gekrönt," Beijing Rundschau 23, no. 44 (November 4, 1986): 6. In the English version, BR 29, no. 44 (November 3, 1986) there is only a short summary of Hu's statement.

79. Berner, "China in der kommunistischen Weltbewegung," p. 355ff. See footnote 3.

80. Closing statement at the normalization talks with the PCE, BR 23, no.48 (December 12, 1980): 5.

81. Cf. the conversation between Hu Yaobang and the Swedish Communist leader Lars Werner, <u>BR</u> 26, no. 16 (April 18, 1983): 6.

PART TWO

Introduction

In the spring of 1977 the leaders of the so-called
Eurocommunist parties--the Communist parties of Italy,
France, and Spain--met at a summit conference in Madrid.
Many observers saw the meeting as the beginning of a
development in which the three parties would act as a
dynamic bloc in Western European Communism, winning
increasing influence in the politics of their countries and
the Western community as a whole.

The programmatic and political collapse of
Eurocommunism and the failure of the Union of the Left in
France has since corrected these fears (or hopes). Instead
of the Communists it was the Socialists whose fortunes rose
in southern Europe, until they finally took over
governmental positions almost everywhere. Some of the
Communist parties experienced severe reverses. The PCF
dropped to 11.3 percent of the vote in the 1984 European
elections and to 9.8 percent in the 1986 parliamentary
elections, pulling back into its traditional "fortress;" the
Spanish Communist party (PCE) was marginalized in the
1982 Cortes elections with 3.8 percent. It improved its
vote only negligibly in the 1986 elections, when it participated in a heterogeneous electoral alliance called the
"United Left" that gleaned 4.6 percent.

Certain Communist parties were however quite
successful: the Portuguese party (PCP) was able to maintain
its strong position in the opposition, and the Cypriot
Communist party even gained strong influence in the
government during 1981-1985, before meeting defeat in the
1985 elections. The record of the Italian party has been
mixed. Forced into the opposition by a five-party coalition
led by the Socialists, it nevertheless emerged in the 1984

European elections as the strongest party in Italy, with
33.3 percent of the vote against the Christian Democrat
33.0 percent. However, it dropped back to a bare 30
percent in the parliamentary elections of 1985. Thus overall
predictions about the Western European Communists are
more problematic than ever. Contrary to many projections,
no generalized correlation can be shown to exist between
the programmatic and political positions of these parties
and their place in the domestic political area in their
countries.

An example for this is the relation of the Communist
parties to the CPSU and the Soviet Union. The PCI made
gains in Italian politics with its westernization, which was
linked to severe criticism of the Soviet system, while the
PCF owes a good part of its historic decline to its renewal
of close ties to Moscow. The Portuguese party, the Greek
party (the Moscow-oriented one, as opposed to the
Eurocommunist Interior party), and Cyprus' AKEL still draw
additional strength precisely from their good relations with
Moscow. The Communist parties of Finland (SKP) and Spain
(PCE) are in a state of confusion, in part because of
internal disagreement about Soviet policies.

Another example of this difficulty of general predictions that seek to relate party strength to political
positions is the attitude of the parties to industrial
restructuring and modernization and to associated austerity
policies. The PCI basically accepts the necessity of such
policies--on condition that their social and humane aspects
take a progressive form. Election results show that this
line meets voter acceptance. The Portuguese party, on the
other hand, fights on principle against the government's
austerity policies, and thereby wins equally stable voter
support.

Both examples make it clear that meaningful
assertions on the trends and goals of the Western European
Communist parties can, more than ever, be made only by
bearing in mind a party's history and the national
conditions in which it operates. Increasing "nationalizing"
of the October revolution by the CPSU is not the least
factor in an inevitable process whereby the fraternal
parties fit themselves in one way or another to the national
conditions and traditions of their countries.

If one can yet make a generalization in all this, it is
that the relatively united and strong Communist parties are
those which have followed a fairly clear line over a long
period of time. With all their differences, the Communist

parties of Italy, Portugal, Greece, and Cyprus can be grouped together here. Those parties which adopted opportunist tactics without drastic programmatic revision or are beset by endemic inner conflicts often had dramatic setbacks. In the first category is the PCF, which today has neither a well-grounded program nor a convincing strategy. The PCE and the SKP belong in the second category: the former broke apart because of inner divergences, while the latter suffered massive interference (from the CPSU) that led to a split in all but name.

Against the background of party histories, the following chapters will examine the structure and organization, program and political strategy, foreign policy and internationalism of relevant Western Communist parties (including the Japanese and Chilean ones), and take a look at their futures. Special emphasis will be given the PCI: it has taken the largest part in smashing the myth of the world Communist movement, and plays a significant role in the national and European scene.

1

The Italian Communist Party

When the Italian Communist party (PCI) held its Seventeenth Congress in Florence in April 1986, all alarm bells were ringing for this largest and most influential Communist party in Western Europe. Despite the PCI's 1,544,000 members and thirty percent of the national vote, the party leadership had to contend with urgent problems: stagnating or diminishing voter potential, political isolation, and a membership aging and dropping away. Was there not a grain of truth in the thesis of journalists and students of the party that the world around it was changing faster than the PCI? Had the Communists, in their determined struggle to achieve continuity, not held on too long to out-of-date ideologies, unsuitable patterns of action, and the rigid structure of the traditional workers' parties? High-ranking party leaders like Luciano Lama, for many years chairman of the Communist-Socialist CGIL trade union, pointed to the French Communist party (PCF), which having opposed any change in its analyses, policies, and internal structure, had in the course of only eight years lost more than half its electorate--from 20 percent of the electorate in 1978 to 9.8 in 1986. [1] Was the PCI in danger of gambling away its historical heritage, and becoming marginalized like its fraternal parties in Western Europe?

The Historical Heritage

The PCI was founded in 1921, when a left-radical group led by Amadeo Bordiga and Antonio Gramsci, under pressure from the Communist International, split off from the Italian Socialist party and formed the Partito Comunista d'Italia. Prior to 1926 the party passed through a revolutionary-sectarian phase, but under Gramsci and Palmiro Togliatti (de facto leader from 1926 on, formally secretary general from 1947 to 1964) it developed the theoretical, strategic, and organizational basis to become the strongest force on the Italian left, a position reinforced by its leading role in the anti-fascist resistance struggle.[2]

Gramsci's theory of revolution departs from the idea that the hegemony of every ruling class in Western Europe rests on two pillars: domination (dominio), the capacity for violent repression of the hostile classes, and direction (direzione), the capacity to create a broad consensus in society. If the bourgeoisie loses its capacity for "direction" (or in modern terms, control of public opinion), its hegemony inevitably enters into crisis. Thus Gramsci saw the task of the working class and its Communist party as widening societal support for the Communists in the framework of bourgeois hegemony, in order to create a new "historical block," (i.e., a new stable class alliance), so that it might take over first "direction" and then "hegemony" in state and society. Gramsci's state is not Lenin's machinery of oppression, to be destroyed in one revolutionary thrust, but rather an embattled organism, offering in its complex articulation an opportunity to the working class for change from within in a socialist direction.

Togliatti's "New Party"

Togliatti, and his successors as party leader Luigi Longo (1964-1972), Enrico Berlinguer (1972-1984), and Alessandro Natta (1984-) took their program from these Gramscian conceptions with important lessons drawn from the experience with fascism. In Togliatti's analysis, fascism owed its impact to the fact that it had won a mass base. The Communists must therefore overcome their traditional sectarian and temporizing positions, characterized by verbal maximalism, and draw the masses to their side by advocating constructive reforms in the existing state.[3]

Thus even in exile and resistance Togliatti consciously conceived of the PCI--in contrast to the Stalinist "party of a new type"--as a "new party" (partito nuovo), thereby opening the gates to the future. In party organizational terms, this meant the transformation of the PCI from a cadre party into a mass party with broad support in the middle classes as well. In time the PCI developed from a class party centered on the workers to a peoples' party. The goal, as Togliatti put it, was to "penetrate into all pores of society" and change it from within. The party was most successful at first in the Red Belt of central Italy, with its small industries and cooperatives (Emilia-Romagna, Tuscany, Umbria), where circa forty percent of PCI members are still concentrated today.

Strategically, this line rejected the "Greek way" of taking power by force in favor of cooperation in building "progressive democracy." This course would provide the necessary consensus-oriented framework for the gradual introduction of far-reaching political, economic, and social reforms that would ultimately change the state system. The charter of this progressive democracy was the Italian constitution of 1947, drafted with the active cooperation of the PCI and still valid today. The demand to fulfill its progressive economic and social-political mandate is almost the essence of the "Italian road to socialism" of that time, and of the "third way" to which the PCI aspired under Berlinguer. In its alliance policies the PCI desired a long-term, stable cooperation not only with the Socialists, but also with the Christian Democrats (DC) as representatives of the broad Catholic popular masses. (This policy explains Communist approval of the integration of the 1929 Lateran agreements into the 1947 constitution.) The PCI believed that a common effort by the three ideological-political currents of democracy in Italy was the only way to prevent a revival of fascism and overcome the ideological split in the country--and was also a means to push the societal and political axis to the left.

Conceiving of itself as a "party of government" that wished to "engage in politics," as Togliatti said, the PCI cooperated actively in the first post-war cabinets until it was pushed out of government in May 1947. Whatever the variations in its alliance policies (the popular front pact with the Socialists in 1948-1956, the "historic compromise" with the Christian Democrats of 1973-1980, and the "democratic alternative with the Socialists since 1980), the PCI has consistently hewed to this basic line. The most recent examples of it are the governments of "national solidarity" in 1976-1979, when the Communists supported DC-led governments from outside and were finally brought into the formulation of the government's program as partners in a de facto coalition in parliament.[4]

A Program of Fundamental Social Reform

The present PCI line has as its central reference point the "programmatic declaration" of 1956, made after a period when the PCI had reluctantly submitted to Cominform discipline. As a mark of destalinization, the party leadership expressly took its distance from the idea of doppiezza (deliberate or deceitful ambiguity), the idea cherished by many that the party's innovations were only a clever tactic, which at the proper moment would give way to a revolution of the Soviet variety.

The most salient point in the line pursued since 1956 is the demand for democratic economic programmation. (Given the relatively large existing public sector, the PCI does not call for further nationalization.) It desires instead to work out goals for all sectors of the economy on the basis of long-term projections, fulfilling them through a flexible system of state framework planning.

This strategy incorporates Berlinguer's idea of building "elements of socialism" into state and society today. Political democracy (including the free formation of majorities) since 1956 has been for the PCI the basis of the road to socialism and of socialism itself. The party also declares its unconditional belief in political and social pluralism. In this it has cast aside the idea, still present in Gramsci's thought, that the party has all-inclusive, or as Direzione member Pietro Ingrao phrased it, "totalizing" claims in society. The party thus expressly recognizes itself as "a part" of society--the most progressive one, desiring hegemony. This position is an expression of the conviction that "under socialism varying interests continue to exist and various spiritual, political, cultural, and religious orientations and traditions will preserve their meaning and value." Thus social-political groups must have the chance to articulate their interests and to settle "the conflicts which arise in a pluralist society" in the framework of democratic institutions.[5]

On the basis of these principles, the PCI advocates stronger ties between representative democracy and the grass roots levels in communities, enterprises, schools, universities, etc. In this, a major PCI motive is the desire to provide the necessary impetus to its parliamentary activities by sinking deeper roots in society--in the unions, the "productive" middle classes, and the scientific-technical intelligentsia.

The PCI as a Non-Class Peoples' Party

The structure and organization of the PCI underline its character as a class and a peoples' party. Of the 1,544,000 members in 1986, workers remain the backbone of the party, with 39.4% of the membership. After this come manual laborers, tradesmen, small businessmen with 9.3%; employees and cadres 7.6%; farm laborers 3.6%; peasants and share-croppers 2.8%; teachers, students, and liberal professions 2.7%; housewives and pensioners 27.6%.[6]

The higher the level of party organ, the lower the proportion of workers to members of the intelligentsia. Of the thirty-six members of the PCI Direzione in 1979, for example, at least eighteen were university graduates, while most of the others had finished secondary school, often with additional university study. Women make up 28.5 percent of party ranks. The whole organizational structure is held together by a hard core of some 180,000 cadres who are the pillars of the party's political and social presence--not least in the jobs they hold as elected or other officials in the communities.

An important indication of the character and image of the party is the composition of its nearly 13,000 basic organizations (1985 figures). There are 11,800 residential sections. Beside them, the 1,200 party enterprise organizations have a subordinate role.

The most important flanking organization of the PCI is the CGIL, the largest of the three Italian trade union confederations, with a strong Socialist minority. Under the chairmanship of Luciano Lama it achieved for itself a certain freedom of action vis-a-vis the party, and even exerts pressure on the party to emphasize its reformism. Another important pillar of the PCI is the National League of Cooperatives--also with a strong Socialist presence, with some 9,000 member cooperatives. Aside from their activities in agricultural production and consumption, they are active in construction, industry and crafts, in transport and in the service sector. Finally, among other organizations close to the PCI there are the women's movement with 91,850 members (in 1975), the partisan veterans with 160,000 members (in 1977), the farmers' league with some 160,000 farmers (in 1976). L'Unità, the PCI central organ, is with a circulation of nearly 300,000 still one of the biggest Italian dailies.

A Contradictory Balance

Despite its broadly based political and social support, the PCI today is in a difficult situation.[7] On the one hand, the "pregiudiziale anticomunista" has nearly disappeared-- that agreement of the Center-Left parties to consider the PCI as subject to international Communist discipline, hence undemocratic and too unreliable to participate in the government or parliamentary majority. The success of the PCI's rehabilitation effort is doubtless connected with its marked aloofness from the Soviet model of society and from Moscow's foreign policy, especially after the suppression of Solidarity in Poland in December 1981.[8] Ciriaco de Mita, head of the Christian Democratic party, has since entering in office in May 1982 frequently referred to the PCI as a party which essentially conforms to the Italian democratic system and represents a real alternative to the DC and to its political ideals. But he also refers to it as a party which because of its antagonistic position inside the Italian "bipolar system" must be opposed by the DC and kept in the opposition.

The national consensus that marked the election of the Italian president in June 1985 was a concrete expression of the acceptance of the PCI as a respectable constitutional opposition party. The Christian Democrats, who claimed the presidency at the end of outgoing Socialist president Pertini's mandate, took care to include the Communists at an early stage of the consultations on a candidate acceptable to all. And in fact the Christian Democrat Francesco Cossiga was elected with Communist support on the first ballot-- something Italian politics had not seen since 1948. PCI Secretary General Alessandro Natta could well emphasize on this occasion that inclusion of his party in the "broad constitutional majority" had confirmed its political weight and its character as a "great democratic force, one of the founders of the republic."[9]

On the other hand, the Italian Communists were not successful in using this admitted legitimacy to strengthen their party or work out specific governmental alternatives to overcome the forty-year hegemony of the Christian Democrats. If one seeks the reasons for this inability-- aside from objective obstacles, especially the political and programmatic barriers raised by the Center-Left parties against the PCI--then subjective insufficiencies must also be listed, and in particular the party's inability to put to use Italy's rapid socio-economic transformation and the changes in attitudes and values that have accompanied it.

The Communists themselves openly discussed these questions at their Florence party congress in 1986.[10] Problems mentioned were the lack of any specific political program for the "democratic alternative," insufficient attention to the changes taking place in the working class, too little contact with technical cadres and with the rising class in the growing education and service areas, inadequate links with the new social movements, the still rather ritual character of internal party discussion, and the resulting difficulty in accepting alternative concepts. All of these inadequacies were said to have had strongly negative consequences for the party in their several areas.

The Electoral Losses of Summer 1985

The setbacks of the May 1985 regional and municipal elections took the party leadership by surprise. The party suffered severe reverses in a series of big cities in the industrial north where both workers and the new groups of technicians and educational and service personnel are heavily concentrated. The PCI share of the vote in Turin, for example, sank from 34.3% in the parliamentary elections of 1983 to 33.8%, in Milan from 27 to 25.7%, in Genoa from 38.5 to 36.3%. As a result, coalition shifts cost the PCI the mayor's office in several large northern cities and Rome. Soon thereafter, in June 1985, the PCI also lost the referendum it had demanded to block the government's reduction in the value of the automatic escalator clause (scala mobile) in wage agreements, by 47.7% to 54.3%.

Their uncompromising strategy and its resultant defeat posed serious problems for the Communists. For one thing, it sharpened their differences with the Socialists, whom they needed for the policy of a "democratic alternative." But it also threatened to disrupt the federation of the three main trade union confederations and even the unity of the CGIL itself, as the non-Communist components were inclined to compromise with the government's measures to slow down inflation and unwilling to follow the confrontational course urged by the PCI on the CGIL's Communist majority.

Finally, the results of the referendum made it plain that workers could no longer be mobilized for wage goals alone. As a result of the rise of the service over the industrial sector, workers' needs and values were changing. This was perhaps the strongest alarm signal of the referendum. In any case, the two quickly succeeding defeats in the regional elections and the referendum were setbacks for the PCI compared with the results of the parliamentary elections of 1983 (31.2% percent) and the European elections of 1984, in which for the first time the Communists had narrowly surpassed the Christian Democrats (33.3 to 33 percent.)

No Possible Alliances

Over and above these losses at the polls, the entire situation seemed more and more complicated for the Communists, for in their quest for parliamentary alliances they had reached a dead end. The broad coalition with the DC designed to achieve the "historic compromise" had fallen apart in 1979; the plan for a "democratic alternative" with the Socialists pursued since 1980 had led to no result. On the contrary, the formation of a five party coalition (pentapartito) by Prime Minister Bettino Craxi (with the DC, the Social Democrats, the Republicans, Liberals, and his own Socialists) again placed the Communist in political isolation.

For the Communists, who since the end of World War II and the experience of fascism have sought the broadest possible alliances with all anti-fascist forces, this isolation was basically new, and therefore extremely worrisome. Even after the dissolution of their unity of action pact with the Socialists in 1956 they had kept ties to the PSI throughout the 1960s, and in the 1970s had also begun a relationship involving growing cooperation with the DC under Aldo Moro. They now had to watch Craxi pursuing quite different objectives in tying the PSI to the pentapartito. He planned over time to marginalize the PCI, with a strategy of "modernizing" by "dominating change" and assuring the "governability" of the country. He would thus change the balance of power on the Left in favor of the Socialists and so improve their chances as governments based on programmatic alternatives succeeded each other inside the center-left spectrum. As Craxi sees it, the PCI like all historical mass parties of the workers' movement has entered into crisis. With their ponderous bureaucratic apparats, their traditional roots among industrial workers and their unions, and with their fixation on the state, they are incapable of dominating socio-economic change and including new needs for individual development and freedom in their conceptions.

Communist isolation was deepened when the Socialists under pressure from the DC broke off most alliances with the PCI in major cities and in the regional governments. Coalition governments had existed in 1978 in most of the regions and in the big cities of north and central Italy, i.e. in the more prosperous and better developed parts of the country: in Emilia-Romagna and its capital Bologna, in Tuscany and Florence, in Umbria and Perugia, in Piedmont and Turin, in Liguria and Genoa, in Lazio and Rome. The year 1986 saw the PCI thrown back to its traditional bastions in the Red Belt in Emilia-Romagna, Tuscany, and Umbria, where it rules in some places alone and in others with the Socialists. This transfer of the national coalition pattern to the regional and municipal level was a particularly severe setback for the PCI. The exercise of governmental responsibility at these levels had always been considered by the Communists as a proof of their capacity to govern and as a prologue to participation at the national level.

A Shrinking Social Base

Finally, it is the situation of the PCI itself that must most disquiet the Communists. The party ranks are diminishing: they reached a new high in 1976, with 1,814,000 members, sank in 1980 to 1,750,000, to 1,630,000 in 1983 and 1,544,000 in 1986, i.e. a loss of 270,000 members in a decade.[11] Qualitative developments were even more troublesome. The PCI has failed to recruit younger members. In the age groups of 18 to 24 they make up only 3.2% of PCI members (against 14.3% of the population), among those 25 to 29 years old the figures are 7.1% party members against 9.3% of the whole population. Membership has stagnated in the new middle classes of the technical intelligentsia, employees and teachers, who make up some 9% of party members, while female membership dropped from 435,000 in 1976 to 430,000 in 1984. The core of PCI membership remains industrial workers with 39.4% of the membership, followed by pensioners with 21% and housewives with 6.6%.

This picture changes significantly when one looks at the electoral preferences of the different age groups and social categories. Here investigations have shown that the PCI takes first place in the preferences of younger voters aged 18 to 34, while the balance shifts progressively toward the Christian Democrats in older age groups, with the Socialists showing a pattern like the PCI's. It is further demonstrated that the new middle classes are more strongly represented among PCI electors than among party members, while the exact opposite is true among workers, pensioners, and housewives.

Discrepancies of social class and age between PCI party members and voters can certainly be traced in part to objective developments which can also be seen in other Western European countries. In general, the younger generation shows little readiness for party political commitment. Its voting pattern overall corresponds less than in earlier years to party identification stemming from cultural or familial background (voto di appartenenza). Instead, voting derives increasingly from rational calculation based on the program of a given party (voto di opinione). The extensive PCI presence among "post-materialist" voter groups is a sign that the social and generational composition of the party does not necessarily and immediately determine voting behavior. The PCI is far removed from the danger of terminal decline exemplified by the French Communist party.

At the same time, the Italian Communists must reflect on new possibilities of tying the "post-materialist" population groups to the party, particularly if they think that the political capabilities of their party depend on its increased dynamism as a mass party broadly represented in society, and do not see politics as basically media events and/or patronage and clientelist relationships. The historic roots among trade unions, cooperatives and the cultural front organizations of the workers' movement have indeed contributed, together with the robust structure of the party, to preserving the PCI's character as a party of social reform against all temptations to adapt itself to neo-liberal concepts. In this it resembles the social democracy of north and central Europe more than the Socialists in southern Europe. But like the former, in its fixation on its traditional values and on narrow corporatist interests, it runs the danger of paying insufficient attention to new needs and aspirations among the population. The PCI could thus in the long run not only risk losing its claim to a share in government, but lose the status it has for decades enjoyed as a force which even in the opposition can exert an influence to shape events.

Elements of Programmatic and Political Renewal

Against this background, and after its defeats in the regional and municipal elections and the referendum, the party leadership decided in the summer of 1985 to hold the national party congress scheduled for 1987 a year earlier, in order to consider a far-reaching "renewal in ideals, program, and organization." Here the tendency toward "preaching for its own sake, mere declamation, propagandism" was to be overcome in favor of a line that would direct discontent toward "positive concrete goals" and aim at "actually attainable political results."[12] In this spirit, the congress theses defined the PCI as a "great modern reform party," constituting an "integrating part of the European Left."[13]

As a result, the various rubrics of the congress program underwent a number of revisions and innovations. Though tightly knit in the original, they will be discussed separately here for analytical convenience.

Ideological Revisions. The PCI had already undertaken far-reaching ideological revisions of its program at the Fifteenth Party Congress in 1979. For example, the previous obligation for all members "to acquire and deepen knowledge of Marxism-Leninism and use its lessons in solving concrete questions" was struck from party statutes. Instead, the current statute refers to the "secular and rational character" of the party and notes that adherents belong to it exclusively "on the basis of the political program." However, at the same time the PCI emphasized that it is "anchored in the ideal and cultural tradition which has its roots and inspiration in the thought of Marx and Engels, and which has received an impulse of historical importance from the renovating ideas and the work of Lenin."[14]

Particularly worthy of note here was the continued reference to Lenin, who had always fought bitterly against bourgeois democracy in general and the social democrats in particular. Party leader Berlinguer later made clear in repeated utterances that this reference to Lenin did not apply so much to his state and party theory as to the Russian revolutionary leader's insistence on action to overcome the passive expectation characterizing the Second International. But doubtless this reference also served at the same time to underline the fundamental political diversity between the PCI and all non-Communist formations which Berlinguer had just emphasized, and to distinguish the PCI, a party intending to change the system, from other parties merely meaning to improve it under capitalism.

The Florence Congress held to the goal of "surmounting the capitalist system," but at the same time made it plain that this change should "not as in the past take place as a great traumatic break," but rather "as a complex interaction of economic models in which one model of production and activity wins out over another."[15] In the key discussions and documents of the Florence congress there is no mention of Lenin and only occasional references to Marx. The third-way concept was upheld only by representatives of the party left wing like Pietro Ingrao and the union leader Bruno Trentin. Secretary general Natta however declared that the bitterly fought "old dispute about reform and revolution and maximalism and reformism" had been transcended; he no longer even spoke up for the fundamental diversità of the PCI.[16]

Finally, the Italian Communists disavowed Marxist dogmatism even further by defining the society they desire as a "non-crystallized socialism."[17] They meant by this that the determinist vision of a socialism with definite stages, specific final goals, and eternal truths had been rejected in favor of a conception stressing the importance of the process of the way to socialism as well as the necessity of using guiding principles quickly to correct unavoidable errors and mistaken assessments. Alessandro Natta remarked that the PCI did not consider "the present capitalist society as the last stage of history," nor did it believe in "final goals which mark the end of human history." Nevertheless, in planning for the future one must "preserve a sense of Utopia and the major values," since holding to such utopias in no way poses a greater risk than "mere orientation on what exists, with politics as mere spectacle."[18]

The emphasis dating from 1979 on the "secular" (laicista) attitude of the PCI, i.e. its conscious turn away from a "sectarian" and "clerical" conception of politics and of the party, was again stressed. The theses of the congress emphasized not only the "heritage of the history and ideals of the workers' movement," but also the importance of the "liberal and democratic revolutions" of the nineteenth century. The single reference in the theses to Marx--to his notion of the goals of society in which "the free development of one is the condition for the free development of all"--notably applies not to his analysis of capitalism but rather serves to bind the achievements of the bourgeois revolutions to the ideals of the modern workers' movement.[19]

Thus it is only logical for the PCI to overcome the Marxist monism of its founding years in favor of a "political and cultural pluralism"[20] that applies to the party itself, while still striving toward socialism. Its political action will thus increasingly orient itself toward certain values, above all freedom, equality, justice, solidarity. Thereby, over and above specific programs, the PCI demonstrates increasing convergence of its ideals with those of the Western European social democratic and socialist parties. They too are changing; they too base their policies on similar "fundamental values" which include a touch of Marxism. The PCI's intensified search in recent years for contacts with social democratic parties, in particular the SPD, is based on this convergence.

Programmatic Change. The trend toward a pluralism oriented toward basic values, which began before the Florence Congress, creates the preconditions for PCI development as a "great modern reform party" of the Western European variety. However, the symptoms of crisis noted above demonstrate that the party has not yet succeeded in combining allegiance to these values with a convincing strategy of modernization that might broaden its voting potential. Nevertheless, the Florence congress was accompanied by some noteworthy initiatives.

The PCI was able to work out a basically positive approach to the restructuring of the economy which has resulted from the diminished importance of big industry and the expansion of the service sector. The Communists pronounced themselves in favor of the introduction of new technologies, to raise productivity and promote individual capabilities. They warned that the party, which had "arisen, grown, and been shaped in industrialism and its culture" as a part of the Western European workers' movement, must not let itself be forced into a corner and "be tied to the residual elements in the world of production," as PCI Turin federation chief Piero Fassino emphasized to the congress. "Industrialism today is undergoing a rapid and drastic transformation," in which "the classical model of industrial society is giving way to a 'neo-industrial society', more articulated, less rigid and compact, more elastic and dynamic."[21]

At the same time, the PCI concept of modernization objects to the notion of a neutral technology and stresses the human and social aspects of the restructuring that follows from technological change. There can be no return to the "concept of socialism as total nationalization of production and exchange and as administrative direction of planning," East European style.[22] The PCI also opposes the policies of the government parties, accusing them of neoliberal and unsocial passiveness in regard to ongoing diversification and innovation. It favors instead a flexibly exercised state piloting "a third way between liberalism and statism."[23] The intent is to "direct overall development of the economy in a market where private initiative, a public sector, and a stronger cooperative and association sector are all active."[24] The piloting involves not only distribution but also includes measures to guide investment (i.e. "the process of accumulation").

Quite logically, the PCI is also interested in proposals for constitutional reform. It believes that a successful outcome to the crises of economy and society is largely dependent on the success of attempts to modernize the indecisive and frequently inefficient state structure of Italy. A party minority around <u>Direzione</u> member Ingrao has even argued for the priority of forming a "constituent government composed of all democratic parties," with the goal of using united forces to free up a "blocked democracy" with "institutional innovations"--and not without a sidelong glance at the PCI hope for a "democratic alternative."[25]

This proposal found no concurrence at the party congress, which did however stress the urgency of constitutional reform and renew the PCI's detailed proposals for it: reduction of the bicameral system to a single chamber with fewer deputies, strengthening of the executive with more effective awareness of its tasks, broader competence and greater financial resources for regions and municipalities.[26]

The PCI has nevertheless been reproached (not least by its own members) for failing to provide detailed proposals to elaborate its general ideas, especially where economic and social problems are concerned. The main stress of the PCI program is to introduce greater justice into the fiscal system and to direct resources from tax-favored gains into productive investment, thus ending a situation in which "the paper economy devours the real economy."[27] The PCI believes that targeted investment would not only reduce mass unemployment but would also help Italy's endangered international competitiveness. Finally, such measures would also check the rise in the public debt. Expected in 1986 to overtake the value of the gross domestic product, the debt acts as a brake on modernization of infrastructure and qualitative improvement in social services.

The Florence congress created a new party "Program Bureau" to compensate for its lack of new ideas. Under Natta's presidency and coordinated by former union chairman Lama, it is supposed to work out propositions that could be realized within one five-year legislative term. Experts from outside the party are to be drawn into the process. It remains to be seen whether the Program Bureau can work out realistic and feasible proposals, or whether it is just an attempt to paper over the lack of consensus within the party by creating still another committee.

Integrating New Values. The PCI effort to come to terms with changes in consciousness and values that have accompanied socio-economic change has moved faster than the drafting of programs. The problems alluded to earlier show that the party, traditionally sensitive to social movements, has in the last few years incurred the danger of becoming a "simple support framework for institutional activities," turning into a "purely electoral organization," and thus losing its "independent presence in society."[28]

The party is further confronted with the difficult problem of integrating the interests and values of two clienteles. It seeks on the one hand to appeal to a more or less production-oriented but increasingly heterogeneous labor force, but also to groups with a "post-industrial" orientation, which frequently have ties to the new social movements. A symptom of this is the disagreement on the peaceful use of nuclear energy, which came to a stormy vote at the Florence congress. A motion supporting its continued development was upheld with difficulty by a vote of 457 to 440 (fifty-nine delegates abstaining), with members of the party leadership on both sides of the question.

In its approach to social problems the PCI is trying to give new definitions to traditional concepts of the workers' movement such as "reform" and "progress." Party theses call for a linkage of economic growth with the quality of life; the creation of new jobs must go together with protection of the environment. Defeat in the scala mobile referendum of June 1985--later conceded to be a mistake by senior party figures like Luciano Lama[29]--spurred first the CGIL and then the party to draw far-reaching conclusions. A corporatist drive for national wage agreements with the state and employers' associations is to give way to a flexible strategy aiming at extensive worker codetermination in the introduction of new technology. This strategy would look increasingly to small and medium enterprise, take account of differences in workers' qualifications, and give the "base" a role in decision-making. Here the Communist hope is to strengthen their weak presence in medium-sized industry, remotivate their followers in big industry, and win over the growing ranks of technical and administrative cadres. This latter group handed the PCI a severe defeat in 1980 when a counter-demonstration wrecked a Communist-backed strike at FIAT opposing restructuring.

The new orientation did not merely take account of changes in the labor force; it went on to question the traditional thesis of the centrality (centralità) of the working class in the PCI's strategy of change. Given social change and new cultural needs, said party leader Natta, a party that bases its policies only on class conflicts is condemned to decline. A "modern Left" must be able "to meet other cultures and experiences: with women's and youth movements, with ecologists and environmentalists, with the peace movement, with religiously motivated progressive forces, with all currents that strive for more freedom and against marginalization and discrimination."[30]

In this spirit the PCI had in 1984 granted its youth movement (membership in 1976: 142,000; in 1985: 47,000) organizational and political autonomy, freeing it from narrow party concerns to give it a better chance of voicing and integrating the specific interests and needs of the younger generation. The Florence congress went farther than the party theses on the "women's question," speaking explicitly of "overcoming patriarchal conceptions" and the need to draw the consequences from the fact that "the women's revolution has changed and continues to change relations between the sexes." To give force to these new accents the congress decided to form a new Central Committee commmision to work out "analyses, proposals, and initiatives for women's emancipation and liberation." The commission is composed of all the female Central Committee members.[31]

Effective legitimation of dissent in the party aims in this same direction. The Florence congress gave every party member the right to express dissent not only in party meetings but also in public, without fear of expulsion. The PCI had liquidated democratic centralism of the traditional type in its Sixteenth Congress in 1983, legitimizing the existence of (long existent) currents and the principle of free formation of majorities within the party. Since then the party has stressed the openness of its decision-making at all levels, freedom for party organizations to communicate horizontally, and the availability of the party press to print all positions. In reducing democratic centralism to a means of maintaining party solidarity and capacity for action, the PCI won a victory over the Leninist "sectarian" and "clerical" interpretation of a Communist party.[32]

Thus for the Italian Communists little remains of the Leninist principle of democratic centralism in internal decision-making--another symptom of the "secularization" of the party. The only real residue is the practice of coopting members into the Central Committee and Direzione. As an expression of the pursuit of unity and constriction, democratic centralism paralyzes the effort to agree on clear alternative courses and promotes a tendency to prefer internal bargaining, compromise, and indecision to clear political statements.

An excellent example is the alliance strategy for a "programmatic government" (governo di programma). Controversial in the party but approved by the Florence congress, the strategy is mainly designed as a step toward the "democratic alternative" with the Socialists. But it leaves a great deal of room for different interpretations, and makes it easier for the other parties to brand the PCI line as contradictory and confused, hence unsuitable for any solution to the country's problems.

Foreign Affairs: The Pro-European Option

It is interesting that the criticism of the other Italian parties is today directed more toward PCI domestic policy than to its foreign policy ideas. The PCI's international relations are marked by a concept of "new internationalism" in which the basis for foreign and security policy is a critical but constructive option for the West. The party has since 1956 rejected the notion of a leading state and party in the world Communist movement. After the events in Afghanistan in 1979 and those in Poland in 1981, the PCI declared that "real socialism" of the Soviet

Communist type had "lost its propulsive force." Marxism in Eastern Europe had become the "closed dogma" of a "state ideology," lost its inspirational force, and had degenerated into an ideology of legitimation that serves to preserve the powers that be. In domestic and bloc policy the basic structures of the Soviet system had stayed faithful to the model Stalin built, with recurring crises in Eastern Europe as a result. Moscow's foreign policy, characterized by power politics and a desire for spheres of influence, had made a notable contribution to the icy temperatures of the East-West climate.

After a long and contradictory phase in the struggle for autonomy designated by Togliatti's formulas of "polycentrism" and "unity in diversity," the PCI leaders decided in 1982 on the spectacular step of dropping any privileged character from their relations with the CPSU and other Communist parties. The PCI thus officially exited from the narrow system of the Moscow-oriented Communist movement, in which it had found its central ideological and political reference point since the October revolution. It considers itself today, according to the theses of the Florence congress, "neither as part of an ideological camp nor of an organized movement on the European or global plane." It therefore strongly opposes participation in a new world conference of Communist parties, such as Polish party chief Jaruzelski proposed in June 1986.[33]

Against this background, Natta affirmed in Florence his party's intention to determine its relations with Moscow according to "political, not ideological criteria."[34] Berlinguer had earlier termed unconditional support for Soviet foreign policy downright "suicidal," announcing that the PCI would decide future problems case by case, determining its decision by examining Moscow's particular position and action.[35] Speculation in the Italian press that the PCI's positive appreciation of Gorbachev's disarmament proposals marks abandonment of the strappo (ideological rift) of 1981 is not necessarily correct. The PCI appears to be reacting to new Soviet orientations in foreign and security policy, and taking note that in intra-Communist relations the CPSU now puts less stress on preserving ideological orthodoxy than on winning political support for its diplomatic offensive against the West.

The PCI follows similar pragmatic political considerations in its appreciation of the U.S. and NATO. Since the 1970s it has accepted Italy's ties to Western European and Atlantic cooperation; in 1977 it signed parliamentary resolutions to this effect together with the other parties of the Italian <u>arco costituzionale</u> (i.e. all major parties except the neo-Fascists). Furthermore, a parliamentary delegation from the PCI entered the North Atlantic Assembly in May 1984 and has since played an active role there.

This line was contested in the preparations for the Florence congress by 38.6 percent of party members. They are not to be confused with the "pro-Soviet" group led by Armando Cossutta, whose resolutions on foreign policy questions were supported by only 12.4 percent of the members. It is clear that positions sharply critical of U.S. policy cannot in their majority be identified with basically pro-Soviet feeling.[36] Natta led the party leadership's counterattack to this challenge, successfully arguing that the PCI as a party with governmental aspirations must maintain a reasoned relationship with the Atlantic alliance and its leader, the U.S.[37] The congress did however sharpen the draft theses by condemning the "conservative offensive...led and backed on the world level by the Reagan administration."[38] But it also affirmed that this line is under attack in the U.S. itself and can therefore be reversed--among other things with help from without.

It is just in this context that the unity of Western Europe assumes ever greater importance for the PCI. It considers that the European Community must use the framework of the Atlantic alliance to uphold specific European interests, must assert Europe's weight and self-confidence, and in the interest of compromise and cooperation must undertake not only regional but also global responsibilities. The PCI's aim here is to exert an active influence on the crisis behavior of both superpowers, hoping to increase East-West detente. But it also has in mind creation of a partnership of equals with the countries of the Third World, largely as an alternative to their dependence on one of the two superpowers. Thus Europe and the Western European workers movement would grow in a role which would make of them "the epicenter of the new phase of the struggle for socialism."[39]

As partners of a "dialogue of equals" with the U.S, the West Europeans have the task, according to the Florence theses, "of working inside the alliance for a policy of "worldwide mutual security...in which political factors win out over military factors."[40] But the Europeans must stick together in other areas too. Given the internationalization of the economy and of technological challenges, the European Community can only perform its worldwide tasks if it develops further into a "supranational political unit."

If the PCI here termed itself for the first time an "integrating" and not just a passively "integral" part of the Western European Left, this denoted its taking distance from the concept of Eurocommunism--and especially from the French Communist party, and making a notable political and programmatic rapprochement with international social democracy, which itself is caught up in a process of change. It is interesting that after earlier concentrating its attention on the French Socialists, the PCI has now turned to the German Social Democrats, who for the first time dispatched an official delegation to the PCI congress. A series of top-level meetings (Natta with Willy Brandt, Giorgio Napolitano-Horst Ehmke, Achille Occhetto-Peter Glotz) strengthened the PCI leaders' impression that the two parties had many interests and points in common.

This similarity can be seen in the reworking of their party programs, where the PCI theses and the SPD "Draft for a New Basic Program" show many resemblances. One might cite the turn to basic values, a changed emphasis on the relations of state, economy, and society, an envisaged reconstruction of the welfare state, the problem of changes in society and values and their effects on the party, as well as aspects of security policy, East-West relations, and European policy. The PCI is also much interested in the dual role of the SPD as a programmatic party which is also at federal and state level a reform-oriented party of government, always prepared for dialogue and compromise. The Italians intend to learn what they can from both the positive and negative experiences of the SPD as a governing and as an opposition party.

The PCI has rejected the proposal made by high-ranking members of the PSI that it should, if it wishes to be logical, request entry into the Socialist International.[41] It would however like observer status, at least as a first step. The PCI leaders are also seriously considering the idea advanced by Giorgio Napolitano that they cooperate in working out a common program of the European Left for the 1989 elections to the European parliament.[42] In any case, Napolitano's designation to oversee PCI foreign relations makes clear the political direction in which Italy's Communists are going. Both he and Luciano Lama, coordinator of the new Program Bureau, are considered convinced advocates of a rapprochement with Western European social democracy.

Current Situation and Prognosis

With its program for permanent constructive change in the infrastructure of society, the PCI has undoubtedly plotted an original path between classical social democracy (construction of a "counter-society" as the foundation of future socialism) and classical Leninism (radical structural change after the takeover). PCI acceptance of the central values of constitutional democratic societies and its self-designation as "a great modern reform party" show that the strongest and most influential Communist party in the West is rapidly approaching the views of the changing social democracies. At any rate, the Florence congress makes it very plain that the PCI has gone a long way toward solving the special problems that stemmed from its affiliation with that part of the world Communist movement that is linked politically and ideologically to Moscow. It has thereby avoided the fate of the French Communist party, which in its competition with the Socialists has met historic defeat. Since the unanimous election of Natta (born 1918) as secretary general, the PCI now has a fully legitimized and capable leader. (His election by the Central Committee after Berlinguer's sudden death in 1984 had only a provisional character.) Natta emerged in Florence as a clearly dominant figure, whose general line found overwhelming agreement.

Yet after overcoming its special historic problems the PCI faces new difficulties. Like the structurally comparable social democratic parties of Northern and Central Europe, it must take account of rapid change in society, the economy and in values, while simultaneously furthering its ambition to rule by working out a detailed and convincing reform program. The PCI was unable to exploit the difficult crisis of the five-party coalition in summer 1986 to break out of its isolation. On the contrary, the least common denominator of the pentapartito turned out to be the effort of all its members to keep the PCI out of power. The Christian Democrats, who have gained votes under De Mita (32.9 percent in 1983; 35 percent in 1985), are not interested in reviving the grand coalition of 1976-1979. Their attention is rather directed to the objective of retaking the prime minister's office from the Socialists, thus reinforcing their hegemony inside the existing governmental alliance. The Socialists, for their part, are exploiting the strategic position given them by the blockage of the PCI by the DC (or, in some future contingency, PCI blockage of the DC). After the traumatic experience of the popular front period of 1947-1956 they now prefer a coalition with the Christian Democrats to an uncertain junior partnership with the Communists, which is in any case at present an arithmetic impossibility. This difficult situation for the PCI may certainly be traced in part to the programmatic problems already mentioned. The specific content of its concept of a "programmatic government" leading to a "democratic alternative" does not emerge clearly enough. But another reason for the PCI's difficulties is the surprising capacity for regeneration of the hegemonic culture of the Catholic social-christian element of the "political class" embodied in the DC. As a result, the PCI finds little room for a decisive breakthrough to a left or "laic" alternative. It may thus continue to exert a strong influence on the political fate of the land, from the opposition. But its prospects for participation in government in the relatively near future appear scarcely improved, despite its mutation into a "modern reform party" of a Western European variety.

NOTES

1. Speech to the Seventeenth Congress, l'Unità, April 11, 1986.
2. I cite here from the extensive literature on the PCI only Aris Accornero, Renato Mannheimer, and Chiara Sebastiani, L'Identità comunista: I militanti, le strutture, la cultura del PCI (Rome: Editori Riuniti, 1983); Joan Barth Urban, Moscow and the Italian Communist Party (Ithaca and London: Cornell University Press, 1986); Wolfgang Berner, "Die Italienische Kommunistische Partei: From Togliatti to Berlinguer," in Heinz Timmermann, ed., Die Kommunistichen Parteien Südeuropas (Baden-Baden: Nomos, 1978); Donald Blackmer and Sidney Tarrow, eds., Communism in Italy and France (Princeton: Princeton University Press, 1975); Massimo Ilardi and Aris Accornero, eds., Il Partito comunista italiano: Struttura e storia dell'organizzazione 1921-1979 (Milan: Feltrinelli, 1982); Donald Sassoon, The

Strategy of the Italian Communist Party (London: Frances Pinter, 1981); Michael Strübel, Neue Wege der italienischen Kommunisten (Baden-Baden: Nomos, 1982); Heinz Timmermann, "Die KPI--Profil einer eurokommunistichen Partei in der Regierungsmehrheit," Osteuropa 28, nos. 5 and 6 (1978); Lawrence L. Whetten, New International Communism (Lexington, Mass.: D. C. Heath and Company, 1982).

3. Cf. Urban, Moscow and the Italian Party, passim.

4. Cf. Timmermann, "Die KPI," Osteuropa no.6: 519ff.

5. Theses of the Fifteenth PCI Party Congress, in La politica e l'organizzazione dei comunisti italiani, (Rome: Editori Riuniti, 1979), pp. 3-146.

6. Direzione del PCI, eds., Organizzazione-Dati-Statistiche (Rome: Editori Riuniti, 1986), p. 38.

7. On the current party constellations in Italy in general and the PCI in particular, see Dieter Boden, "Italien unter Craxi: Neue Perspektiven der Stabilität?," Beiträge zur Konfliktforschung 16, no. 2 (1986): 77-92, and Günter Trautmann, "Italien in den achtziger Jahren," Aus Politik und Zeitgeschichte, no.8 (1986): 28-46.

8. Cf. my article "Die italienischen Kommunisten gehen auf Distanz," Osteuropa 32, no. 6 (1982): 443-460.

9. L'Unità, June 25, 1985.

10. The speeches at the congress, including Natta's opening and closing remarks, can be found in l'Unità, April 10-14, 1986. Cf. also the controversial Central Committee debates over the draft theses for the congress, ibid., December 8-11, 1985.

11. See Organizzazione-Dati-Statistiche, also Giuseppe Caldarola, "La galassia comunista," Rinascita 41, no. 13 (1984): 7ff.; Renato Mannheimer and Roberto Biorco, "Autoritratto dell'elettore comunista," Rinascita 42, no. 10 (1985): 12-14; Michelangelo Notarianni, "La metà è venuta dopo il '68," Rinascita 42, no. 44 (1985): 20-22; idem., "Il partito di massa per una nuova fase politica," Rinascita 43, no. 15 (1986): 6.

12. From Natta's opening speech at the Seventeenth Party Congress, l'Unità, April 10, 1986.

13. The draft theses were printed in l'Unità, December 15, 1985. Texts of theses noted hereafter were adopted without changes. Cf. Tesi, Programma, Statuto. I Documenti approvati dal 17 Congresso del PCI (Rome: Rinascita Documenti, 1987), pp. 7-86.

14. "Statuto del Partito comunista italiano," in Documenti per il Congresso (Rome: Edizione Rinascita, 1986), pp. 149-189.

15. Draft thesis no. 1.

16. From Natta's introductory speech, l'Unità, April 10, 1986.

17. Draft thesis no. 1.

18. See Osteuropa 36, no. 7 (1986): 529-533 for the discussion on Natta's March 1986 speech at the Bundesinstitut für ostwissenschaftliche und internationale Studien, Cologne .

19. Draft thesis no. 1. Cf. the similar SPD "Entwurf für ein neues Grundsatzprogram" of June 1986, Presse-und Informationsabteilung der SPD (1986), p. 10.

20. Draft thesis no. 45.

21. L'Unità, April 11, 1986.

22. Draft thesis no. 1.

23. Cf. the article by Direzione member and Central Committee secretary Achille Occhetto, "Il programma e il movimento," Rinascita 43, no. 24 (1986): 3ff.

24. Draft theses, thesis no. 1.

25. Cf. Ingrao's alternative proposal for the draft theses, in Documenti per il Congresso, p. 137ff.

26. See the section "The Reform of the State and Democratic Institutions" of the "Proposed Program" accepted at the Seventeenth Congress, l'Unità, December 17, 1985. For details of PCI views on this question see the report on a Central Committee discussion in October 1984, especially the introductory speech by Direzione member Renato Zangheri, l'Unità, October 3, 1984.

27. From an interview with Direzione member Alfredo Reichlin in La Repubblica, July 8, 1986. Interest rates in Italy are among the highest in the world.

28. Cf. Natta's Central Committee speech, in which he explained the reasons for advancing the Seventeenth Congress by a year, l'Unità, July 23, 1985.

29. Cf. the interview with Lama in the Corriere della Sera, October 4, 1985.

30. Concluding speech at the Seventeenth Congress, l'Unità, April 14, 1986.

31. Ibid.

32. Cf. my article "Die genetischen Mutationen der KPI," Die Neue Gesellschaft 30, no. 5 (1983): 449-458.

33. Cf. the views of Direzione member Antonio Rubbi, l'Unità, July 1, 1986. Jaruzelski made the proposal in his speech to the Tenth PZPR Party Congress. See Trybuna Ludu, June 30, 1986.

34. Natta's introductory speech, Seventeenth Congress.

35. L'Unità, January 24, 1982.
36. La Repubblica, April 8, 1986.
37. See Natta's remarks in the Central Committee discussion on the draft theses, l'Unità, December 9, 1985.
38. L'Unità, April 14, 1986.
39. See Berlinguer's Central Committee speech on the events in Poland, l'Unità, January 12, 1982.
40. Draft theses, no. 2.
41. PSI deputy-chairman Claudio Martelli, quoted in la Repubblica, November 23, 1985 and in l'Espresso 31, December 1, 1985.
42. L'Unità, May 10, 1986.

2

The French Communist Party

In June 1972, two days after he had signed a "Common Program of Government" with the French Communists, Socialist party First Secretary François Mitterrand announced at a meeting of the Socialist International in Vienna:

> Our basic objective is to rebuild a large Socialist party on the terrain occupied by the Communist party itself, in order to demonstrate that out of five million Communist voters, three million can vote Socialist. [1]

In the course of the next ten years Mitterrand succeeded in doing this. In 1972 the Communists were clearly the dominant factor on the Left; today the balance is heavily weighted in favor of the Socialists. The Communists, however, are caught up in a process of decline that may be irreversible.

The symptoms of sickness in the French Communist party (Parti Communiste Français-PCF) are the loss of half its electorate, from twenty percent in 1978 to 9.8 percent in 1986 (the lowest point since 1924), and a declining membership, which has dropped by 100,000 in three years even according to official figures. Calculated by the party in 1986 at 608,000, membership was thought by outside experts to be closer to half that figure. Added to this is what the party terms a crisis in militancy, meaning an increasing disinclination by members to take a strong stand for party policies. Even when the PCF left the Socialist-led government in July 1984, taking a militant stance that attempted to draw new force from opposition, it had no success. Today the chief question about the PCF is not what it can do in French politics, but what it can do about its own problems.

What has caused this marginalization of a famous Communist party, which in the 1930s assumed the heritage of the German Communists as the strongest Western party, whose postwar vote, surging in 1946 to 28.6 percent, powerfully influenced the politics of its country? To understand the process, a brief review of PCF history is needed.

The Historical Conditions

The PCF was founded in Tours in late 1920, when a majority of the French Socialist party (Section Française de l'Internationale Ouvrière-SFIO) decided against the resistance of a minority, led by Léon Blum, to enter the Communist International.[2] This schism in the French workers' movement had historic importance, because the victory of the revolutionary current was unique in Europe. The Congress of Tours remains today a central point of reference in the ideological identity of the PCF, legitimizing the PCF's claims to leadership in the process of social change.

From 1920-1930, the Comintern was unable to remake a loosely organized, ideologically diverse mass party into a satisfactorily Leninist cadre party, tightly centralized and monolithic. Though it had not been fully bolshevized, the PCF pursued a sectarian line that rapidly reduced its influence. Weakened by repeated purges of its leaders, the party saw membership drop by 1933 to 28,500.[3] Support of Stalin's social fascism thesis directed against the Socialists did not help matters.

Maurice Thorez became leader of the PCF in 1930, a post he held until the year of his death in 1964. Champion and symbol of a hard line, Thorez presided over the full transformation of the PCF into a Leninist party, a character it has retained through all the changes and vicissitudes of its political existence, including the Eurocommunist phase of the 1970s.

The Leninist character of the PCF influenced the Popular Front alliance with the Socialists and the left-bourgeois Radical Socialists in the mid-1930s, which in PCF eyes was only a temporary antifascist association with limited goals. The PCF granted its allies only a conditional parliamentary support which later turned into partial opposition to the Blum government. However, the PCF did lay the foundation for its later success as a mass party: its membership rose to 328,000 in 1937. After the reunification of the trade union movement in 1936 the PCF occupied key positions which it holds to this day. The reconciliation at that time of the "Internationale" with the "Marseillaise" and the red flag with the tricolor had more than symbolic importance. In this way the Communists demonstratively let it be known that they had emerged from the political wilderness. Yet with their approval of the Hitler-Stalin pact, they soon maneuvered themselves back into it.

The PCF had a second chance to break out of the ghetto during the Resistance and in the period of postwar reconstruction. By 1946 it claimed 800,000 members, won its highest vote (28.6 percent in the November 1946 elections), and became the largest party in France. The PCF joined the governments of General de Gaulle, the MRP leader Georges Bidault, and the Socialist Paul Ramadier. In them it supported policies of drastic economic and social reform. In 1946 Thorez even declared that in countries with a glorious democratic tradition like France one might consider other ways to socialism than the Russian one.[4]

This vision disappeared in late 1947, when the PCF followed orders from Moscow's new Cominform to take up cold war positions of frontal opposition against the bourgeois state and the Socialists. It became clear that the "external ties" to non-Communist forces formed during the Popular Front and immediate postwar periods had not altered the party's tight "in-house ties" to Moscovite international Communism. Given the character of a Marxist-Leninist cadre party which the PCF had retained in all phases of broad political alliance, the party could relatively easily reverse poles when the political climate changed in Moscow, adopting a policy of uncompromising confrontation.

Thus in the late 1940s the PCF reverted to its apparently revolutionary but actually sectarian claim to represent the vanguard of the working class in a radical reformation of state and society. Its chief opponents were again the Socialists, accused of being the props under the bourgeoisie. (The same cry was raised when the PCF made its exit from the Left coalition government in July 1984, this time less on a signal from Moscow than out of fear that in participation in a Socialist-led government the PCF had lost its identity as a militant revolutionary party.)

In Communist eyes, the Socialists are the historical representatives of "the social democratic-reformist current in France." They are therefore by nature incapable of proceeding beyond certain social reforms to make a "decisive break with big capital" on a national and international plane, but instead incline "to compromises with the bourgeoisie and class collaboration."[5] Therefore a Left alliance offering hopes for a socialist transformation must presuppose a balance of forces in favor of the PCF. Such a balance existed at the end of World War II when the Communists entered the government (PCF 26.1%; SFIO 17.9%) and again in the early 1970s when the Common Program of Government was drafted (1967 elections: PCF 22.5%; SFIO and allies 19%).

For the PCF, the decisive factor for the success of such an alliance strategy lies in the social impetus provided by extra-parliamentary mass mobilization, which must be inspired, organized, and directed by the Communists. In the party's self-image only the PCF, vanguard of the working class and thus the only authentic revolutionary force, is both able and legitimized by history to determine the dynamics and direction of the revolutionary process. Should this social impetus prove insufficient, and should the balance of power on the Left change to favor the Socialists, then the PCF leaders prefer to withdraw into isolation and defiance, to strengthen their organization while awaiting a more favorable conjunction of the stars.

Firm in the basic conviction that this tactic could be repeated at will, the PCF failed to recognize the dramatic economic changes accompanied by social differentiation that were taking place in France in the postwar years. In its ouvrièriste narrow-mindedness it is fixated on the working class, the lone actor on the stage of revolutionary history. It has rejected any constructive dialectic with the rest of society, any spiritual-political discussion intended to influence and gradually transform it. It has cared more about defending its own position than about flexibility and expansion, more about the stability of society than about its dynamism, or about taking risks.[6]

The epoch-making events of French postwar history have thus quite literally rolled over the PCF. It was taken by surprise in 1958 by Gaullism, which it at first classified as fascism, in 1968 by the May revolt, when the urge to

change the system was directed against the PCF too, surprised, finally, in 1981 when Mitterrand's Socialists seized
the commanding heights of power, forcing an unprepared
PCF against its original intentions into the role of junior
partner in government--because "le peuple de gauche" (the
left electorate) wanted it so.

The internal contradictions of the PCF now began to
break into the open. Did it wish to be a vanguard or a
mass party, an opposition party or a governmental party?
Unable to resolve these and other questions, worried about
increasing organizational problems, the leadership was
alarmed by a diminishing vote and the sense that it had
little control over government policies which were almost
entirely determined by the Socialists. The PCF therefore
seized upon the change of prime ministers in July 1984 to
justify its exit from the government. PCF leaders saw their
return to the opposition not just as the end of a three year
experiment in government, but as "ending a whole period of
French political life," in which "the project and then the
victory of a Left government ⟨grew⟩ from the idea of a
common program of government."[7]

To replace the strategy of a party participating in
government, the PCF elected to return to its traditional
"tribunician function,"[8] in which the party represents the
discontented and the socially disadvantaged. The goal was
to use an oppositional status to sharpen the organizational
weapon in class warfare, basing party strength in the
factories and enterprises. Unity of the left, the previous
slogan, gave way to "a new people's majority muster"
centered on the PCF--suggesting a new strategy with
populist overtones. This empty language could not conceal
the reality--the PCF had no prospective allies and its own
ranks were dwindling. PCF accusations grew shriller, reviving an old accusation that the PS had betrayed the idea
of radical structural reform and was guilty of "capitulation
to capitalist forces."[9] In the crisis, said PCF leader
Georges Marchais in 1985, the Right and the Socialists had
made "the same class choices."[10] His words found no echo
in the Left electorate; in March 1986 hundreds of thousands
more voters deserted the PCF.

An Erosion of Influence

PCF political and social influence has always been
unevenly distributed, with traditional strength in the Paris
area, the industrial departments of the north, the

Mediterranean departments, and some largely agricultural departments in the center. Beginning in 1965, the PCF strongly accentuated a policy of winning new members to increase its presence in the society. According to inflated party statistics, membership grew from 380,000 in 1969 to 702,000 ten years later. (French experts on the PCF estimate membership peaked in 1979 at about 380,000 members.)[11] In the 1979 membership, workers made up the largest group with 49.1%, followed by employees with 28%, cadres (administrative employees) with 7.6%, and teachers with 6.9%.[12] In 1982, the party had 9,500 of its 27,500 basic organizations (cells) in enterprises.[13] These forces, together with PCF control of the Conféderation Général de Travail (CGT), the largest French trade union, give it an powerful industrial bastion. The Socialist party, in comparison, had perhaps 200,000 members in 1979 and though present in all three major union confederations dominated none of them.

Since the end of the 1970s the PCF has seen its zones of influence shrink dramatically. A share of the vote that had hovered around twenty percent dropped to 16.2% in the 1981 parliamentary elections, then to 11.3% in the 1984 European elections, and finally to 9.8% in the 1986 parliamentary elections. Where it had provided mayors in 1977 to 72 of the 221 cities with populations above 30,000, the PCF held only 57 in 1983. Important losses occurred in regional centers like Reims, St. Etienne, and Nîmes. Worse was to come. The 1986 elections saw the end of traditional Communist hegemony in the "Red Belt" of suburban departments around Paris. In its strongest suburban fortress, Seine-Saint-Denis, where the party had received thirty-six percent of the vote in 1981, it sank to 18.6 in 1986. In Paris itself the PCF had less than five percent of the vote and could thus send no deputy to the National Assembly. Overall, the PCF vote exceeded twenty percent only in three small departments in central France.

Party decline became apparent also in PCF membership, which sank even by inflated party estimates to 608,000 in 1984 and has since stagnated. Even the CGT, the most important PCF front organization, was not untouched by the crisis in militancy. In the elections held in 1983 for representatives to the social security boards it lost ground to the moderate Force Ouvrière (CGT 29.2%; FO 25.4%; CFDT 19%). In ten years, its membership sank from a claimed 2,000,000 to an official 1,200,000, estimated by observers at closer to 800,000.

TABLE 1

Parliamentary elections 1973-1986: PS and PCF percentages

	<u>1973</u>	<u>1978</u>	<u>1981</u>	<u>1986</u>
PS	21.2	22.5	37.8	31.2
PCF	21.1	20.5	16.1	9.8

   This process of erosion in the PCF and the CGT, its most important flanking organization, can be traced back to a series of tightly interconnected causes. The party had been hard hit by reductions and restructuring in old industries, such as iron and steel, coal mining, textiles, shipbuilding, printing, and automobiles, where its roots as the party of the industrial working class had sunk most deeply. In addition, the PCF paid too little attention to growing differentiation in the social attitudes, interests, and values of French workers, contenting itself with a generalized denunciation of contemporary French society as uniformly oppressive "state monopoly capitalism." The PCF found little encouragement from the new employee class of the service sector and in the groups referred to in France as "engineers, technicians, and cadres." Both groups found the party's working-class populism (sometimes with anti-foreign overtones) to be rather repugnant.
   The PCF still has a higher percent of workers in its membership than any other party in France. But in elections only twenty percent of workers vote for the "party of the working class." Furthermore, according to recent research, the PCF has held up relatively well precisely in those regions and social groups least characterized by mobility and innovation. The PCF has tended to suffer its highest losses, however, in the more active regions marked by rapid urbanization. These are "signs of a certain archaism, precursors of more losses," suggests a French scholar of Communism. [14]
   This diagnosis is confirmed by the poor reputation of the PCF among the young. Polls taken among students show

that only three percent of them consider themselves close to the PCF, whereas forty-three percent declare sympathy for the Socialists, seven percent for the ecologists, and four percent for the extreme left.[15] Symptomatic of the PCF's loss of contact with the young were the university and secondary student demonstrations in December 1986, which obliged the Chirac government to withdraw its proposed laws on university reform and inflicted a stinging political and psychological defeat on the Right. The Communists, who shortly before had included the youth as active participants in the general "slippage to the right,"[16], were completely surprised by this development (as on other occasions) and had no influence on it.

Excesses of Democratic Centralism

The problems of the PCF come into focus in its strict observance of democratic centralism. The PCF might be characterized as a cadre party with a (shrinking) mass base. Iron control of internal decision-making by the leadership and domination of the party by its own apparatus have furthered its tendency to barricade itself off from the capitalist world around it, making the PCF into a counter-society oriented toward a revolutionary future, "pure and tough," facing an existing order perceived as the enemy.

The excesses of democratic centralism had much to do with the crisis and decline of the PCF. The party was unable to renew itself; forces desiring change were severely disciplined, as was the group around Marcel Servin and Laurent Casanova in 1961, excluded like Roger Garaudy in 1970 or marginalized, in the case of Pierre Juquin and his friends in 1984. Repeated abrupt changes of the party line for tactical reasons disoriented both members and PCF voters. Mobilized for the Union of the Left from 1972-1977, they then witnessed the sabotage of Left hopes in 1977; a savage campaign against the Socialists was followed by entry into the government in 1981, and then by the breakup of the coalition in 1984.

The Communists no longer dominated women's, youth, or even peace movements, as they had in the postwar years. A large number of new activists in such movements, along with members of the small French ecologist movement, rejected French Communism as another aspect of Jacobin centralism, fixated on the state. Communism had once enjoyed a large following among intellectuals. By the end of the 1970s they had come to regard PCF centralism as anti-democratic and repugnant. In those years Aleksandr Solzhenitsyn's Gulag Archipelago finally awakened the French intelligentsia to aspects of the Soviet Union they had long deliberately overlooked. The administrative bureaucracy and narrow-mindedness of the PCF leadership appeared to the intellectuals as a relic of Stalinism, and was a major cause of their turn away from Marxism. Although in 1979 the PCF claimed 70,000 members among intellectuals as a whole,[17] PCF influence among intellectual opinion makers today is about zero.

Given this negative balance, it is not surprising that since the beginning of the 1980s the PCF leadership has encountered increasing internal opposition to its political line and especially to its use of democratic centralism in internal decision-making. It is interesting that protests are now raised not only by intellectuals but primarily by municipal leaders and leading representatives of Communist enterprise groups (Peugeot and Renault)--i.e. down to earth politicians. Since 1984 the main spokesman of this quite unhomogeneous current has been Pierre Juquin, former Politbureau member and party spokesman. Who in the party decides who is right, asked Juquin, referring to the party's zig-zag line. Juquin believes that only a changing party, able to withstand the controversy involved in assimilating new impulses from outside, can become a force for "change, here and today" in French society.[18]

The group of leaders around Marchais understood how to channel this unusually widespread dissidence. At the Twenty-Fifth PCF Party Congress they even tolerated the re-election of some of its members to the Central Committee, including Juquin and former minister Marcel Rigout. This was a novelty for the PCF, where declared critics of the official line have not been tolerated in the Central Committee since the early 1930s.

Marchais made it clear, however, that this was only a tactical measure, not a signal that the leadership was ready in principle, like the PCI, to democratize internal decision-making and legitimize the existence of variant currents in the party. If we give way on this, remarked Marchais, we open the way to an unavoidable "social democratization" of the PCF, i.e. to its adjustment to the capitalist system.[19] In this declaration in defense of democratic centralism, Marchais expressed the belief of French party leaders that party identity cannot be separated from the PCF's Leninist tradition.[20]

When in January 1987 the general secretary referred to the reformers for the first time as "liquidators." i.e. people whose ideas would allegedly lead to the liquidation of the PCF as a revolutionary formation, he made it clear that the party leadership had ended a phase of relative tolerance toward internal dissent, and that the time for drastic purges had arrived. Such administrative measures will however only further hasten the erosion of the PCF. In answer to the accusation "liquidator" hurled at Juquin, Claude Poperen resigned his seat in the Politburo and Central Committee, while in the same month the popular Rigout resigned from the Central Committee.

A Blocked Eurocommunism

Marchais' allusions to Lenin and use of traditional discipline point up the contradictions in a PCF line which has been only inconsistently Leninist. The strategy and program of the PCF, adumbrated under the Stalinist Thorez, was continued into a period of cautious democratization by his successor Waldeck-Rochet in the late 1960s. The plan called for an alliance with the Socialists and progress by way of an intermediate "advanced democracy" to "socialism in the colors of France." Electoral competition created unstable tension between Leninist tradition and the need to appear democratic. Thus in 1976 the party eliminated central theoretical concepts like the dictatorship of the proletariat from its program and replaced the pledge to observe Marxism-Leninism with a commitment to "scientific socialism." The PCF was the last of the three big Eurocommunist parties to say that it accepted political democracy as a principle, not a tactic--including respect for the existence of political pluralism, meaning the possibility that a leftwing government would yield power if it lost an election.[21]

PCF economic programs called for nationalization of the most important firms and remaining private banks. One aim was to deprive the bourgeoisie of an economic power that might replace lost political power. Nationalization was also seen as the condition for effective state framework planning, which together with a demand-oriented left-Keynesianism would stimulate the domestic economy, make available necessary investments for industrial expansion, and simultaneously make the national economy independent of the pressure and influence of international capital. When the PCF in fact got the chance to prove itself in government, it presented itself as a constructive, reliable political force which had decided upon longterm non-revolutionary cooperation with the Socialists and thus on lasting partnership in the coalition. At the PCF Twenty-fourth Party Congress in 1982 Politbureau member Charles Fiterman, who as a Minister of State was the most senior PCF representative in the government, put party ideas thus:

> The Communists are called upon to build, to administer, to govern....There are many among us who, strongly desiring change to continue, see it at the same time in a longterm context. They want the forces of the Left to give proof of their ability to master such a complex situation.... A priori, we conceive our activity today, including our work in the government, as a longterm effort. We are and always will be ready to go as far as possible, as far as the people in this country wish us to go. [22]

After its entry into the government the PCF at first showed itself to be a loyal ally, competently administering the ministries given it (Transport, Health, Public Service, Professional Training). But from mid-1982 on the Socialists, under pressure from rapidly growing budget and foreign trade deficits, moved toward policies of industrial restructuring and drastic social austerity intended to restore French competitiveness by modernizing productive capacity and maintaining full integration in the European Community. The Communists reacted with opposition inside the coalition. In July 1984 they withdrew from the government and soon thereafter declared that the twenty-five year period of Left unity had ended. Since then, Communist polemics against the Socialists have disavowed their participation in the government.

Self-criticism by the PCF leaders of their role in disastrous policies has been limited. The PCF Twenty-fifth Congress stated that the battle for "advanced democracy" gave the Socialists the chance to pass off this intermediate stage as the real goal of the Union of the Left and thus disorient the masses. The new concept must be the immediate task of creating "democratic self-management socialism with a French impress." Agreements at the top with the Socialists had fostered illusions among the masses on the character of the Socialists and the Union of the Left with a demobilizing effect. In future, only a "new majoritarian peoples' muster" under PCF leadership could develop a new dynamic leading to socialism.

Furthermore, said the resolution of the Twenty-fifth Congress in February 1985, "historic delay" caused by previous leaders (during the time of Maurice Thorez and Waldeck Rochet) was responsible for party difficulties. Marchais and his peers explained that their predecessors were at fault for not moving away from foreign models of socialism and outdated ideas of political alliances soon enough, and for not taking sufficient account of the changes in class structure brought about by economic change.[23]

Return to the Soviet Line

The obstinate attempts by the PCF to justify its domestic turnabout ran parallel to the normalization of its relations with the CPSU which had begun in late 1978. PCF renewal of traditional international ties posed relatively few problems for the party. Despite certain differences with the CPSU during the Eurocommunist phase, PCF leaders had always been guided by the traditional "two camps" theory, whereby a fundamentally repressive and war-mongering capitalist imperialism (including its social democratic variant) was faced by a socialist camp led by the Soviet Union, which by its nature was progressive and peace-loving. In all its criticisms of real socialism--insufficient democracy, intervention in Czechoslovakia, at times also insufficient militancy in pursuing peaceful coexistence--PCF leaders consider the balance sheet of the USSR and the socialist community as still "on the whole positive,"[24] and support Moscow's positions in the East-West conflict, on Afghanistan, Poland, and in the Third World.

This behavior has contributed a great deal to the loss of trust in the PCF by French voters, and has weighed heavily in the attitude of French intellectuals, who are by now overwhelmingly critical of the USSR. When PCI chief Berlinguer refused to support Soviet foreign policy after the 1981 crackdown in Poland on the grounds that doing so was "downright suicidal,"[25] Marchais echoed his words in indirect polemic, calling the USSR a "guarantor of peace" and arguing "it would be tantamount to suicide if one were to forget this, or isolate our forces from the other forces which are fighting in the world against capitalism, and for socialism."[26]

In this context the PCF has developed foreign policy ideas tied to what it saw as the "positive aspects" of de Gaulle's foreign policy, a concept accentuating the defense of national sovereignty. It holds that France as a member of the Atlantic alliance must preserve its full freedom of action, particularly by keeping up its nuclear strike force. (But in contradiction to this, the PCF now wants to count French strategic weapons as part of the overall East-West balance.) The PCF also refuses any greater integration into the European Community or any strengthening of its foreign policy functions. In its view such trends will lead to the liquidation of France's national sovereignty, since in the last analysis the alliance follows the U.S. global strategic line, despite all intra-imperialist contradictions.[27]

At this point PCF-PCI divergences become particularly clear--divergences which have recently led the Italian Communists explicitly to criticize the French brother party, and to take their distance from it. Members of the PCI _Direzione_ have diagnosed the causes of PCF decline as the "dogmatic," "sectarian," and "extremist" positions of the PCF leadership, i.e. its inability to take strategic account of social change, or to give a new definition to its relation to Moscow.[28] At the PCI's Seventeenth Party Congress in April 1986, _Direzione_ member Luciano Lama, in a plea for acceleration in his party's adaptation to modern conditions, went so far as to refer specifically to the decline of the PCF as an example of what happens to a party which holds tightly to traditional patterns of thought and behavior. [29]

Relations with the CPSU remain ambivalent, however. It is questionable whether PCF leaders agree with the main elements of new trends in Soviet foreign policy, for example the notion that in an "interdependent" world the "peace question" has priority over the "class question." Also, Soviet readiness in principle to recognize the European Community as a political unit with worldwide tasks (not merely an economic one)[30] must bother the PCF.

Such latent differences with Moscow surfaced at the Twenty-seventh CPSU Congress in February-March 1986, which Marchais did not attend. In his greetings to the congress PCF Politbureau member Gaston Plissonier quoted a passage from the communique of the Gorbachev-Marchais meeting in September 1985, which spoke of the possibility that "differences" and even "divergences" could arise between the two parties. The communique had gone on to say "each party develops its analyses, its policies, ⟨and⟩ its way toward the building of a socialist society in full independence, according to the situation in its own country."[31]

This passage was certainly intended to polish the domestic image of the PCF. At the same time, it can also be understood as a warning to Moscow not to exaggerate any wooing of Mitterrand and the Socialists for foreign policy reasons. Future conflicts seem built into this situation, since Gorbachev will probably give priority to his diplomatic offensive in Western Europe, favoring influential forces which support it over internationalist solidarity with a shrinking PCF. Such policies would be quite in line with those pursued by past Soviet leaders at the expense of their French brother party.

Prognosis

PCF policy is Gallocommunist rather than Eurocommunist. Revolutionary and nationalist elements are intimately mixed in it, against a background of pro-Sovietism, and its prospects are uncertain. There are few hints that the PCF will undergo the "cultural revolution" which Pierre Juquin regards as the indispensable condition for an upsurge by his party.[32] Its history, sense of mission, and organizational character instead suggest that after the failure of its venture into government the PCF will remain in its oppositional fortress for a long time, presenting itself as a "party of struggle", seeking with all means in its conflict with the Socialists to change the balance of forces on the Left in its favor.

Signs of this recourse to traditional behavior are clearly visible. Among others they are the simultaneous pursuit of two political lines--a combat against the Right and the non-Communist Left. Tactics include concentration on a purely oppositional course, against social injustice, curtailment of civil liberties, against any sellout of national interests. They may heat up social conflicts, even by using violent commando methods (alongside CGT activists). The project of the "new majoritarian peoples' muster" is in many ways reminiscent of the policies of the early 1930s, when the sectarian policy of "class against class" led to the isolation of the PCF, a policy characterized by:

refusal of any political compromise or even any contact, autonomy in principle for the 'mouvement populaire' that assured its total control by the party, a corresponding narrowness in its influence, a predeliction for demonstrative action.[33]

One might object here that in previous periods the PCF has repeatedly freed itself from self-imposed bonds of sectarianism and isolation, rising from a small left-extremist party to become an influential mass party. The best example of this came in the Popular Front phase in the mid-1930s. Favored by the nearly unbroken prestige of the Soviet Union, the Communists were then able to draw to themselves large parts of an expanding industrial working class as well as many intellectuals. These favorable conditions no longer exist today, or have even reversed themselves. Industrial workers, the old seed bed for the growth of the party, are reduced in number, while the reputation of the Soviet Union in France--and particularly among the intellectuals--is lower than ever before.

The PCF can probably hold off a decline into meaninglessness by serving as a catch basin for protest, especially as it still has notable reserves of cadres and organizational capacity. It will however be forced to content itself with a minor role in great national decisions, and as reform leader Juquin put it sarcastically, stand "gesturing courageously on the sidelines."[34]

NOTES

1. Le Monde, June 30, 1972.
2. Cf. Jacques Fauvet, Histoire du Parti communiste français (Paris: Fayard, 1977); Annie Kriegel, Les Communistes français 1920-1970 (Paris: Editions du Seuil, 1985); Ronald Tiersky, French Communism 1920-1972 (New York and London: Columbia University Press, 1974).
3. Cf. Philippe Buton, "Les effectifs du Parti communiste français (1920-1984)," Communisme 7 (1985): 8.
4. See Maurice Thorez, Oeuvres choisis, vol. 2 (Paris: Editions sociales, 1966), pp. 451-454 for Thorez's famous interview with the London Times.
5. See Etienne Fajon, L'Union est un combat (Paris: Editions sociales, 1975), p. 117 for Georges Marchais' 1972 speech to the PCF Central Committee defending the Common Program of Government. The speech was kept secret until 1975.

6. Cf. Ronald Tiersky, "Die Französischen Kommunisten in ihrer Gesellschaft," in Heinz Timmermann, ed., Die Kommunistischen Parteien Südeuropas (Baden-Baden: Nomos, 1978), and Georges Lavau, A quoi sert le parti communiste? (Paris: Fayard, 1981).

7. Resolution of the PCF Twenty-fifth Party Congress in February 1985, in Cahiers du communisme no. 3/4 (1985): 363. On the contentious relation between the PCF and the PS, see Frank L. Wilson, "French Communism on the Defensive," Problems of Communism 34, no. 5 (1985): 77-84.

8. This striking phrase was coined by Georges Lavau. Cf. his "Le Parti communiste dans le système politique français," in Frédéric Bon et al., eds., Le communisme en France (Paris: Armand Colin, 1969), pp. 7-81.

9. Cf. Le Monde, July 2, 1985, for a speech by Politbureau member Philippe Herzog which is an example of this polemic.

10. Georges Marchais, in a speech to the Central Committee, L'Humanité, June 25, 1985.

11. Cf. Jean Ranger, "Le déclin du Parti communiste français," Revue française de science politique 36, no. 1 (1986): 57.

12. "Le P.c. en chiffres," France Nouvelle no. 1752, (June 15, 1979): 10.

13. Resolution of the Twenty-fourth PCF Party Congress, in Cahiers du communisme no. 2/3 (1982): 391.

14. Ranger, "Le déclin," p. 50.

15. Le Monde, December 16, 1986.

16. Ibid., for a quote from Politbureau member Pierre Blotin.

17. L'Humanité, April 28, 1979.

18. See l'Humanité, January 10, 1985 for this statement by Pierre Juquin, in the discussion of the draft resolutions for the Twenty-fifth PCF Congress. Also see his speech at the congress, l'Humanité, February 9, 1985.

19. L'Humanité, April 28, 1979.

20. See Part I, chapter 5 for a fuller discussion of democratic centralism.

21. On the PCF program, see Georges Marchais, Le Défi démocratique (Paris: Grasset, 1973); Parlons franchement (Paris: Grasset, 1977); L'Espoir au présent (Paris: Editions sociales, 1980).

22. Cahiers du communisme no. 2/3 (1982): 138ff.

23. See Cahiers du communisme no. 3/4 (1985): 14-81 for Marchais' address to the PCF Twenty-fifth Congress.

25. L'Unità, January 24, 1982.

26. Cf. Marchais' speech to the Twenty-fourth PCF Congress, Cahiers du communisme no. 2/3 (1982): 70. On the PCF-CPSU relation see Brian L. Zimbler, "Partners or Prisoners? Relations between the PCF and the CPSU," Studies in Comparative Communism 17, no. 1 (1984): 3-29.

27. Cf. my article "Die Westeuropakonzeption der Eurokommunisten," in Heinz Gärtner and Günter Trautmann, eds., Ein Dritter Weg zwischen den Blöcken? Die Weltmächte, Europa und der Eurokommunismus (Vienna: Verlag für Gesellschaftskritik, 1985) pp. 245-263.

28. Cf. l'Unità, March 18, 1986 for comments by PCI Direzione member Emmanuele Macaluso on the PCF defeat at the polls, and la Repubblica, March 18, 1986 for similar remarks by Direzione member Giancarlo Pajetta. For a systematic and critical balance sheet of the PCF line, see Augusto Pancaldi, "Rottura Pc-Ps. E torna indietro l'idea di sinistra," l'Unità, April 6, 1986.

29. Speech to the Seventeenth PCI Congress, l'Unità, April 11, 1986.

30. Cf. Part I, chapter four above on Gorbachev's strategy.

31. Pravda, March 1, 1986. The communique on the Gorbachev-Marchais meeting appeared in Pravda, September 4, 1985.

32. Pierre Juquin, Autocritique (Paris: Grasset, 1985), p. 38.

33. Ranger, "Le déclin," p. 62.

34. L'Humanité, January 10, 1985.

3

The Spanish Communist Party

A decade ago, after the transition from dictatorship to democracy in Spain following Franco's death in 1975, the Spanish Communist party (Partido Comunista de España- PCE) had great hopes for the future. The example of the Italian Communist party, which had used the Resistance to turn an active cadre party into a mass party with deep social roots, had nourished hopes that the PCE too could use its leading role in the resistance to Franco to gain hegemony on the Spanish Left, and push the transformation in Spain toward socialism.

These hopes have since disappeared. The leading party on the left--and in the country--is the Partido Socialista Obrero Español (PSOE), which since 1982 has governed Spain under Prime Minister Felipe González. The Communists today are marginalized, split into several factions, and fighting for survival. How did this happen, and what is the prognosis for this prestigious but controversial and self-contradictory party?

The Rise of the PCE

Founded in 1921, the PCE was declared illegal at the end of the Civil War in March 1939.[1] When it was again made legal in 1977, no signs suggested longterm decline. During the period of illegality it had moved toward ideas of political and social pluralism, and begun an intensive dialogue with non-Communist forces. This and other drastic changes in its program were begun when Dolores Ibárruri was secretary general (1942-1960) and carried further by her successor Santiago Carrillo (1960-1982).[2] The innovations made were set forth in the PCE "Program Manifesto" of 1975, one of the central documents of Eurocommunism. The manifesto characterizes the completion of the bourgeois democratic system as a necessary step on the road to socialism. The freedoms achieved by the progressive bourgeoisie and the working class, including party pluralism and the right to strike, were to be maintained after a socialist transformation--along with a key measure: socialization of the key centers of private capital, both productive and financial.[3]

Once the PCE became legal again, Carrillo's programmatic innovations received even greater stress. In the party's search for a democratic reputation, tactical and opportunist considerations played a considerable role.[4] Thus at its Ninth Party Congress in 1978 the PCE struck the expression "Marxism-Leninism" from its statutes, defining itself henceforth as a "Marxist, democratic, and revolutionary party." And as a symbol of its contribution to "national reconciliation," it accepted the institution of the monarchy with its traditional flag.

The PCE's most dramatic move was to draft a strategy of pragmatic consensus with the Center party of Prime Minister Adolfo Suárez, culminating with the signing of economic and political agreements in the "Moncloa Pact" in 1978. Intended as a Spanish variant of the PCI "historic compromise," the pact meant that the PCE would abandon insistence on drastic economic and social reforms, with the strategic goal of assuring Spain's democratic transformation through economic consolidation. But the PCE line also had a tactical side; the PCE was to appear to the progressive bourgeoisie as a constructive and cooperative representative of the Left--thus checking the thrust of a dynamic Socialist party.

After the Soviet intervention in Czechoslovakia in 1968, the PCE began a radical change of course in international relations. One important reason for this change was the long exile of many Spanish Communists in Czechoslovakia. They had learned at first hand that the Prague Spring was in no way a counterrevolution, but rather an attempt to reform and renew the existing system. Party chief Carrillo criticized the Soviet model of society and central aspects of Soviet foreign policy more vociferously than any other Western Communist leader.[5] And in 1982, after the suppression of Solidarnosc, the PCE, like the PCI, declared the propulsive force of Soviet Communism to be exhausted. [6]

In the spirit of a "new" internationalism (not Moscow's "proletarian" type) the PCE wished to entertain relations equally with Communist, socialist, and social democratic parties. With Spain's entry into the European Community, this policy would facilitate creation of a bloc-free "Third Force."[7] The engine of a movement toward an independent Western Europe tending toward socialism was in PCE eyes a seemingly unstoppable Eurocommunism. In March 1977, when Carrillo invited his Italian and French colleagues Berlinguer and Marchais to the first (and only) Eurocommunist summit meeting in Madrid, the PCE leaders intended both to legitimize and strengthen their party at home, and together with the PCI and PCF to clarify the contours of their "new internationalism."

The PCE's combination of active resistance to Franco and adaptation to Western democratic norms and values paid off at first.[8] The party struck deep roots in the industrial concentrations of Barcelona, Madrid, and Valencia, as well as in the industrial regions of Catalonia, the Asturias, Andalusia, and the Basque country. The proof was its dominant influence in the Workers Commissions (Comisiones Obreras-CC.OO.), which had taken shape inside the obligatory Francoist trade union at the end of the 1950s as the authentic voice of the workers, with Socialist and Catholic currents as well as Communists. The PCE had also found a following in the new middle classes, especially among intellectuals and the scientific and technical intelligentsia. Communists frequently occupied leading positions in the official associations of the liberal professions, giving the party hope that the PCE (copying the PCI and the PCF after World War II) could achieve cultural hegemony in post-Franco Spain.

Indeed, the underground cadre party of circa ten thousand members had grown by 1978 to an official figure of 200,000. The Partit Socialista Unificat de Catalunya (PSUC), its autonomous Catalan branch, the advance guard of Spanish Eurocommunism, alone numbered 40,000 members. The leadership had forged what it termed an "alliance of the forces of labor and culture" which seemed successful, as was the transformation of the PCE into a powerful formation--"a mass party, equally of cadres, members, and militants." [9]

Decline

The first two elections in 1977 and 1979 showed that Communist expectations were too high. With 9.2% in 1977 and 10.8% in 1979 the PCE ran far behind the PSOE, which won 29.2% and then 30.8%. In the big cities, largely administered by Socialist and Communists together, the PCE was assigned the role of junior partner, with Córdoba the sole exception. The 1982 elections were a disaster for the Communists: their share of the vote sank to 3.9 percent, while the PSOE won 46.1. The power ratio scarcely changed in the 1986 elections, with 4.6 against 44.1 percent. Membership dropped to an official 68,000 in 1985, even while the Unión General de Trabajadores (UGT), close to the PSOE, moved abreast of the Comisiones Obreras.

TABLE 2

Cortes Elections in 1986 and 1982

Party	Percent		Seats	
	1986	1982	1986	1982
PSOE (Socialists)	44.1	46.1	184	201
AP (Conservatives)	26.0	25.4	105	106
UCD (Center)	9.2	7.3	19	12
PCE (Communists)	4.6*	3.9	7	4
Carrillo group	1.1	-	-	-

* The "official" Iglesias PCE, campaigning in the electoral alliance Izquierda Unida (United Left).

Source: Archiv der Gegenwart 52 (1982): 26,087; ibid. 56 (1986): 30,008.

In addition, a party deeply divided on program and policy lost members from both its wings, by resignation and by exclusion.[10] With the reform-minded Renovadores, who at the Tenth PCE Congress in 1981 had provided twenty-five percent of the delegates, the party lost the larger part of its intellectuals and its best known local politicians. Among highly respected figures were Manuel Azcárate, leading theoretician and foreign policy authority, and Ramón Tamames, economic expert and deputy mayor of Madrid. At the other extreme, the orthodox "prosoviéticos" set up a parallel party in early 1984, led by the former Executive Committee member Ignacio Gallego and entitled "Communist Party of the Peoples of Spain" (Partido Comunista de los Pueblos de España).[11] Immediately recognized and thus "legitimized" by Moscow, it claims 20,000 members, a majority of them organized in the CC.OO.

Finally, Carrillo, forced out of office in 1982 and unable to control the PCE, founded his own Communist party in 1986. (In 1983 the Carrillo forces at the Eleventh Party Congress had forty-five percent of the delegates and elected thirty-five percent of the Central Committee members.) In the 1986 elections his ticket received only 1.1 percent of the vote and won no seats. He did not let this discourage him; his successor Gerardo Iglesias has said that Carrillo's main goal is "to lay the PCE in ashes."[12] What are the causes for this historic decline of Spanish Communism, which retains as its only common symbol the nonagenarian Dolores Ibárruri, the legendary Pasionaria of the Civil War?

The Albatross

An important reason for the unexpectedly weak performance of the PCE after the transition from dictatorship to democracy is surely the distaste of a great majority of Spaniards for the polarizing forces of both left and right. After the traumatic experiences of the past, they preferred groups from the liberal-social and reform-oriented center. On the right, the former Franco minister Manuel Fraga Iribarne suffered repeated defeats at the polls, finally resigning the chairmanship of his conservative Popular Alliance in November 1986.

The record of the Communists in the Civil War hung heavily on their necks. They drew strength from the myth of the Popular Front period, when they had grown from a political sect to a mass party, with a claimed membership of 380,000 in 1937. They had been the most influential factor in the defense of the republic against right-radical, clerical reactionary, and conservative monarchist forces, and after defeat constituted the most active element in resistance to Franco. But close ties to the CPSU dating from Comintern days, and Civil War memories of the liquidation of "Trotskyites," anarchists, and deviationist International Brigaders carried out by PCE and Comintern agents continue to mar the PCE's reputation. The PCE's wartime grab for hegemony against Largo Caballero and the Socialists has not been forgotten. Therefore the Socialists have continually refused Communist overtures, first made in 1965-1966 for a broad anti-Franco alliance, (pacto para la libertad), just as they have rejected Communist offers made since the beginning of the 1980s for a Left alliance.

PCE leaders themselves admit today that it was a serious mistake to leave the reins of power in the 1970s to the old guard around Carrillo. In the first Cortes elections in 1977 the PCE presented returned exiles from the Civil War in a majority of constituencies.[13] In contrast, the PSOE had made radical changes in its leadership in the mid-1970s. Civil War veterans, mostly living in French exile, were replaced by dynamic young activists firmly rooted in contemporary Spain. (In 1974 Felipe González became leader of the PSOE at thirty-two.)

Strategic Errors

Although tactical mistakes made the burden of history even heavier, the party was devastated by another error, this time a major and strategic one. Until the end of the 1970s the PCE leaders assumed that the transition to democracy in Spain could be assured only by a radical break with the Franco regime. In their thinking, no evolution to democracy could take place that involved liberal elements from the regime.[14] In the 1960s the party had expelled the leaders like Fernando Claudín and Jorge Semprun who even then had advocated a gradualist strategy which could take advantage of this eventuality.[15]

The myth of the radical break shows that the Communists basically continued to think in the polarizing categories of the Civil War. They thereby underestimated not only the increasing inner decomposition of the regime, but also the extent of rapid change in society and values, paradoxically set in motion after 1960 by Franco and his Opus Dei technocrats, with their policy of forced draft industrialization. The broad new middle classes and large parts of the working class had little interest in a radical break with the regime, particularly as it had little chance of acceptance by the still influential military, self-elected guardians of stability and order. What they wanted was a gradual dismantling of authoritarian structures and comprehensive modernization.

Significantly, the Comisiones Obreras under the longterm leadership of Marcelino Camacho were able to retain their strong position among the workers just because they concentrated on reformist goals and assured themselves some autonomy vis a vis the PCE. (Camacho resigned from the PCE Executive Committee in 1982).[16] In politics, however, a majority of Spaniards decided at first in favor of Adolfo Suárez' bourgeois Unión de Centro Democratico as the party of democratic transition, and then for the Socialists as the party of socially cushioned modernization. The Communists lost influence, even though they contradicted their proclaimed strategy by showing themselves quite ready for compromise in day-to-day politics (thus without doubt making an appreciable contribution to the stabilization of democracy).

The Communists thus began with an inherent lack of attractiveness. Added to this was their contradictory strategy. The consequence was political isolation, followed by internal splits that threatened paralysis and finally "auto-destrucción".[17] The PCE understood the strategy of revolutionary break to mean the leading role of the Communist party in any alliance, while Carrillo made no secret of his aversion on principle to the reformism of the PSOE. He thus maneuvered the PCE into a blind alley, since the Socialists would not accept a subordinate role. Instead, they made a clear strategic decision in 1979 to shift toward the center, a move symbolized by dropping the definition of PSOE (adopted in 1976) as a "Marxist" party.

Even more serious was the fact that the group of leaders around Carrillo had only slightly modified the model of a militant Leninist cadre party, with all its centralist and authoritarian structures, which they had brought with them from underground work. Every attempt to relax the principles of democratic centralism in internal decision-making, to receive new impulses from the society without, were branded by Carrillo as "liquidative" initiatives that would lead to "social democratization" and dissolution.

This behavior followed from the general PCE line: as an orthodox Communist Carrillo believed that any policy of extensive alliances and openings to society at large demanded energetic measures by the leadership to preserve the identity of the PCE as a revolutionary party. "We were Eurocommunists without, but not within," as Manuel Azcarate, a leader of the "Renovadores" pertinently remarked.[18] Thus the Eurocommunist program of the PCE fell into discredit because it stood in evident contradiction to the party's practice of a centralism that was in fact antidemocratic (an important cause for the parallel decline of the PCF). Moreover, the party itself split into several groups. Carrillo's attempts to preserve the PCE traditional revolutionary identity by using Leninist discipline against dissidence only accelerated decline.

Spain's Communists Today

The present state of Spanish Communism is somewhat confusing, not least in international affairs. The PCE is keeping a very low profile in its relations with the CPSU, especially in comparison with the 1970s. Its chief organ Mundo Obrero has for some time printed little criticism of "real socialism" or of Soviet foreign policy. One reason is certainly Gorbachev's policy of seeking reform at home and the "new thinking" in foreign policy.[19] But the PCE rapprochement with the CPSU and the East bloc can also be traced to the desire of Iglesias' PCE to find a modus vivendi with the Moscow-oriented group led by Gallego and to strengthen its own legitimacy with the Communist base, especially with those militants still under Carrillo's influence.

The normalization and improvement of CPSU-PCE relations, dormant in 1983, began in 1984 with discussions conducted by PCE leaders in Sofia. They were continued in talks in Prague in October and Budapest in November of 1986, which were to pave the way for an Iglesias meeting with Gorbachev in January 1987. The meeting did not take place, however, possibly because of Gorbachev's domestic political problems. Instead, Executive Committee member Simon Sanchez Montero met with Dobrynin in Moscow, and agreed on a "normalization" of party relations.[20] The Soviet leadership is less interested in the ideological loyalty of fraternal parties than in the broadest possible support for its diplomatic offensive against the West. It seems to have accepted PCE overtures largely because an anti-NATO movement in Spain led by the PCE promises more success than do the separate activities of Gallego's uninfluential pro-Soviet sect. When Gallego met Dobrynin in Moscow in late 1986, Moscow quite evidently demanded "on the basis of principle... in the spirit of Marxist-Leninist international solidarity" that Gallego should seek reunion with the PCE. [21]

The rapprochement of the PCE with the CPSU and the Eastern European state parties may strengthen the authority of the Iglesias leadership among Spanish Communists. In the population at large, however, it may excite discordant sentiments. The PCE, clearly the petitioner in renewing party relations with the East, could not hide its vulnerability to Soviet intervention in its internal affairs.[22] Moscow may thus be tempted in future to condition the PCE in the Soviet interest, if necessary by threatening a renewed split in line with the three precedents: 1970-1975 with the Líster group, 1977 with attacks on Carrillo, 1984 with the Gallego group.

The rump PCE remains the strongest of the three Spanish Communist formations, and has the largest following in the Comisiones Obreras. Against bitter resistance from Carrillo, it is trying to find a third way between Soviet style socialism and traditional social democracy. Under the leadership of Gerardo Iglesias (born 1945) and encouraged by the aged Dolores Ibárruri, honorary party chairman, the PCE and the majority in the Comisiones Obreras want to continue the genuine Eurocommunist concept of the 1970s.

The PCE is highly critical of the economic and social policies of the Socialist government, in which it sees an increasingly neo-liberal tendency. [23] At the same time it is ready to agree on a "national solidarity plan" with the government and the employers--but only at a price, for example increases in public investment, provision of solidarity funds to create jobs, a shortened work week, guarantees of social measures, etc. The example of the French party and the tightly associated CGT may have helped teach Iglesias and his followers that a radicalized general line appears to left-oriented voters as largely verbal maximalism and is thus not credible, particularly to the growing new middle classes. The other Communist formations under Carrillo and Gallego still insist on uncompromising economic and social alternatives and on mobilization aiming at stronger pressure on the "bourgeois-liberal" González government. [24]

Rejoining the ideas of the Renovadores, the present PCE leadership is trying to bring both the structure and self-image of the PCE into harmony with a Eurocommunist project of society. For these new leaders, there is no future in Spain for a "dogmatic, sectarian, antiquated

Communist party."[25] The "laic character of the party," "freedom of criticism" and "the largest possible measure of inner-party democracy" constitute an unconditional basis for the success of a multi-class mass party in a complex Western society.[26]

Iglesias' quest for party alliances differs from Carrillo's by rejecting a strategy of confrontation on principle with the PSOE. The new PCE line is to offer the long-term prospect of cooperation as a partner in a left government led by the Socialists. Until this can be worked out, the PCE is trying to form a broad political and social "convergence of the Left," including dissatisfied PSOE followers, parts of the "homeless Left," and the new social movements, in order to break the hegemony of the Socialists as the "unique alternative to the Right." [27] Among these groups are Ramón Tamames' Progressive Federation, the Humanist party, the Socialist Action party made up of dissident Socialists, the Republican Left, an ecologist party and the Carlist party (monarchists who contest the legitimacy of the ruling Bourbon branch). After lengthy negotiations the PCE was even able to conclude an electoral alliance with Gallego's Moscovite party, with which it was bitterly feuding. Both formations want reunification.[28] The Carrillo group, whose tactical opportunism repels the other components of the "United Left," remains outside.[29]

The most important impulse for these tendencies toward rapprochement emerged from the relative success won by the Communists and other NATO critics in the March 1986 referendum on Spain's membership in NATO. The vote was nine million votes or 52.5 percent in favor, seven million or 39.8 percent against. On this issue the PCE can reckon on the future concurrence of an audience reaching far beyond its own ranks, and can hope to condition the government accordingly. (The main points are adherence to Gonzalez' three pledges: no nuclear weapons on Spanish territory, no military integration within NATO, and reduction of the American military presence in Spain.).[30]

Another factor for unity lies in gains by the Comisiones Obreras (in which the three Communist tendencies together hold a majority position). The CC.OO. campaigns against the negative results of Socialist austerity and restructuring. Spain leads Europe with three million unemployed (21.8 percent of the labor force). The situation of the UGT, which is close to the PSOE, is thus particularly shaky; it is often placed in the difficult position of remaining true to its own union principles while yet attempting to defend PSOE policies of economic adaptation and modernization. In the enterprise council elections of October 1986 the CC.OO claimed 28,937 votes, against 26,865 for the UGT and 16,572 for other groups.[31] The Communists are thus much stronger in the unions than in parliament. Significantly, the general strike called in June 1985 by the CC.OO. to protest pension reform, the first general strike since the return of democracy, found a surprisingly large echo in the population.

Prognosis

Thus the PCE and the CC.OO. have proved that they can still mobilize large groups for specific actions. But the question remains whether Iglesias' PCE can in the medium term convert widespread dissatisfaction with certain aspects of PSOE policies into lasting support for its own line and so become a real rival to the Socialists.

The demoralizing scissions of the last few years have cost the party many members throughout the country.[32] The rapprochement with Moscow and the way in which it was carried out can only have a negative effect on the PCE image. Finally, one may doubt whether the PCE electoral alliance, the "United Left," which reaches from pacifists and Greens to Gallego's Moscovites, can agree on a united and constructive program capable of exciting enthusiasm. In any case, the meager result of 4.6 percent in the 1986 elections, less than a tenth of the PSOE vote, hardly suggests a rapid turnaround.

NOTES

1.On the history of the PCE, see Guy Hermet, The Communists in Spain. Study of an Underground Political Movement (Westmead and Farnborough: Saxon House, 1974), and Eusebio Mujal-León, Communism and Political Change in Spain (Bloomington: Indiana University Press, 1983).

2. On this point, see Carrillo's books, especially Demain l'Espagne. Entretiens avec Regis Debray et Max Gallo (Paris: Editions du Seuil, 1974), and Le communisme malgré tout, interview avec Lilly Marcou (Paris: Presses Universitaires de France, 1984).

3. Manifiesto Programa del Partido Comunista de España (Paris: Colección Ebro, 1975).

4. Cf. Carrillo's much cited book, violently criticized by Moscow: Eurocomunismo y Estado (Barcelona: Editorial Critíca, 1977).

5. Carrillo, Eurocomunismo, pp. 99ff and 179ff.

6. "Resolución del C.C. del PCE". El País, January 13, 1982.

7. On such "Third Force" ideas, see the unsigned article "La tercera posición," Nuestra Bandera 44, no. 103(1980): 4-8. This article in the PCE's theoretical journal was written by its then director Manuel Azcárate, later a leader of the "Renovadores".

8. Cf. my article "Spaniens Kommunisten auf dem Weg in die Legalität," Osteuropa 26, no. 2 (1976): 125-145.

9. Carrillo, Eurocomunismo, p. 129.

10. Cf. Eusebio Mujal-León, "Decline and Fall of Spanish Communism," Problems of Communism 35, no. 2 (1986): 1-27, an excellent account.

11. See Pravda, May 23, 1984 for the communique on the meeting of Gallego with Boris Ponomarev and Vadim Zagladin.

12. El País, November 26, 1985.

13. Author's conversation with a leading representative of the PSUC in September, 1985.

14. Cf. Mujal-León, "Decline and Fall," p. 2ff.; and Harald Wilkens, "Politische Konzeption und innere Struktur der KP Spaniens 1956-1964," Berichte des Bundesinstituts no. 1 (1983): 16ff.

15. See Wilkens, "Politische Konzeption," p. 46ff. for a full account of the Claudín-Semprun affair.

16. On the structure and policies of the Comisiones Obreras see Harald Wilkens, "Die spanischen 'Arbeiterkommissionen' in der Krise: Zum III. Kongress der KP-nahen Richtungsgewerkschaft," Aktuelle Analyse des Bundesinstituts no. 40 (1984).

17. Mundo Obrero 4, no. 208 (1982): 17. Quoted from Iglesias' report to the PCE national conference in December, 1982.

18. See the Azcárate interview "Unsere schwerste Krise seit dem Stalinismus," Der Spiegel 36, no. 25 (1982): 124.

19. Cf. Part I, Chapter 4, above.

20. "PCE-PCUS: Gorbachov e Iglesias se reuniran en enero," Mundo Obrero 7 no. 415 (1986): 45; and "Normalisación de relaciones entre ambos partidos," and "Comunicado PCE-PCUS," both in Mundo Obrero 7, no. 427 (1987): 48ff.

21. Cf. Pravda, November 2, 1986, for the joint communique of the meeting between Dobrynin and Gallego.

22. The joint CzPC-PCE communique explicitly states that the resumption of party relations took place "a petición de la dirección del PCE." See Mundo Obrero 7 no. 409 (1986): 42. The PCE had broken off relations in 1968 after the Soviet military intervention in Czechoslovakia.

23. Cf. the resolution of the PCE Executive Committee "El P.C.E. contra la politica economica del Gobierno," Mundo Obrero 7, no. 410 (1986): 19.

24. Cf. El País, June 29, 1983 on Carrillo. Cf. also Mujal-León, "Decline and Fall," p. 15ff.

25. El País, June 18, 1982, quoting Nicolás Sartorius, one of the two vice-secretary generals of the PCE.

26. El País, December 9, 1983, quoting Iglesias. Also see Mujal-León, "Decline and Fall," p. 6ff.

27. "Resoluciones del Comite Central," Mundo Obrero 7, no. 408 (1986): 46.

28. See "Encuentro PCE-PCPE," Mundo Obrero 7, no. 407 (1986): 15, for an account of the talks between Iglesias and Gallego.

29. Cf. Thierry Maliniak, "La gauche non-socialiste se rassemble autour du PCE," Le Monde, May 2, 1986.

30. "O.T.A.N., por la puerta falsa," Mundo Obrero 7, no. 407 (1986): 10. The article was signed only "C.M."

31. "Elecciones sindicales: el fraude se generaliza," Mundo Obrero 7, no. 413 (1986): 33. Article signed only "A.B. P.".

32. Cf. the statement by the PCE organization secretary: "Francisco Palero: 'Estamos decidos a innovar el Partido,'" Mundo Obrero 7, no. 413 (1986): 56ff. However, the PCE noted that its membership had risen from 68,000 in 1985 to 93,000 in early 1987.

4

The Finnish Communist Party

The Finnish Communist Party (SKP, from its Finnish title <u>Suomen Kommunistinen Puolue</u>) was founded in Moscow in August 1918 by Finnish Socialists who had fled to Russia. Illegal during the first decades of its existence, at times crippled by factional struggles, it became legal only after the Finnish-Soviet armistice of September 1944. In the period after the war its strength nearly equalled that of the Social Democrats, with about 50,000 members and an electoral following hovering around 20 percent.

Zones of Political and Social Influence

The social base of the SKP lies among the industrial workers of southern Finland (about 70 percent of membership) and the peasant population of the thinly settled north (about 10 percent).* It has had difficulty recruiting in the middle classes (some 15 percent of membership). Its influence in Finland's unitary trade confederation corresponds to its strength in the working class: five of the twenty-eight branch unions are controlled by Communists, among them the powerful construction workers.

---

*The statistics cited here on the SKP in Finnish society and in the SKP's subsidiary organizations reflect the situation before the formal split of June 1986 which saw the emergence of the dogmatist faction in the SKP as a separate party. Accurate figures reflecting the new situation are not yet available, except for those of the 1987 parliamentary elections. See Table 3, below.

The Communists also enjoy strong minority positions in a series of other federations, for example with 47 per cent in the governing body of the powerful metal workers' union. The Communists' problem is that social change has shrunk the basis for the party's strength. Skilled workers and the new middle strata in the growing service and information industries turn more easily to the Social Democrats than to a Communist party crippled by power struggles and factional disputes.

At the parliamentary level the SKP is represented by the Finnish People's Democratic League (SKDL), founded in October 1944, which for decades has been a recognized front organization for the SKP. Originally conceived as a movement that would gather together all forces on the Left, the SKDL consists of Communists and left Socialists as individual members (1984 figures: 36,000 members, 22 percent Communists). As a roof organization it also takes in all of the SKP (except for the dogmatists, after the 1986 split) plus a small left-socialist group, together with a series of groups close to the SKP, such as organizations for women and youth, war veterans, etc.

From 1944 to 1948 and--with interruptions--since 1966 the SKDL has participated in the government with the Social Democratic and Agrarian (now Center) parties.[1] In the second period, however, it had to be content with "divided" ministries or with lesser portfolios below the level of the key ministries, such as Social Affairs, Transport, Public Works, or Justice.

Since the beginning of the 1970s the SKP has undergone a process of slow erosion that reduced its membership by 1983 to 33,000, while the Social Democrats had 101,000 members. Its voting strength sank from 18 percent in 1979, providing 35 parliamentary seats of the total 200, to 14 percent and 27 seats in 1983, and 13.7 percent and 20 seats for the now divided Communists in 1987.

The levels of the 1983 parliamentary elections were confirmed in the local elections of October 1984, when the SKP obtained 13.9 percent. The Communists left the government in December 1982 and have since then been in opposition.[2]

TABLE 3

Finland: Parliamentary elections in 1983 and 1987

Party	Percent		Seats	
	1983	1987	1983	1987
Social Democrats	26.7	24.2	57	56
Conservatives	22.1	23.1	44	53
Center	17.6	17.7	38	40
Communists	14.	-	27	-
-SKP	-	9.4	-	16
-Democratic Alternative (Sinisalo dogmatists)	-	4.3	-	4
Small Farmers	9.7	6.3	17	9
Swedish Peoples' Party	4.6	5.3	11	13
Christian Union	3	2.6	3	5
Greens	1.4	4	2	4
Constitutional Right	0.1	0.4	1	0

Source: Helsingin Sanomat March 18, 1987

The Special Relation with the CPSU

The rise of the SKP at the end of World War II, as well as its present problems, are closely related to its special historical relationship with the CPSU.[3] The Communist Party of the Soviet Union views itself as the SKP's patron, with extensive rights of interference in its internal affairs. Because they saw the SKP as an important guarantee of the neutrality of a country that lies within the Soviet sphere of influence, the Soviets constantly pushed for its inclusion in Finnish government.

The Finno-Soviet relationship found its symbolic expression in the person of Otto Kuusinen (1881-1964), for many years leader of the SKP, who functioned in 1918 and again in 1939 as head of a Soviet-supported Finnish puppet government, but served in 1952-53 under Stalin and again in 1957-64 under Khrushchev as a member of the CPSU Presidium (Politburo).

For decades the SKP drew its strength from the Soviet myth, which was deeply rooted among Finnish workers. The myth goes back to the period of the common Finnish and Russian revolutions of 1905 and 1917/18, and remains unforgotten in the older generation of SKP members. But as it faded, and as a reformist leadership and majority took over the SKP, first under Aarne Saarinen (1966-1982) and since 1984 under Arvo Aalto, the special relationship with the CPSU created serious problems for the SKP. It has made a major contribution to the decline of the SKP, which after 1969 was a united party only in the formal sense, but in fact was split into reformist and dogmatic factions. Each had its own apparatus, base organizations and central press organs--for the majority, <u>Kansan Uutiset</u>, <u>Tiedonantaja</u> for the minority.[4]

The CPSU supported the reformist majority insofar as it guaranteed the Soviet policy of continuing a coalition government of Social Democrats, Centrists, and Communists. But it opposed the reformists' programmatic innovations and their criticism of Soviet policy--for example on Czechoslovakia in 1968 and Poland in 1980 and thereafter. The real sympathies of the CPSU lay with the minority dogmatists, who rejected participation in government but held fast to Lenin's theory of revolution and upheld unconditional solidarity with the Soviet Union.

Through massive personal interventions by Soviet Politburo members (Brezhnev, Suslov, Pelshe, Romanov, Zaikov) and with operational "supervision" by the Leningrad party organization, the CPSU leaders repeatedly forced the two hostile SKP factions to preserve party unity, taking care to ensure that the dogmatists would be well represented in the leading organs of the party. This "shotgun marriage" (Saarinen's phrase) was held together with difficulty by external pressure. Characterized by daily factional trench warfare interrupted by only formal compromises, it paralyzed the SKP and considerably reduced its power of attraction, particularly for the younger generation.[5]

Majority and Minority in the SKP

The bastions of the reformist majority of the SKP are in the capital, Helsinki, and in the north. Its position is actually stronger than one might suppose from a slight superiority in the number of party federations under its control before the split (nine of seventeen) and delegates to the 1982 SKP Party Congress (196 out of 347).

The majority has a stronger following among the SKP members of the unitary trade union movement; many of its leaders, including Saarinen, come from union backgrounds. Moreover, the reformists are reinforced by the non-Communists in the SKDL, who under the leadership of the left socialist Ele Alenius (1965-1982) eliminated their dogmatists and with the vogue of Eurocommunist concepts won increased importance as a distinct group. Their role has become more important since the SKDL Socialists organized themselves in late 1982 as an independent country-wide group inside the mother organization, and introduced new themes for discussion such as ecology and criticism of unrestricted growth.

The SKP majority continued to support the general line of Soviet foreign policy, with particular emphasis on Moscow's interest in continuing the Paasikivi-Kekkonen line in Finnish-Soviet relations. It has however energetically rejected Soviet pretensions to a leading role among fraternal parties; even small CP's like the SKP have, as Saarinen put it, the right to "their own identity and self-respect."[6]

Under the banner of a "Finnish road to socialism," the SKP majority bade farewell to the Leninist theory of revolution, and under the strong influence of the SKDL leadership moved toward Eurocommunist positions. They emphasized their intention to realize socialism with peaceful and democratic means. In coalition politics the majority group aspires to a longterm "historical compromise" with the Social Democrats and the Center (ex-Agrarians) to achieve specific social improvements for the workers and, in Aalto's words "to steer investment to change the industrial structure and strengthen and enlarge the sector of enterprises with state participation."[7]

The dogmatic minority under Taisto Sinisalo considered itself the guardian of the revolutionary task of the radical Finnish workers' movement, handed down from the years of illegality. It is most strongly represented in the southern industrial regions, with its fortress in the city of Turku. Considering itself a militant revolutionary party, it unconditionally backs the international policy of the CPSU, as in the case of intervention in Czechoslovakia, and advocates even closer Finnish ties with the Soviet Union-- joint military maneuvers, for example.[8]

The minority opposed the reformist policy of the majority as a right-revisionist national-Communist deviation from the universal principles of Marxism-Leninism. With its traditionalist analysis of the bourgeois liberal state, it considers parliament at best a tribune for class struggle. Taking a position more dogmatic than that of the Soviet leaders, it condemns the coalition policies of the majority that aim at governmental participation, finding them inimical to worker interests and fit only to strengthen the capitalist system. The consistent opposition and obstructionist tactics of the dogmatists inside the SKDL parliamentary group complicated the task of SKDL ministers and directly or indirectly brought about the fall of several governments. The minority regards this as a means to hinder creeping "social democratization" of the SKP by preventing it from losing its character as a militant revolutionary party.

Schism and Prognosis

The outlook for the SKP is rather poor, especially since the failure of the attempt to avoid a split carried out in 1982-84 under the leadership of Jouko Kajanoja, who sought to create a new party majority with the slogan of "a third line." In fact, the programmatic and political boundaries inside the Finnish Left have long since ceased to separate the Social Democrats from the SKDL and the Communists, particularly since the Social Democrats gave up their anti-Communism (and anti-Sovietism) in the mid-1960's and moved to the left. Instead, the frontiers run straight through the Communist camp. In normal conditions this situation would have favored a new constellation of forces, with a large democratic-socialist reform movement on one side, and on the other the Marxist-Leninist dogmatists from the former SKP minority, doomed to meaninglessness. In the trade union movement, the women's organization, and in the big workers' athletic league this is already a reality.

Because of the special geographical and political situation of Finland, however, the SKP reformers for years shied away from such a reorientation. The CPSU repeatedly told the SKP leadership that it could maintain ties only with a "revolutionary" Communist party, and that such a relationship was an important guarantee for the continuation of good neighborly relations between the USSR and Finland. The resulting paralysis of the SKP was one factor in the party's inability to attract new voters from the growing middle classes and new social movements, even as the traditional CP electorate was shrinking. Many indications suggest that the power ratio between Social Democrats and Communists will continue to move toward the former inside a Left electorate that counts roughly forty percent of the voters.

Not until after the Twentieth Party Congress of the SKP in May 1984 did the SKP reformist majority decide to push its own ideas without regard to the traditionalists in the party (and in Moscow), and thereby risk a formal split. The election of Aalto, the leader of the reformists, as party chairman against Kajanoja and the successful establishment of the majority's own party organizations in the industrial bastions of the traditionalists in southern Finland began a series of steps that moved ever more resolutely toward a party split. At the extraordinary Party Congress of March 23, 1985 the dogmatists rejected any further collaboration, whereupon a Central Committee was elected consisting entirely of members of the reformist wing. In October 1985 the Central Committee excluded from the party eight federations controlled by the minority. Its response was to constitute a "Committee of the SKP Party Organizations for Unity, against Schism," with Sinisalo as chairman and Kajanoja as general secretary. In a conference in Tampere in late April 1986 this group made a last attempt to win a majority in the SKP and bring in a central committee and politburo to its liking.

Finally, in June 1986 the reformists excluded the dogmatists from the common parliamentary group (where they had had ten of the twenty-seven members.) Thereupon the dogmatists created their own formation under the name of "Democratic Alternative," thereby completing the schism into two separate Communist parties. The new party has given itself a front organization imitating the SKDL's relation to the SKP. Sinisalo is party chairman, Kajanoja general secretary of the front group.

The weakening of the SKP resulting from the party split is probably of minor importance to state relations between Finland and the USSR. The CPSU has come to have such good relations with the Social Democrats, as well as with the peasant-middle class Center party (both sent guest delegations to the Twenty-Seventh CPSU Congress in 1986) that in the Soviet view the Communists have lost much of their relevance as important guarantors of Soviet-Finnish friendship.

On the party level, both the purged CP and the "Democratic Alternative" maintain relations with the CPSU. The SKP claims that it alone is recognized by the Soviets as the true fraternal party, while the CPSU relationship with the "Democratic Alternative" corresponds to relations with "other democratic forces." It is hard to decide whether this is wishful thinking, or perhaps designed to please Communist voters. So far the CPSU has not taken an official position on the split in the SKP.

The future of the two Finnish Communist groups is also uncertain. Despite the fact that the combined score of the two currents in the 1987 election (13.7%) nearly equalled the results of the 1983 elections, Sinisalo's dogmatists will in the long run probably not escape the fate that overcame other Communist dogmatist groups in Denmark and Norway, which dwindled away into insignificant political sects without parliamentary representation. On the other hand, one can only speculate whether enough political space remains alongside the Social Democrats for Aalto's reformists to maintain themselves as an influential force advocating significant structural reforms.

NOTES

1. Cf. John H. Hodgson, "Finnish Communism and Electoral Politics," Problems of Communism 23, no. 1 (1974): 34-45.

2. On the SKP's disappearing voters, see Hermann Beyer, "Finnlands Kommunisten vor grossen Problemen," Osteuropa 34, no. 5 (1984): 357ff.

3. An excellent description of this special relation is given in Jyrki Iivonen, "State or Party? The Dilemma of Relations between the Soviet and Finnish Communist Parties," Journal of Communist Studies 2, no. 1 (1986): 5-30.

4. On the origins of the schism, see Ulrich Wagner, Finnlands Kommunisten: Volksfrontexperiment und

Parteispaltung (Stuttgart: Kohlhammer, 1970) pp. 81ff. See also Seija Spring and D.W. Spring, "The Finnish Communist Party: Two Parties in One," in David Childs, ed., The Changing Face of Western Communism (London: Croom Helm, 1980).

5. Beyer, "Finnlands Kommunisten," p. 353ff.

6. Aarne Saarinen, Suomalaisen kommunistin kokemuksia (Experiences of a Finnish Communist (Helsinki: Tammi, 1984) p. 138.

7. Interview with l'Unità, June 14, 1978.

8. Frankfurter Allgemeine Zeitung, September 16, 1978.

5

The Portuguese Communist Party

Founded in March 1921, the Portuguese Communist party (Partido Comunista Português-PCP) led an underground existence from 1921 until the end of the Salazar-Caetano regime in April 1974. Many of its leaders were sentenced to life imprisonment, among them Alvaro Cunhal, from 1936 the most important PCP leader, and since 1961 the secretary general.[1]

Despite repression, the tight organization of the PCP as a cadre party enabled it to become the strongest and most militant force resisting the dictatorship. In the transition years 1974-1975 it won an appreciable head start over other parties, thanks to its prestige, its intact and powerful organization, and the network of agents it had infiltrated into all apparatuses and institutions of the regime. But after early successes its characteristics of strict, militant Marxism-Leninism, shaped in clandestinity, did much to ensure its defeat in late 1975 and its subsequent isolation. The hard sectarian line of the PCP is however not entirely attributable to its ideological and political dependence on the CPSU. Instead, it finds its origins in the forms of struggle and strategy which the party itself developed from its experiences in clandestinity, and from the precedent of the October revolution.

Political and Social Influence Zones

The structure and organization of the PCP stem from its self-image as the revolutionary vanguard of the working class, a cadre party with a mass base. Tightly organized and ideologically corseted in the principles of Marxism-Leninism, the party is directed by a hard core of leaders formed by underground work, often owing their positions and legitimacy to the long years they served in the Salazar regime's prisons. Only very recently has any number of young cadres been brought into the leading organs. In the Ninth Party Congress in 1983, for example, forty-eight new members were brought into the 165-person Central Committee.[2]

In the eyes of PCP traditionalists careful selection of cadres represents the best guarantee that rapid growth in membership and active participation in the institutions of parliamentary democracy do not endanger the revolutionary character of the party. The number of PCP members has in fact steadily risen, according to official party statistics. From two to three thousand in the clandestine period it went up to over fifteen thousand in 1974, 115,000 in 1976, 164,000 in 1979, and in 1984 to 200,000. The self-image of the party demands that the party give priority to recruiting workers, who in 1983 made up 57.4% of the membership (45.4% industrial workers, 12% agricultural laborers) outdistancing employees at 20%, the intelligentsia at 6%, and peasants, 1.9%.

With circa 45% of its members under thirty, the party is relatively young, if one counts the thirty thousand members of the Communist youth movement. It is also recruiting more women, whose ranks went up from 28,000 in 1978 to 45,000 in 1983. The PCP had 8,155 basic organizations in 1978, including 1,729 enterprise cells. Its central organ is the weekly Avante, its theoretical one the monthly O Militante, with a circulation of 30,000. The daily O Diario (circulation 40,000) is close to the PCP.

The PCP's principal zones of influence are in the industrial belt around Lisbon--where it won 27.5% in 1985 municipal elections--and in the southern agricultural areas long dominated by great landowners--especially in the Alentejo with its rural proletariat. The north of the country, where two-thirds of the population lives, is largely lower-middle class and under strong Catholic influence. The Communists have so far had great difficulty advancing there. An exception is the northern metropolis of Porto with 25,000 PCP members and a 20% Communist vote.

The regional nature of PCP strength helps to explain the party's lag behind the nationally well-represented Socialists (PSP) and free enterprise "Social Democrats" (PSD). In the municipal elections the PCP, with its front alliance APU, regularly wins around 20%: 20.6% in 1979; 20.7 in 1982; 18.9% in 1985. It does worse in national elections, now ranking only as the fourth strongest party in the country.

TABLE 4

___

Portugal: 1985 and 1983 parliamentary elections

Party	Percent		Seats	
	1985	1983	1985	1983
PSD (Social Democrats)	29	27.02	88	75
PS (Socialists)	20.8	36.6	57	100
PRD (Eanes list)	18	-	45	-
APU (PCP electoral alliance)	15.4	18.2	38	44
CDS (Democratic-Social Center)	9.8	12.4	22	30

Source: Archiv der Gegenwart 53 (1983): 26,567; 55 (1985): 29,248.

The PCP draws its real strength from its dominating role in the trade union confederation Confederação Geral dos Trabalhadores Portugueses-Intersindical Nacional (CGTP-IN), which according to its own statistics in 1983 included 146 unions and 1,400,000 members--actually about 900,000. Even allowing for exaggeration, comparison with the rival Uniâ Geral dos Trabalhadores (UGT) founded in 1979 (close to the Socialists), evidences the dominating role of the Communist-lining CGTP-IN in the Portuguese labor movement. The UGT claims 1,300,000 members but actually has circa 450,000.[3]

The strong position of the CGTP-IN is explained by the fact that the Communists early penetrated the union apparatus of the Salazar regime, played an important role at the founding of the roof organization Intersindical in 1970, and after April 1974, supported by the ruling military government, had it recognized as the unitary trade union confederation. (The constitution of 1976 re-established the possibility of multiple confederations.) Considering itself a class-conscious trade union, the CGTP-IN rejects the idea of social agreements, but after a transitional phase of revolutionary agitation in 1975 it has usually worked for standard workers' objectives.

Aspects of the Strategy for Change

The political line of the PCP after April 1974 was determined by the strategic goal of becoming the leading ideological force which could guide the process of democratic change through the phase of anti-monopolistic democracy and into socialism. Together with the increasingly radical Armed Forces Movement (MFA) the Communists were able to win important successes: nationalization of all power over productive and finance capital, agrarian reform and creation of a cooperative system in the latifundias of the Alentejo, and considerable control and codetermination for workers. In the constitution of 1975 the building of socialism was set down as a social and political goal. This strategy, which had originally found broad agreement, ran into determined resistance from the other political forces, including some in the MFA, as it revealed itself as a barely concealed plan by the PCP to take over power. The PCP then sought to hasten the revolution by instrumentalizing the state machinery, hoping to break all resistance with its organizational influence in state apparatuses and organs.

In consequence, the PCP considered democratic elections as "bourgeois democratic methods," with far less legitimacy than what Cunhal termed the "revolutionary process with its dynamic, popular and revolutionary power."[4] Cunhal announced after the Communist defeat at the polls in April 1975 that Portugal, with its outmoded economic and social structure, was unsuited to "neo-capitalist development" and had in any case left the stage of bourgeois democracy far behind it. (The PCP had just received 16.6% of the vote, the Socialists 37.9%, the Social Democrats 26.4%.) For the PCP leaders, recognition of the electoral process as the central criterion for distributing power and determining future policies meant the danger of a successful counter-revolutionary movement.

Changing Alliances and Their Results

The PCP's alliance policies were marked by a Manichean view nurtured in the long years of clandestinity: only two alternatives exist--forward to socialism or back to fascism. In its extremes this view underlines the PCP's operational ideas on the conquest of power and the inability of its leaders to make a realistic analysis of the power balance and use it to form lasting alliances.

Tacking as power shifted, the Communists worked first with the Socialists (until April 1975), then viewed alliance with the Armed Forces Movement as the "revolutionary motor" from April till July 1975, and turned in early autumn to the populistic base element of the MFA, but also to the ultra-left splinter groups which they had previously condemned. After the Portuguese Thermidor of November 1985 they presented themselves as an entirely constitutional opposition party, and made a popular front style offer to the Socialists.

Two elements contrived to isolate the PCP, what Nikos Poulantzas called their narrowly conceived "partisan policy"[5] and the opportunistic alliance policy which followed it. The PCP's failed power bid made a major contribution to the shift to the right in the Portuguese party spectrum and to the consequent partial withdrawal of structural reforms, such as return of tracts to great landlords, dismantling of worker control in the enterprises, dissolution of the MFA revolutionary council, and strengthening of the government's prerogatives at the expense of the president.

Without changing its long-range strategy, the PCP has since the end of 1975 adopted a middle-range defensive position, fighting to defend the political and economic accomplishments of the April revolution. It has sought alliance with the Socialists, but not with Mario Soares' majority current, which Cunhal has termed a central part of the "counter-revolutionary process."[6] However, when in February 1986 Soares faced the conservative Christian Democrat Freitas do Amiral in the second round of the presidential race, the Communists did back him. PCP votes were decisive in Soares' hairline victory of 51.28 percent. His second round vote jumped in Communist strongholds, reaching 76% in Beja and 70% in Evora, where before it had been 18% and 14%.

Even before the second round, however, Soares made it clear that he had entered into no engagements with the Communists, i.e. that he would not let his behavior be conditioned by them. The Communists for their part stressed that they had chosen to support Soares only as the lesser of two evils. Thus no great rapprochement is in sight for the feuding Left. The PCP sets more hope on convergence with the Party of Democratic Renewal (PRD), a formation founded in February 1985 by followers of former president Eanes. The PRD has a generally nationalist and leftist tone. Cunhal has said that the advent of this party could change the power balance in Portugal, create chances for "new social and political alliances," and become a basis for the realization of a "democratic alternative."[7] The anti-Socialist thrust of these remarks is plain--and in its maiden race in the parliamentary elections of 1985 the PRD won 18% of the vote, largely at the expense of the Socialists.

Following Soviet Foreign Policy

PCP foreign relations are closely tied to the CPSU. The Soviet Union, says Cunhal, is the country which through "its achievements, its example, its influence, its economic and military power, and in its consequent international policy remains the most important vanguard of the workers and progressive forces of the planet, the chief guarantor of world peace, the main factor in revolutionary progress."[8] There have been occasional differences between the two parties. In the summer of 1975 the Soviet leaders recommended that the PCP moderate its drive for power, fearing complications in the CSCE negotiations.[9] But the PCP has consistently backed the CPSU in its quarrel with the Chinese party. It defended Soviet intervention in Czechoslovakia in 1968, in Afghanistan in 1979, and approved the suppression of the reform movement in Poland, which it judged counter-revolutionary. It most conspicuously aided the Soviets by backing the MPLA in Angola against rival liberation movements.[10]

PCP relations with Eurocommunism are strained, particularly with the Spanish and Italian parties. Responding to criticism, it accused both parties of treasonable deviation from Marxism-Leninism, of liquidating proletarian internationalism by their distant behavior toward the CPSU, and indeed of splitting the world Communist movement.[11] For the PCP, the true independence of a Communist party consists in its ability to withstand ideological pressures from the bourgeoisie and social democracy and practice active solidarity with Soviet-style "real socialism."[12]

Portugal's membership in NATO has not yet been questioned by the PCP--but it has substantial reservations. The party has fought "against the NATO states' policy of military bases, against the appearance of the Pentagon's atomic weapon submarines in the country's ports, and the intent to build a rocket observation station that will serve U.S. plans to militarize space."[13]

The government's policy of entering the European Community--which took effect on January 1, 1986--found bitter Communist opposition. The PCP saw this as a reinforcement of Portugal's dependence on international capital and further liquidation of the remaining achievements of the April revolution.[14]

Summary and Prognosis

The PCP has thus far been an exception in its ability to bridge the central contradiction affecting the Communist parties of Western Europe: the contradiction between national interest and proletarian internationalism of the traditional type. With its 15 to 20% of the vote and its dominant role in the trade union movement it remains an important factor in Portuguese politics. The historic decline of the Communist parties in France and Spain will presumably immunize the PCP against any Eurocommunist temptation and strengthen its drive to proclaim itself the tribune of the workers and champion of national independence, in short to show itself, in the words of PCP leader Octavio Pato, "the party of hope and the future."[15]

In the deepening economic and social crisis, Cunhal and his friends seem to hope for a new revolutionary situation. The policy of austerity and revision of the results of the 1974-1975 revolution followed by all other parties gives the PCP the opportunity of presenting itself to the working class as the only authentic defender of the "achievements of April." A tactical variant of this course, after the victory of the Left in the 1986 presidential elections, is a "democratic alternative" made up of the PCP, PSP and PRD. Though Cunhal shows interest in this idea, the other parties do not.

The PCP is however suffering from a certain strategic and organizational stagnation. Strategically, it is on the defensive, as a party of protest rather than a real alternative in the present system. The new middle classes are closed to it, offering no base for wider social and political alliances, despite considerable PCP effort. They have in any case a new outlet besides the PSP and the Social Democrats in the Eanes PRD. There are signs of a crisis of militancy in the PCP, visible in a slower growth of the membership--whose numbers are in any case exaggerated by the leadership and subject to considerable fluctuation. There are fewer factory cells, and less active ones, the CGTP-IN has problems mobilizing its troops, and the party press is ailing. Even the PCP alliance with the small but well-established Democratic Movement of Portugal (MDP) fell apart in November 1986, entailing the collapse of the electoral alliance APU. The MDP, an ally of the Communists even in the days of the dictatorship and sometimes called "the second Communist party," has now accused the PCP of "sectarian behavior" and "hegemonic practices." In consequence, it broke off its alliance with the PCP and is moving closer to the Socialists and Eanes forces.[16] Obviously, the PCP has still to face the identity crisis of its Western European fraternal parties.

NOTES

1. Cf. Eusebio Mujal-León, "The PCP and the Portuguese Revolution," Problems of Communism 26, no. 1 (1977): 21ff; and Keith Middlemas, Power and Party: Changing Faces of Communism in Western Europe (London: André Deutsch, 1980) p. 210ff.

2. Interview with Alvaro Cunhal in Avante, December 29, 1983.

3. See Hans-Ulrich Bünger, "Portugal," in Siegfried Mielke, ed., Internationales Gewerkschafts-Handbuch (Opladen: Leske und Budrich, 1983) pp. 922-928.

4. Interview with Cunhal in l'Humanité, June 4, 1975.

5. Nikos Poulantzas, Die Krise der Diktaturen: Portugal, Griechenland, Spanien (Frankfurt am Main: Suhrkamp, 1977) p. 134.

6. Interview with Cunhal in Avante, December 29, 1983.

7. Alvaro Cunhal, "Unsere Plattform ist die demokratische Alternative," Probleme des Friedens und des Sozialismus (hereafter PFS) 28, no. 1 (1985): 170.

8. PFS 20, no. 12 (1977): 1607. Cf. also Alex McLeod, "Portrait of a Model Ally: The Portuguese Communist Party and the International Communist Movement," Studies in Comparative Communism 17, no. 1 (1984).

9. Middlemas, Power and Party, p. 196.

10. Ibid., p. 201.

11. Cunhal, in his speech to the Eighth Party Congress of the PCP, in A Revolução Portuguesa (Lisbon: Avante, 1976), p. 430ff.

12. Avante, December 21, 1978; also in Cunhal's article "Die unvergängliche Aktualität unserer Lehre," PFS 22, no. 3 (1979): 335.

13. From remarks made during a trip to the DDR. See Neues Deutschland, February 25, 1985.

14. Cf. also Veronika Isenberg, "Die Kommunisten Spaniens und Portugals und die Europäische Gemeinschaft," in Heinz Timmermann, ed., Die Kommunisten Südeuropas und die Europäische Gemeinschaft (Bonn: Europa Union Verlag, 1981) pp. 147-218.

15. Title of an article by PCP Politburo member Octavio Pato, PFS 22, no. 10 (1979): 1318-1326.

16. Le Monde, December 3, 1986.

6

The Communist Party of Cyprus

The Progressive Party of the Working People (Anorthotikon Komma Ergazomenou Laou-AKEL) was founded in 1941. It is the successor to the Cypriot Communist party, founded in 1926, declared illegal in 1933. Again declared illegal by the British from 1955 to 1959, AKEL demanded Cypriot independence rather than reunion with Greece (Enosis), and consequently opposed EOKA, George Grivas' anti-British guerrilla movement.[1]

After Cyprus became independent in 1960, the Communists were rapidly able to lose any stigma of "national betrayal." The majority of the bourgeois camp under Archbishop Makarios moved away from the idea of union with Greece toward a policy of independence and non-alignment. AKEL was thus offered the chance to confirm its national legitimacy in increasingly close cooperation with the national-liberal bourgeoisie and win strong support in the population as a socially progressive anti-imperialist party.

Organization and Zones of Influence

With fifteen thousand party members, an equal number in its youth organization EDON, and a voting strength varying from thirty to thirty-five percent, the exclusively Greek AKEL is the strongest political group in the country. (The Greek part of Cyprus has about 540,000 inhabitants). This strength is the result of intensive political work combining both traditional and modern concepts of the workers' movement. [2]

AKEL is bolstered by a network of flanking organizations: the farmers union EKA, the extensive leftwing cooperative movement, and especially the trade union league PEO, which unites in its sixty thousand members more than a sixth of the active population and circa eighty percent of organized labor. The party has also successfully kept its doors open to both old and new middle classes-- craftsmen, small businessmen, tradesmen, as well as service and teaching personnel, and professionals. AKEL has thus transformed itself to all intents and purposes into a leftwing people's party, but without losing the impetus that derives from its traditional social roots.

Because of the low level of industrialization in Cyprus, AKEL is organized on the basis of residential cells. It possesses a daily newspaper, Haravghi, with a circulation of circa 13,000, and a central party school in Nikosia. The secretary general since 1949 has been Ezekiel Papaioannou, a veteran of the Spanish Civil War and of the British Communist party. The membership of PEO union chief A. Ziartides assures easy party control over the influential union confederation.

Program and Political Strategy

For all its Marxist-Leninist rhetoric, AKEL's practical policies rather resemble the reformism of Mediterranean socialism.[3] In economic policy it advocates restraints on foreign capital and increased aid to small and medium-sized private enterprise, especially in labor-intensive and export oriented areas. Its social policy calls for improvement in working conditions and extension of social services for the under-privileged. The main thrust of its policies indeed is to assure Cypriot independence and non-alignment, and to create a unitary federative state of peacefully coexisting Greeks and Turks on the island.

These interests have determined AKEL's alliance policies since 1960. In their endeavor to isolate nationalist and/or pro-Western right-wing forces the Communists concluded agreements with the national-liberal bourgeoisie, leaving top political offices to them. Thus AKEL supported both Archbishop Makarios and later Spyros Kyprianou for the presidency. In the first three parliamentary elections (1960, 1970, 1976), after discussions with the Makarios forces AKEL did not insist on a representation equivalent to its voting strength. (In 1970, for example, AKEL won 39.6% of the vote, but fearing negative reactions from the Cypriot guarantor powers, Great Britain, Greece, and Turkey, AKEL contented itself with only nine of the thirty-

five seats in parliament.) In 1981 AKEL signed an
agreement on a "minimal program" with DIKO, the centrist
party close to President Kyprianou. The agreement later
became a governmental program and was also supported by
the left-socialist EDEK party led by Vanos Lyssarides.

Despite its 32.7 percent share in the parliamentary
delegation after the 1981 election, AKEL was not directly
represented in the government. However, the Communists
exerted considerable indirect influence on it through a
committee of AKEL and DIKO leaders. AKEL, as a reform
oriented force with "a considerable ability to compromise"
has in practice "acquired the characteristics of a governing
party."[4]

TABLE 5

1981 and 1985 parliamentary elections

Party	Percent		Seats	
	1981	1985	1981	1985
AKEL (Communist)	32.80	27.43	12	15
DISY (Conservative)	31.89	33.56	12	19
DIKO (Centrist)	19.50	27.65	8	16
EDEK (Socialist)	8.17	11.87	3	6

Source: Archiv der Gegenwart 52 (1982): 25,529;
Ibid. 55 (1985): 29,425.

In December 1984 President Kyprianou unexpectedly
broke off cooperation with AKEL, stating that he wished to
form a new government with "a larger political spectrum."
AKEL criticized this unilateral conclusion to the
cooperation of "two friendly parties," expressing a fear that
this could only serve "American and NATO imperialism, the
chief enemy of our people."

Behind Kyprianou's decision lay a deep conflict over
the solution to the Cyprus problem which had been
presented at meetings in New York sponsored by UN
Secretary General Perez de Cuellar between Kyprianou and
Rauf Denktash, leader of the Turkish ethnic group on
Cyprus. AKEL and the conservative DISY party wanted a

compromise, fearing that the current division of the island might be perpetuated. Kyprianou however opposed the secretary general's plan for creating a transitional Greek-Turkish government. Supported by Greek prime minister Andreas Papandreou, he insisted that all Turkish troops must leave the island before any agreement could be reached.

Since then AKEL has opposed the president. Its forces and DISY's do not constitute the two-thirds parliamentary majority needed to remove him, however. And in December 1985 the party suffered a severe defeat in parliamentary elections, losing 5.5 percent of the vote and sinking for the first time in decades below thirty percent. One cannot yet say whether this reverse was due to its willingness to compromise on the national question, or should be seen as a result of the social and structural change in the prosperous Greek part of Cyprus.

International Relations

AKEL's foreign policy, like its domestic policy, can be termed refusal of the double Enosis--neither union with Greece nor with the West. It desires a unitary, independent, nonaligned and demilitarized Cyprus.[5] Its main target is the United States and its NATO allies, accused of meaning to pull the island into Western defence dispositions without regard to the interests of its population. AKEL therefore demands the removal of British military bases and the withdrawal of British, Greek and Turkish troops stationed on Cyprus.

From this optic AKEL sees the Soviet Union as Cyprus' natural ally in the struggle for national independence and territorial integrity, because Moscow for Soviet policy reasons takes the same line.[6] The only foreign policy controversy between AKEL and the CPSU came in 1965, when Moscow's policy took a momentarily pro-Turkish turn. AKEL's foreign policy will presumably continue to be the main reason for the pro-Soviet orientation of this party in the world Communist movement and in the World Federation of Trade Unions--despite a domestic line which is rather Eurocommunist.

NOTES

1. For the history of AKEL, see Anna Focà, "Zyperns Kommunisten und die zypriotische Gesellschaft", in Heinz Timmermann, ed., Die kommunistischen Parteien Südeuropas (Baden-Baden: Nomos, 1979) pp. 359ff. See also T.W. Adams, AKEL, the Communist Party of Cyprus (Stanford: Hoover Institution Press, 1971).

2. The following facts are cited in part from Western publications, but principally from details appearing in articles by AKEL members in the Prague periodical Probleme des Friedens und des Sozialismus (PFS): Ezekiel Papaionnou, "Der Wille des unbezwingbaren zyprischen Volkes," PFS 20, no. 1 (1977): 76-79; Donis Christofinis, "Das patriotische Programm des Parteitags--Richtschnur des Handelns," PFS 25, no. 10 (1982): 1332-1337; Idem, "Einheit an der Basis ist die Grundlage von Bündnissen," PFS 29, no. 10 (1986): 1333-1340.

3. Focà, "Zyperns Kommunisten," p. 362ff.

4. Ibid., p. 371.

5. On Cyprus's situation in foreign policy, see Semih Vaner, "Chypre: Petite île, grandes puissances," Politique étrangère 50, no. 1 (1985): 158ff.

6. Ibid., p. 168ff.

7

The Chilean Communist Party

The Opposition to the Pinochet Regime

In 1983-1984 the Pinochet military dictatorship in Chile appeared to be coming to an end.[1] Its monetarist economic policies had ruined the country's industrial base. With a foreign debt of twenty-three billion dollars (against a four billion dollar debt in 1973), an unemployment rate of thirty percent, and a wage rate that had regressed to the 1960 level, the Chilean economy was on the brink of ruin. The military, who had justified their putsch in 1973 in part by the necessity of liberating the economy from the chains of collectivism imposed by Salvador Allende's Unidad Popular government, now saw themselves pushed toward ever more drastic state intervention in the economy. To prevent economic collapse the state was obliged to take over the private banks, now without liquidity, and with them that part of big industry dependent on them. But this did not solve the problems of the Chilean economy.

The economic decline of the country was accelerating in the early 1980s, with drastic political consequences. The crisis shrank the social base for the regime; increasing portions of the middle class which had originally supported the 1973 putsch found themselves threatened by the failing economy and turned against the dictatorship. The Christian Democratic party, the most important representative of this middle class, moved from the rather passive resistance of the 1970s to active opposition, with increasing support from the Catholic Church, including Cardinal Juan Francisco Fresno, archbishop of Santiago de Chile. Opinion polls taken in Santiago in 1985 showed that circa eighty percent of the population desired a return to democracy before President

Pinochet's term ends in 1989, while only fifteen percent supported the dictator and his regime.

Thus the Pinochet regime since 1983 has found itself increasingly isolated. Large sections of the middle class which had supported the putsch now made common cause in resistance with the parties and organizations of the workers' movement. Beaten down in 1973, these parties had regrouped in illegality and, like the unions, gradually found a narrow beachhead from which they could exert legal influence. This resistance found its most impressive expression in the "national protest days" of 1983-- a mass non-violent movement fed by demonstrations, strikes, and civil disobedience, calling for the return of freedom and democracy.

The most important inspiration for these protest days was provided by the unions, which in 1983 came together in a loosely organized roof group called the National Workers' Commando (Comando Nacional de Trabajadores-CNT).[2] In the same year, the illegal parties formed groups to provide political orientation and organizational reference for the growing resistance. The two most important party alliances were the Democratic Alliance, (Alianza Democratica-AD) led by the DC, and the Popular Democratic Movement (Movimiento Democratico Popular-MDP), led by the Communists. The dynamics of the opposition movements seemed strong enough to push the regime from its controlled opening (begun in part because of American pressure) toward Pinochet's resignation and a return of democracy.

By the end of 1984 this hope had turned out to be an illusion. Pinochet replied to the first general strike organized by the CNT by proclaiming a state of siege, thus frustrating all opposition hopes for a quick transition from dictatorship to democracy after the example given by Argentina, Brazil, and Uruguay. A more important reason-- perhaps the most important one--for the relative stabilization achieved by the regime is the difference in views between the two party groups over the character of the transition to democracy, and especially the attitude of the Chilean Communist party and its role in this process. This difference has until today prevented the creation of a united resistance to the military dictatorship.

The Communists reject on principle any negotiations with Pinochet for peaceful transition. Furthermore, they demand an equal share in resistance front decisions. In contrast to their previous traditions, they no longer reject violent action. They are supported in this by their partners in the MDP, the Movement of the Revolutionary Left (Movimiento de la Izquierda Revolucionaria-MIR) and parts of the Socialist party under Clodomiro Almeyda.

A majority of the Christian Democrats, on the other hand, together with the representatives in the AD of the conservatives critical of Pinochet, want a transition negotiated with the regime, and make any common action with the MDP dependent on Communist rejection of the principle of violence.[3] The ideas of this group actually aim at marginalizing a Communist party which is by Latin American standards influential, creating a stable middle class democracy, and preventing any far-reaching social transformations along the lines attempted by Allende.

Here their ideas differ from those of other members of the Alianza Democratica, like the Radical party (PR), a member of the Socialist International, and the Socialists led in Chile by Allende's Interior Minister Carlos Briones and from exile by the former Socialist party chairman Carlos Altamirano.[4] This faction of the Socialists has allied itself in the AD with the left-Catholic Movimiento de Acción Popular Unitaria (MAPU) group as the "Socialist Bloc." The Radical party and the Briones Socialists are also opposed to violent action, but together with representatives of the DC Left advocate a cooperative relationship with the MDP and believe that the Communists should be drawn into the political process after the restoration of democracy.

Thus the Communist question is at the center of Chile's future political development. The Communist party is at once an active factor in resistance to the dictatorship, and a means for Pinochet to justify and maintain repression against "Marxism." The dictator can thus assure himself of at least minimal acquiescence from the upper and middle classes (as well as from the Reagan administration) who fear a new version of Unidad Popular.

What sort of party is this, whose presence in the society has survived the brutal repression of the military regime? Where are its political and social zones of influence, and how did it behave in the Unidad Popular period? What can be said of its current positions and its prospects, viewed in the light of its history?

Political and Social Influence Zones

The Chilean Communist party was formed in 1922, when the ten year old Socialist Workers' Party under Luis Emilio Recabarren changed its name and requested admission to the Communist International.[5] Despite long periods of illegality (1927-1931; 1948-1958; again since 1973) the Chilean party grew after an early sectarian phase to become in the 1930s the best-organized and strongest CP on the South American continent. With considerable influence in the country's politics, it participated twice in government: in 1946-1947 under the presidency of the Radical González Videla, with the portfolios of Transport, Agriculture, and Public Works, and in 1970-1973 under the Socialist Salvador Allende, with the Economy, Labor, Public Works ministries and later Justice also. With its Popular Front policy of a peaceful road to socialism, which it had followed since 1935/36, the Chilean CP was in the 1960s one of the most prominent opponents in Latin America of the Cuban concept of guerrilla actions leading to violent overthrow.

The Chilean CP reached the high point of its political influence and organizational strength in 1970-1973, during the period of Unidad Popular.[6] At that time the party claimed two hundred thousand members--in fact probably about one hundred twenty thousand--organized in ten thousand cells. Workers with 46.6 percent were the best represented, followed by farmers with 16.1 percent, employees and intelligentsia 8.1 percent, tradesmen 4 percent, housewives 2.9 percent, and pensioners 2.8 percent. Its most important adjunct was the Chilean Unitary Workers Center (Central Unica de Trabajadores de Chile-CUT), founded in 1953, which with its million members (in 1973) and forty member unions was the largest union confederation in the country. From this position the CP exerted control over a series of key unions, such as the miners, copper production workers, and railroad workers. The CUT was dominated by the Communists, who provided its president, Central Committee member Luis Figueroa. It included Socialists, with the secretary generalship, and in its later phases also took in the Christian Democrats, who had the vice-presidency. Thus the CUT reflected a social model for Communist popular front ambitions. Other front organizations were the farmers union Ranquil, with ninety thousand members, and the Chilean Communist Youth, particularly strong in the universities, with fifty thousand members. The central organ was the daily El Siglo.

The Communist share of the vote wavered around fifteen percent (in 1965, 12.2%; 1967, 15.1%; 1969, 16.6%), which in 1969 won them six of the fifty senatorial seats and twenty-two of the one hundred fifty congressional ones. The party nevertheless exerted strong influence in Unidad Popular, since the Socialists were not much stronger, while the combined Left was always a minority. (It won 39 percent in the presidential elections of 1964, 36.2 percent in 1970, and 43.8 percent in the legislative elections of 1973).

The Chilean party's program had since 1936 called for a peaceful way to socialism effected by gradual socialist changes, in which the existing system of plural parties and parliamentary democracy would be supplemented by thorough-going economic and social reform. The Communists warned against haste, saying that the first task of the Left was not the socialist revolution but the democratic revolution against American political and economic "imperialism" and the native oligarchy of great landowners.

In the spirit of this "unity of action of all progressive forces against reaction," a slogan coined by party secretary Luis Corvalán, the Communists concluded an alliance in 1958 with the Socialists called the Popular Action Front (Frente de Acción Popular-FRAP), and in 1958 and 1964 supported Socialist Salvador Allende's presidential candidacy. In 1969 the FRAP was enlarged by the inclusion of the middle-class leftist Radical party, the left-Catholic MAPU, which had just split off from the Christian Democrats, and several small leftist groups. It now took the name of Unidad Popular. The Communists meant by this opening to sections of the left-social bourgeoisie to strengthen their reform platform and undercut right-wing counter-revolutionary forces. However, the Communists continued against Socialist objections to attempt a dialogue with the Christian Democrats and the Catholic Church.

The Communists in Unidad Popular

The basic program of Unidad Popular, signed on December 17, 1969, largely corresponded to Communist conceptions and was used as the party's own program. It criticized the reformism of Eduardo Frei's Christian Democratic government as insufficient and promised to end "imperialist exploitation" and reduce the influence of "latifundism" and "monopoly capitalism." The political system was to be democratized by creation of a monocameral popular assembly to replace the bicameral Congress, and complemented by institutionalizing decision-making by the base. The economic plank of the program called for nationalization of foreign capital and basic industry controlled by native monopolies, but left other areas in private hands.

The land reform which had languished under Frei was to be pursued, with the accent on forming cooperatives. In foreign policy the program stood for the complete political and economic independence of Chile and for replacement of the Organization of American States, dominated by the United States, with a new organization representing Latin America's interests. The program also promised to respect the plural party system and the rights of the opposition in the framework of constitutional legality.

The destruction of Unidad Popular by Pinochet's putsch in September 1973 was certainly in large part the result of extensive destabilizing measures by the U.S., which saw its economic interests endangered and feared extension of the Chilean model in Latin America. The strategy of destabilization was however a success because it could fasten onto the mistakes of the Left and the polarization they caused in the country.

Unidad Popular was able at first to carry out important points in its program, particularly the nationalization of American monopolies and amelioration of working class conditions. However, the left-radical MIR--which was not a part of Unidad Popular--together with some elements in the Socialist party pushed a more leftist program which included illegal takeovers of land, creation of parallel structures in the enterprises, and introduction of far-reaching nationalizations. This so-called dynamizing of the revolution led to a crisis which in the opinion of the Communist party and the CUT union, both loyal to the government and assuming a responsible attitude, could be checked only by a return to the basic program and a priority for stimulation of production. The inflation caused by the crisis encouraged the formation in 1972 of a compact rightwing bloc including the Christian Democrats, with a policy of uncompromising opposition to the government.

More decisive for the failure of Unidad Popular, however, was the loss of an inner cohesion that had proved transitory. It lost an important component with the departure of the Radicals, a party of the progressive bourgeoisie. At the end, Unidad Popular was not only opposed by the larger part of the middle class, but suffered increasingly from mutual mistrust between Socialists and Communists. This mistrust had roots going back to the 1930s. The Communists occasionally charged that Socialist radicalism was merely verbal; the latter accused the CP of obedience to Moscow and suggested that its pragmatism was purely tactical. These differences became plain during the Trilateral Conference sponsored by Fidel Castro in 1966 and the Cuban-inspired Latin American Solidarity Organization conference in 1967, both of which took place in Havana. Whereas the Socialists then saw the Cuban idea of guerrilla revolutions as a model for all Latin America and termed the Chilean Communists' popular front strategy outmoded and unsuitable, the latter agreed with the CPSU in calling the attempt to generalize Cuban experience adventurous, and held to their traditional concept of a peaceful road to socialism for Chile.

In 1969 Secretary General Luis Corvalán said of his party's relation with Moscow:

> Some of us like vodka, some not; someone may agree with this or that opinion of the Soviet comrades and another not. But one may not forget that the Soviet Union is the outpost of popular liberation, and that the role that it and its party played and is playing in the history of our century is a decisive one. Without the Soviet Union, without its economic and military power, its political weight in the world and its daily struggle against imperialism, the great successes of the peoples, the revolutionary perspectives which unfold before the whole world would be unthinkable.[7]

Little has since changed in the Chilean CP's appreciation of the Soviet Union.

Suppression and Self-Criticism

The Communist party and its organisations were shattered by the military putsch of September 1973, with many of its militants jailed or killed. This state-sanctioned terror of the first years of the dictatorship has now been declared illegal. It has not entirely ceased, as is shown by the murder of three CP functionaries by the police in early 1985. (General Mendoza of the Carabineros, was however held responsible for the murders by Pinochet and compelled to resign.)[8]

The Communists blamed the defeat of Unidad Popular in the first instance on resistance by foreign capital and the Chilean oligarchy to the government's policies. This is correct insofar as the U.S. government itself later confirmed its active role in destabilizing the leftist government. However, the Communist leadership has also criticized the mistakes and failures of Unidad Popular, especially the lack of a leadership acting on common principles, and the activities of ultra-left groups inside and outside the coalition. The main target here was the MIR, and secondarily some members of the Socialist party. The chief reproach to the ultra-leftists was their denial of the importance of the changes made by the government and their reliance on the "abstract postulate of the 'socialist character' of the revolutionary process," as well as their attempt to "make an artificial leap over necessary stages of revolutionary development."[9]

This criticism of the non-Communist Left reflects the basic historical position of the Chilean CP and is thus of great importance for any appreciation of the present and future line of the party. Its detailed thrust concentrates on the economic and alliance policies of Unidad Popular. The ultra-left had used the slogan "increases in production are the affair of the capitalists...not of the people," instead of "giving priority to the task of growth in production and productivity." "Wishful thinking and subjectivism in the government's own economic apparatus had also led to ignoring the objective laws of development of the economy, in which the market continues to play an essential role."[10]

Communist criticism of the ultra-left went on to say that it had pursued a "primitive policy of unconditional conflict with small and medium-sized business" marked by "sectarian handling of the intermediate classes," so that these classes had ended by joining the forces of reaction. Ultra-leftist behavior had expressed their "condemnation of

any compromises or alliances." They had also set themselves against "an alliance of the popular movement with
patriotic officers loyal to the constitution," thus weakening
the position of these potential allies inside the military and
playing into the hands of the putschists. Particularly disastrous was their appreciation of the DC as a "unitary reactionary mass," whereas it is a "mass...and multi-class party,"
influencing parts of the population reaching from members
of the monopolist bourgeoisie and the middle classes to
proletarians and farmers. The Communists concluded in
their review of the three years of Unidad Popular that the
counter revolution had succeeded in isolating the working
class from its allies and defeated the Left not only militarily, but also politically. "Our military defeat was above
all possible because we were defeated politically."[11]

Rebuilding and Fighting the Dictatorship

Since the 1973 putsch the Communists have organized
worldwide solidarity meetings against the Pinochet dictatorship. Secretary General Corvalán (freed from prison in
a 1976 exchange for the Soviet dissident Vladimir Bukov-
sky) took up residence in Moscow. The Communists built up
a clandestine network of party organizations inside the
country, even holding their first "national conference" in
June 1984. Jaime Inzunza, a forty-one year old history
professor from Santiago, was elected leader of the internal
organization. [12]

The Communists have become the strongest force in
the Left opposition, not least because of Socialist quarrels
on policy and organization that have led factions into two
distinct party groupings, the AD and the MDP. The
Communists have much influence in the unions, among students, and in a series of professional associations. With the
MDP they control one of the two main currents of resistance against the dictatorship. The MDP chairman, Manuel
Almeyda, is a brother of Clodomiro Almeyda, Allende's
foreign minister.

The immediate goal of the Communists and their allies
is the overthrow of the dictatorship by a "popular rebellion." The new government would bring back freedom and
democracy, abolish the dictator's repressive machinery,
purge the judicial system of regime supporters, bring all
democratic forces including the anti-Pinochet Right into an
all-party government, replace Pinochet's 1980 constitution
with a new one drafted by a constituent assembly, nation-

alize all state-subsidized big industry and banks, assure
civilian control over the military and work out a "democratic doctrine of national defense," i.e. nullify the officer
corps' thesis that it is the guarantor of domestic order.[13]

These immediate goals for the restoration of bourgeois democracy are in essential accord with the ideas of
the DC and its allies. Consequently the Communists (in line
with their traditional search for an "historic compromise"
with the Christian Democrats) are pushing for close cooperation between Democratic Action and the MDP in order
to work out a minimal program. They support the demands
of the "national pact for the transition to full democracy,"
signed in August 1985 by eleven parties ranging from socialists to conservatives and inspired by Cardinal Fresno.
The points the Communists stressed were "the demand to
respect human rights, to reestablish democracy, to permit
the return of all political emigres to Chile, to assure the
rights of all parties without exception to participate in
political life."[14]

The Communists and Violent Action

If the Communists have not thus far achieved the
unity of the opposition they desire, a major factor has been
the disagreement already emphasized concerning the character of the transition to democracy. The "national pact"--
which the CP was not allowed to help draft--carefully ig-
nored this problem. Its signators thus let it be understood
that they were ready to cooperate with the regime if it
would open the road to restoration of democracy. The Communists and their allies would accept the presence of officers in a provisional government. But they reject talks
with the Pinochet forces as illusory--and as a maneuver
directed against the Communists.

The differences between the AD and the MDP over the
transition to democracy are not inappreciable, reflecting as
they do different views on the content of the democracy
which is to be reestablished. A graver disagreement di-
viding the opposition arose in 1980, when the Communists
proclaimed the "right of the people to rebellion against
tyranny," for a "militant and resolute mobilization of society, expressing itself in an unprecedented variety of
combined peaceful and violent forms of action."[15]

This plea for the use of force to overthrow the dictatorship did not mean merely the understandable self-defense of the poblaciones in the poor quarters of big cities

against the often brutal raids of the security police. The Communists were in fact calling for intensification of sabotage actions, for example against the power net or the supply depots of the security police. Such acts were practiced by the "Manuel Rodriguez Patriotic Front," founded in 1983.[16] According to its own statements, the Front includes Communists, Socialists, MIR members, former and even active members of the armed forces. The Communist leadership denies that the Front is the armed force of the party, but makes no secret of active Communist membership in it.[17]

The Front does not propose creation of a guerrilla force to overthrow the regime by civil war. Its most spectacular action has been the attempt to get rid of the dictator himself as the chief obstacle to a return to democracy, a goal narrowly missed on September 7, 1986.[18] The dictator used the attempt on his life to undertake severe repressive measures. Many details of this assassination attempt are still cloudy and cannot yet be analyzed. It is clear, however, that this attempted tyrannicide has at least in the short run stabilized the regime and polarized the opposition.

Advocacy of force as the necessary lever of political change contradicts the traditional strategy of the Chilean CP, based on peaceful transition to power. One can refer back to the CP's polemic against the MIR tactics of revolutionary power during the Unidad Popular period, or against Che Guevara's model of a revolution kindled on the hearth of a guerrilla movement. The Communist leaders argue that their present call for violent action is a necessary counter-force against the terror of the dictatorship. Beyond this, they see violence--flexibly combined with civil resistance--as a means of accelerating the breakup of the regime. Corvalán has said that if the Communists had neglected the use of force alongside peaceful resistance, "Pinochet and his clique would never be uneasy, and the Center-Right opposition would pursue its dilatory disposition." [19]

Do these arguments signal a fundamental change in Chilean Communist strategy, possibly influenced by the 1979 success of the Sandinistas in Nicaragua against the Somoza regime? Or is it rather a tactical course correction which seeks both to keep a contact with the radical Left and to demonstrate that the Communists are indispensable in bringing any return to democracy?

This question has no easy answer. But it is reasonably clear that prospects for success in deposing Pinochet and returning to democracy have not been improved by the Communist argument that violence is a useful tactic. Disagreement here paralyzes an already badly splintered opposition. Its divergences on the use of force keep it from political exploitation of the social impetus visible in the mass mobilization of the "national protest days." The Communist line here even gives Pinochet a chance for an at least temporary consolidation of his shaky regime, by playing on widespread upper and middle class anxiety over revolutionary upheaval.

He can thus keep order in his army and security forces--the real props of the regime--despite disagreements in their ranks and continue to present himself to the United States as the only alternative to chaos and Communism. The Communist leaders had glimpsed this danger before 1980, warning against "private terror," "adventurism," "putschism", and "civil war." At that time the Communists were saying that the putschists would be pleased if the people were to adopt such tactics, for "they would thus have a justification for their own policy of terror on which they base their power."[20]

There are no present signs that the Communists will reject violence and return to their strategy of peaceful change. It is true that in a May 1985 letter to Gabriel Valdés, the Christian Democratic chairman, the Communist leadership defended itself against the charge that it saw no exit from dictatorship but in a "long military confrontation" or even civil war. Recalling the history and the special role of the CP in Chilean society, it condemned "narrow-minded sectarianism, putschism and adventurism." It expressly concurred with Valdés' view that "the regime understands only the language of disobedience and protest action." But it also reiterated its belief that the mass struggle must find its expression in "a broad and creative combination of peaceful and violent combat."[21]

Thus a contradictory situation prevails in Chile today, much conditioned by the change in Communist views since 1980. Deep disagreements among the regime's opponents block the onset of a process of democratization, although the dictatorship has ever less latitude and the social base for change is widening. Without doubt the Communist party will again have an important role in political life once democracy is reestablished.[22] Its attitude toward the use of violence thus has great importance-- not just for the prospects of ousting the dictatorship, but for the character of the party itself.

NOTES

1. On the current situation in Chile see Jorge Rojas Hernandez, "Chile, ein Land ohne Rechte," Sozialismus 11, no. 12 (1985): 55-59; Edgardo Boeninger, "The Chilean Road to Democracy," Foreign Affairs 63, no.4 (1986): 812-832, and the contribution by Paul E. Sigmund on the Chilean CP in Yearbook on International Communist Affairs 1985 (Stanford: Hoover Institution Press, 1985), pp. 59-61.
2. Cf. Hernandez, "Land," p. 57ff.
3. Cf. the interview with DC President Gabriel Valdés in the Italian Communist daily l'Unità, November 27, 1985.
4. Cf. the resolution of the Socialist party's first national plenum of June 30-July 1, 1984, Pensiamiento Socialista no. 32 (1984): 23ff.
5. On the history of the Chilean Communist party see Boris Goldenberg, Kommunismus in Lateinamerika (Stuttgart: Kohlhammer, 1971).
6. Cf. Klaus Esser, "Die chilenische Revolution," Berichte des BIOst no. 39 (1971); Paul E. Sigmund, "Chile: Two Years of 'Popular Unity,'" Problems of Communism 21, no. 6 (1972): 38-51; Carmelo Furci, The Chilean Communist Party and the Road to Socialism, (London: Zed Books, 1984); and the entries on the Chilean party in Yearbook on Communism 1970-1985.
7. Speech to the third World Communist Conference in Moscow, June 1969, in Internationale Beratung der kommunistischen und Arbeiterparteien Moskau 1969 (Prague: Verlag Frieden und Sozialismus, 1969) p. 330. On the foreign policy of Unidad Popular see John C. M. Ogelsby, "Chile unter Allende: auswärtige Beziehungen und innere Probleme," Europa Archiv 27, no. 16 (1972): 581-588.
8. See Gabriele Invernizzi, "I fuochi di Santiago," L'Espresso 31, no. 39 (1985): 34.
9. Hugo Fazio, "Analyse der Lehren aus der Vergangenheit für die Zukunft," Probleme des Friedens und des Sozialismus, (hereafter PFS) 69, no. 4 (1976): 509. Fazio is the Chilean party's representative on the magazine's editorial board.
10. Idem.

11. René Castillo, "Lehren und Perspektiven der Revolution," PFS 15, no. 7 (1974): 956 ff. An editorial note presents Castillo as a member of the Chilean party leadership. Cf. also Gladys Marin, "Lehren der Ereignisse in Chile: die Arbeiterklasse und ihre Bündnispolitik," PFS 20, no. 7 (1977): 920-929.

12. Invernizzi, "I fuochi," p. 34.

13. Cf. Hugo Fazio, "Kurs auf Rebellion des Volkes," PFS no.10 (1984): 1352-1359; Luis Corvalán, "Die Ereignisse in Chile," Neues Deutschland, October 22, 1985; "Die kommunistische Partei Chiles über ihr Verhältnis zu den Streitkräften," answers of leading Chilean Communists to questions by Chilean and foreign newsmen, Informationsbulletin (Vienna) no. 1 (1985): 40-47; Luis Corvalán, "Einheit gegen die Diktatur--Wege und Formen des Kampfes," PFS 29, no. 1 (1986): 19-27.

14. "Il est grand temps d'engager une lutte hardie et décisive," appeal of the Chilean CP, Bulletin d'Information (Prague) 23, no. 22 (1985): 29.

15. Corvalán, in Neues Deutschland, October 22, 1985.

16. On the Front see Sigmund, in Yearbook, 1985 p. 60. The Front is named for a guerrilla leader against the Spaniards in the early nineteenth century.

17. Interview with Inzunza, l'Espresso 31, no. 39 (1985): 38.

18. Cf. "Uccideremo Pinochet così il Chile sarà libero," interview with the Roman representative of the Manuel Rodriguez Front, la Repubblica, September 10, 1986, and Fernandez Colino, "El Frente Manuel Rodriguez, por dentro," interview with Roberto Torres, the official responsible for the Front's external relations, Mundo Obrero 7, no. 412 (November 20, 1986): 52.

19. Neues Deutschland, October 22, 1985.

20. Volodia Teitelboim, answers to readers' questions, PFS 23, no.3 (1974): 374 ff. Teitelboim is a member of the party leadership. Cf. also René Castillo, "Lehren und Perspektiven der Revolution" Part II, PFS 17, no. 8 (1974): 1112.

21. The letter is printed in Informationsbulletin No. 9 (1985): 47-55.

22. Boeninger, "The Chilean Road," p. 827ff.

8

The Japanese Communist Party

Facing Isolation and Stagnation

From November 19-24, 1985 the Japanese Communist party (JCP), the largest and most influential of Asia's non-ruling Communist parties, held its Seventeenth Party Congress near Tokyo. The congress, attended by representatives of twenty-four fraternal parties (including the CPSU), came at a critical time for the JCP. In many ways its situation is comparable to that of the French party, which after a short-lived new dynamism in the 1970s now clearly shows signs of longterm decline. The JCP's problems are complex; they concern in equal measure its domestic and alliance policies, its external relations and the internal state of the party itself.[1]

Japan's Communists have no domestic allies. Under its new chairmen Masashi Ishibashi (1983-1986) and Takado Doi (since 1986) the Japanese Socialist party (SPJ) has given up its traditional unity of action with the JCP. The strongest opposition party, the SPJ holds eighty-six lower house seats of a total 512. Together with the Democratic Socialists and the Buddhist-inspired Komeito party, the SPJ is seeking an alternative to almost forty years of unbroken Liberal Democratic party (LDP) rule. This desire for new alliances results from a reoriented program; the SPJ has increasingly moved away from its heritage of orthodox Marxism, set its sights on a modern economic program, and adopted a more positive approach to Japan's Self-Defense Forces and to the country's alliance with the U.S.

In the eyes of the JCP this pragmatic and flexible adjustment by the SPJ to Japan's domestic and foreign situation amounts to a radical break with the party's socialist tradition and a de facto "grand coalition" with the

Liberal Democrats.[2] For the moment, the JCP has had to write off the Socialists as a potential ally. Symptomatic of the break was the refusal by the JCP leadership to admit reporters from the SPJ press to the JCP congress.

But JCP international relations in the Communist party system are also extremely precarious. Despite the normalization of relations with the CPSU in late 1979 which foresaw a resumption of regular contacts and Moscow's renunciation of the pro-Soviet splinter group led by Yoshio Shiga, a number of disagreements on principle have not been settled. Difficult discussions with the Chinese Communist party (CPC) on resuming the relations broken off in 1966 have only just begun. The JCP's real problem is that as it is isolated in domestic politics, so is it more or less isolated among its brother parties in Asia. Socialism has made great strides in that region since 1945, as JCP party chairman Kenji Miyamoto remarked significantly in a talk with Yugoslav Communists, but its present realization contradicts its ideals and is not very helpful for JCP strategy.[3]

Examining the condition of the JCP, its leaders complain of "serious weaknesses" in party work, evident particularly in bureaucratic tendencies, waning enthusiasm, and a decreasing ratio of younger members.[4] JCP membership has been stagnant for some years at around 470,000 (the Socialists in 1984 had 64,000), and the party has recently been unable to push its vote above ten percent. What are the current and historical causes for the strengths and weaknesses of the JCP, what are its programmatic and political ideas, and what does its future look like in the wake of the Seventeenth Congress?

History, Roots, and Organization

The JCP was founded in 1922, under the pressure of a Comintern which was then expanding in Asia.[5] After a long period of suppression it was legalized by the American occupation authorities in 1945 as a strong force for anti-militarism. Under the leadership of Sanzo Nosaka (born 1892, now honorary chairman) the JCP set itself the goal of completing the bourgeois democratic revolution by peaceful means. Its membership rose to over 100,000, and in the lower house elections of 1949 it won a limited but real success, with ten percent of the vote and thirty-five seats (out of 466).[6]

Accused in January 1950 by the Cominform of "naturalizing Marxism-Leninism" and pledged to a line of violent revolution by Stalin in person, the party agreed to change its line. After the outbreak of the Korean war in June 1950 the JCP swung over to a Chinese-style guerrilla campaign with acts of sabotage and terror, was again banned (this time by order of the American occupying authorities), and lost all its lower house seats in the 1952 elections.[7] Two basic memories remain from that time: the U.S. ranks as the JCP's main enemy (even ahead of the national bourgeoisie and the Liberal Democrats, its parliamentary representatives). And for large parts of the population, extending to the right wing of the JSP, the JCP remains an unreliable force in the nation, the representative of foreign powers--the USSR or China. In the 1960s the JCP drew the lesson from the change of line that had been forced upon it--never to become dependent on a hegemonic party, whether it be the Soviet "great power chauvinists" (a JCP phrase from 1982)[8] or the Chinese "social colonialists" (language used in 1986).[9]

Led in an authoritarian and centralist manner by Kenji Miyamoto, the JCP had its structure and organization shaken by repeated purges which led to the exclusion of pro-Soviet elements in 1964 and pro-Chinese ones in 1966 (and to the establishment of corresponding splinter parties).[10] The JCP was nevertheless able to keep recruiting, its membership rising from 87,000 in 1961 to 300,000 in 1966, 370,000 in 1976, 466,000 in 1985.[11]

JCP leaders are intellectuals like Nosaka, Miyamoto (born 1908, Central Committee chairman since 1982) and the theoretician Tetsuzo Fuwa (born 1930, chairman of the Central Committee presidium since 1982). The JCP possesses a powerful apparatus. (In 1984 1,000 persons were employed in headquarters; there were 10,000 full-time functionaries in the provinces.) An extensive network of party newspapers and periodicals helps to support this burden; the central organ Akahata (Red Flag) with a press run of circa 600,000 copies daily and 2,700,000 Sundays (1985 figures) is the largest newspaper belonging to any Japanese party and is bigger than any other paper owned by a non-ruling Communist party. Akahata has a professional appearance; its Sunday edition in particular attracts middle class academic and pro-Socialist readers (the JSP lacks anything comparable). The JCP finances about ninety percent of its expenses from Akahata's profits

--in 1981 it made public a yearly budget of ninety-five million dollars. The party is thus financially independent.

Besides this, the JCP controls about a dozen front organizations, including a youth league (200,0000 members), a peasants' federation, organizations comprising farm cooperatives, small businesses, and trade associations, as well as groups of leftist scientists, writers, journalists, doctors, and finally the Japan Peace Committee and the Japan Council against Atomic and Hydrogen Bombs. JCP influence among the unions is weak, however. While Sohyo, the biggest confederation (four and one-half million members) is controlled by the Socialists, the other unions are neutral, like the influential teachers' union Nikkyoso, or even hostile to the JCP.

The JCP was able to recover from its 1952 low, raising its vote in Diet elections from 4.8% in 1967 to 10.9% in 1972 and 10.7% in 1976. It was more successful on the local level, where the Left (JCP plus SPJ) has often supplied mayors to the biggest cities in Japan. Since the end of the 1970s, however, the JCP has experienced electoral stagnation or reverses which have frustrated its strategy of using grass roots democracy, programmatic innovation, and extensive alliances to win national responsibilities. In the 1983 and 1986 lower house elections its share of votes sank to 9.3 and then to 8.8 percent. Among causes for these losses are the lack of a convincing economic and social program, the unwillingness of Socialists, Democratic Socialists and the Komeito party to conclude alliances with it, and the growing acceptance by the population of an American alliance strongly opposed by the JCP. The isolation of the JCP and the associated impotence of the opposition make up the principal reason for the permanent hegemony of the ruling Liberal Democrats.

Domestic and Foreign Programs

In the 1970s the JCP gradually accepted the ideas of Eurocommunism.[12] It has abandoned the doctrine of the dictatorship of the proletariat and intends to take scientific socialism (instead of Marxism-Leninism) as its future guide. In the Manifesto of Freedom and Democracy it adopted at its Thirteenth Party Congress in 1976 the JCP affirmed its intention to defend basic bourgeois rights and freedoms, including political and social pluralism, both on the road to socialism and after a socialist society had been achieved.[13] The heart of the manifesto is its vision of an "independent democratic" and ultimately "socialist" Japan, culminating in a broad "democratic coalition government" achieved via an "anti-imperialist and anti-monopolist revolution." Key industries are to be nationalized, but small and medium ones would remain in private hands.

TABLE 6

Elections to the House of Representatives   1986 and 1983

	seats won 1986	seats at dissolution	votes won July 6, 1986	votes won in 1983
LDP	300***	250	29,875,496 (49.4%)	25,982,785 (45.8)
JSP	86	111(1)*	10,412,583 (17.2)	11.065,082 (19.5)
Komei	57(1)*	58(1)*	5,701,277 (9.4)	5,745,751 (10.1)
JCP	27(1)*	27(1)*	5,426,968 (9.0)**	5,439,480 (9.6)**
DSP	26	37	3,895,857 (6.4)	4,129,907 (7.3)
NLC	6	8	1,114,800 (1.8)	1,341,584 (2.4)
USDP	4	3	499,670 (0.8)	381,045 (0.7)
others	0	0	120,627 (0.2)	62,323 (0.1)
IND.	6***	5	3,401,320 (4.6)	2,631,740 (4.6)
(vacancies)		11		
total	512	511	60,448,598 (100%)	56,779,700 (100%)

LDP	Liberal Democratic Party
SPJ	Socialist Party of Japan
Komei	Komeito Party
JCP	Japanese Communist Party
DSP	Democratic Socialist Party
NLC	New Liberal Club
USDP	United Social Democratic Party

N.B.* Figures in parentheses represent independents forming intra-Diet groups with the parties indicated.
    ** The number of votes cast for the JCP includes votes cast for two progressive independents to form an intra-Diet group with the JCP.
    *** Four independents have joined the LDP, bringing the number of its seats to 304 and reducing the number of independents to 2.

Source: Bulletin: Information for Abroad   No. 571, 1986.

Following this line, the Seventeenth Congress of the JCP undertook an important revision of the party program, eliminating the thesis of a "general crisis of capitalism." It acted in part because this cliche, repeated and proved false since Comintern days, stands in all too flagrant contradiction to the brilliant development of capitalism in Japan and has no credibility. The Communists themselves have had to admit that Japan's GNP takes second place in the West only to the GNP of the United States.

Another reason for revision of the party program was to provide a better theoretical foundation to an autonomist JCP . The JCP gloss on history ran as follows: since Stalin's time, Moscow has increasingly employed the thesis of the "general crisis of capitalism" to show that the socialist countries are the decisive force in deepening this crisis everywhere and changing the power relation in favor of socialism. The autonomous revolutionary role of individual national parties was consequently underestimated, and they succumbed to increasing dependence on the strategy of the socialist countries--countries which by their hegemonic actions had helped "to aid and prolong the life of monopoly capitalism, playing a serious negative role contrary to world progress." The analysis ended by stating that today it is clear that:

the law-determined basis of development from capitalism to socialism in Japan and other countries of the capitalist world today is to be found in the internal contradictions of the capitalist society of each individual country...and the subjective strength of its revolutionary forces.[14]

For the JCP a precondition for the success of its program is restoration of national self-determination, i.e. termination of the American-Japanese security pact signed in 1951 and extended in 1960, thus giving Japan the status of a bloc-free neutral power. The party accuses the Liberal Democrats of increasingly integrating Japan into U.S. global strategy, thereby bringing the 1936 anti-Comintern pact up to date. The Nakasone government, by allowing Japan to be drawn into militarism and imperialism dependent on the U.S. and making Japan (in Nakasone's words) an "unsinkable aircraft-carrier" for the U.S. has become, says the JCP, the "worst reactionary cabinet since the end of the War." [15]

The JCP presents a counter-program, with the goal of an "independent, democratic, peaceful, bloc-free and neutral Japan," laying emphasis on nuclear arms control and disarmament.[16] A major motive is to appeal to a Japanese anti-nuclear sensibility dating from Hiroshima and Nagasaki, which renders public opinion relatively favorable to arguments against indirect integration of Japan into American nuclear defense dispositions. Along these lines, the JCP advocates a unitary anti-nuclear front on a national and international level analogous to European efforts to create a unitary anti-Fascist front in the 1930s. Here there are convergences with the Moscow line--but only insofar as the Soviet leadership calls for global destruction of nuclear weapons and does not consider them instruments of the global equilibrium between the super-powers. In any case, the Seventeenth Party Congress confirmed the JCP's rejection of the doctrines of mutual destruction and equilibrium, and spoke out against Soviet acceptance of such ideas.

The JCP in the International Communist Party System

The positions of the JCP in the world Communist movement were determined into the 1960s by close ties to the Soviet and Chinese parties. In the Moscow-Beijing conflict the JCP in 1964 at first sided with the Chinese, whose hard anti-American line suited the JCP better than the Soviet policy of peaceful coexistence, symbolized in 1963 by the treaty ending atomic tests in the atmosphere. JCP leaders also had close personal ties with the Chinese party, which had harbored them in exile, both during the Yenan period in 1940-1945 and later during the years of repression in 1950-1952. Mao's Cultural Revolution and his refusal of anti-American cooperation with the Soviets in the Vietnam war nevertheless led to a break with the Chinese party in 1966.

Now as before, the JCP leaders believe that socialist states are superior to capitalist ones especially for their social achievements, but also in their institutions.[17] Nevertheless, in the late 1960s they declared total independence in the world Communist movement, acting on the lesson drawn from international ties which in the Cominform period repeatedly ended in fiasco and proved extremely harmful in domestic politics. Coupled with this policy is an attempt to present their party as the consistent champion of national interests, outdoing the LDP itself. Both Moscow and Beijing have been accused of "great power chauvinism," "striving for hegemony," and a tendency to collaborate with Washington to the detriment of third parties. The Seventeenth Congress even passed a resolution writing the struggle against "hegemonism" Soviet and Chinese style into the party program as "not only an essential task for the future of the Japanese revolutionary movement, but also an important international duty so that the historic mission of socialism may properly be given full play."[18]

Relations between the JCP and the CPSU remain strained even after the 1979 agreement to normalize them. A summit meeting in Moscow between Miyamoto and CPSU General Secretary Chernenko in December 1984 did produce considerable agreement on the intentions of both parties to intensify the struggle to get rid of nuclear weapons, mobilizing not only Communists but the people of the whole world to this end.[19] Contentious questions were, however, excluded from the discussion--Soviet policies toward Afghanistan and Poland as well as the claims of the CPSU to lead the Communist party system. And in fact at its Seventeenth Party Congress the JCP again condemned the Soviet intervention in Afghanistan, after it had earlier refused to consider participating in the fourth world Communist conference which the Soviets are planning. But most important of all is the persistent Japanese Communist demand that the Soviets return the islands north of Hokkaido annexed in 1945, not limiting themselves to the four islands of Habomai, Shikotan, Kunashiri, and Etorofu, but demanding, alone among Japanese parties, the return of the whole Kurile chain. According to a commentary in Akahata in May 1986:

> The Soviet occupation of Habomai-Shikotan and the Kurile islands after the war, which were historically Japanese territories, was against the principle of "territorial non-expansion," as well as against the principles of scientific socialism. It is in conformity with international justice and the principles of socialism that the JCP calls for the immediate return of Habomai-Shikotan Islands, which are part of Hokkaido, as well as all the Kurile Islands, by abrogation of the article in the San Francisco Treaty renouncing the Kurile Islands, which the Japanese government signed.[20]

The JCP also expressed these views to Soviet Foreign Minister Eduard Shevarnadze when he visited Tokyo in January 1986. The Soviet answer to the Japanese brother party had been given years before in noteworthy language-- that this strange request would in practice mean "the forcible separation of territory of a socialist state, for the benefit of a bourgeois state."[21]

JCP relations with the Chinese party are even worse. The JCP was the only Japanese party to object to the peace treaty with China in 1978, seeing the danger of an American-Japanese-Chinese alliance in its anti-hegemony clause, which it interpreted as an "anti-hegemony international united front" directed against the Soviet Union.[22] Party leader Miyamoto did announce at the Seventeenth Congress that discussions about resumption of JCP-CPC relations had begun (on Chinese initiative, Miyamoto emphasized). But he expressed pessimism about their outcome.[23]

The real obstacle to resumption of Japanese-Chinese Communist party relations is not just variant positions on the American military presence in Asia in general and Japan in particular (both viewed positively by the CPC, sharply opposed by the JCP). The two parties are in substantial agreement on the character of a "new internationalism" based on the equal rights of all Communist parties. The main differences arise rather from a JCP demand--repeated at the Seventeenth Party Congress-- that the CPC assume the blame for the break in party relations in 1966, expressly condemn the subsequent Maoist splitting tactics used against the JCP, and drop support of the still existent pro-Chinese groups.[24] CPC negotiations on resumption of party relations with a series of Western European parties showed that Beijing is not prepared to make concessions on a matter which has become a prestige question for both sides.[25] At the end of 1986, normalization talks were suspended for the time being.[26] Renewal of JCP-CPC relations will thus probably be delayed for some time.

Given these problems with the Soviet and Chinese parties, it is hardly accidental that the closest JCP foreign relations are not with Asiatic parties but with the Yugoslavs and Eurocommunists, as shown by visits to Japan by Berlinguer, Marchais, and Carrillo, as well as by multilateral theoretical conferences with Western Communists in Tokyo in 1972 and 1979. Besides discussion of common problems over the "peaceful way to socialism" in highly developed industrial democracies, the JCP sees in such contacts two tactical uses--they raise its reputation for democracy in Japan, and help overcome its isolation in the Communist party system.

Prognosis

As the JCP sees it, Japanese politics are moving toward a situation like that of the 1930s, in which the ruling conservatives and the various parties of the non-Communist opposition are coming closer together to restore Japan's traditional influence in the Asiatic-Pacific region-- this time in alliance with the U.S. The Communists see themselves as ostracized, excluded from an enemy citadel, fighting alone against forces that are reducing democracy at home and encouraging a display of imperialist power abroad. The Seventeenth Congress, with the Popular Front strategy of the Seventh Comintern Congress of 1935 in mind, therefore concentrated on the idea of creating a united front of all those forces which demand dissolution of the American alliance and desire nuclear disarmament.[27] The JCP hopes that a grass roots mass movement of this type could develop a dynamic toward change in the political fortunes of the Communists and further their aims.

In fact, however, it is not only the conservative and strongly anti-Communist social environment which led to the stagnation and increasing isolation of the JCP; in the 1970s it was able to make remarkable gains. Quite evidently its strategic line is to a considerable degree responsible for its lack of success. Despite its programmatic renewal, the party has missed a rendezvous with the changes in society and values linked to Japan's economic dynamism. Furthermore, its strongly anti-American line runs counter to the increasing acceptance found by the alliance far beyond Liberal Democratic circles. The impression produced is an inclination to pro-Sovietism, which the party's nationalist campaign for recovery of the "northern territories" and emphasis on its independence cannot remove.

With its powerful apparatus, impressive press empire, and wide spectrum of front organizations the JCP remains a formidable organization in the political life of Japan. But it is also in critical condition--an aging party lacking the ability to focus on the transformation of Japan into a middle-class society. The party congress of autumn 1985 developed no convincing ideas to overcome stagnation at home and isolation abroad.

NOTES

1. Cf. Philippe Pons, "Le Parti communiste japonais au creux de la vague," Le Monde, December 10, 1985. See also the reporting on the congress in the Japan Times.
2. Cf. "Resolution of the 17th Congress of the Japanese Communist Party," Akahata, November 24, 1985, and the Central Committee report by Tetsuzo Fuwa, chairman of the presidium of the Central Committee, Akahata, November 20, 1985.
3. Akahata, November 1, 1985.
4. "Resolution of the 17th Congress."
5. On the history of the JCP, see Manfred Pohl, Die Kommunistische Partei Japans (Hamburg: Institut für Asienkunde, 1976), and the official party history, Central Committee of the Japanese Communist Party (eds.), Sixty-Year History of the Japanese Communist Party (Tokyo: Japan Press Service, 1982).
6. Cf. Paul F. Langer, Communism in Japan: A Case of Political Naturalization (Stanford: Hoover Institution Press, 1972).
7. Pohl, Kommunistische Partei Japans, p. 77ff; Sixty-Year History, p. 157ff.; and Tetsuzo Fuwa, Stalin and Great Power Chauvinism (Tokyo: Japan Press Service, 1984) p. 37ff.
8. Title of a book by Fuwa. See footnote 7.
9. "What does the Renmin Ribao Article say?" Akahata, September 14, 1986.
10. Cf. Margarete Donath, "Die Kommunistische Partei Japans zwischen Peking und Moskau," Berichte des Bundesinstituts für ostwissenschaftliche und internationale Studien no. 28 (1985); and Peter Berton, "The Japanese Communist Party," Studies in Comparative Communism 15, no. 3 (1982): 266-287.
11. See Peter Berton, "Japanese Eurocommunists: Running in Place," Problems of Communism 35, no. 4 (1986): 2ff.
12. Cf. Peter Berton, "Japan: Euro-Nippo-Communism," in Vernon V. Aspaturian, Jiri Valenta, and David P. Burke (eds.), Eurocommunism between East and West (Bloomington: Indiana University Press, 1980).
13. Cf. Bulletin: Information for Abroad no. 359, October 1976.
14. Cf. the Report on Amendments to Party Program (sic) given by Yoshinori Yoshioka, member of the Standing Presidium of the Central Committee, Akahata, November 22, 1985. Emphasis added.

15. "Resolution of the 17th Congress." Cf. also Fuwa's Central Committee Report.

16. "Resolution."

17. "Resolution."

18. Quoted from Yoshioka, "Report on Amendments."

19. The "Common Declaration" appeared in _Pravda_, December 18, 1984.

20. Yogi Kogiso, "Last-Ditch efford (sic) of Anti-Party Shiga Clique, blind followers of the Soviet Union," _Akahata_, May 26, 1986. Cf. also the extensive explanation of the JCP position in "Japan-URSS (sic) Relations," _Akahata_, October 26, 1986.

21. "Vopreki interesam mira i dobrososedstva," _Pravda_, June 12, 1977.

22. Miyamoto, in _Akahata_, October 17, 1978.

23. _Akahata_, November 20, 1985.

24. Yoshioka, "Report on Amendments." Cf. also "What does the _Renmin Ribao_ Article say?"

25. Cf. the chapter in this book on the Chinese Communist Party and the Communist party system.

26. Cf. _Akahata_, November 15, 1986, and the press conference given by Hiroshi Tachiki, chief of the JCP Central Committee Department for International Relations, _La Stampa_, November 15, 1986. Tachiki accused the Chinese party of pursuing a policy of "hegemony" and "interference" in the internal affairs of the JCP.

27. Hiroyuki Okamoto, "Lessons of the Seventh Comintern Congress and Anti-Nuclear International Front," Speech at the Theoretical Conference in Commemoration of the 50th Anniversary of the Seventh Congress of the Comintern, _Akahata_, July 22, 1985. Cf. also Berton, "Japanese Eurocommunists," p. 23ff.

Appendix One:
Chronology of Communist Events

2-6 March 1919	Founding congress of the Communist International. Participants: 51 Communists from 30 countries.
31 July 1919	Destruction of the Soviet republic in Hungary.
19 July-7 August 1920	Second congress of Communist International Agreement on 21 conditions for acceptance into Comintern.
March 1921	Defeat of the Communist-led rising in central Germany.
22 June-12 July 1921	Third World Congress of the Comintern. Swing to the right--united front tactic.
5 November-5 December 1922	Fourth World Congress of Comintern. Keeps to united front tactic. Sixty-six member parties with 1,200,000 members.
October 1923	Failure of the Comintern plan for revolution in Germany. Isolated rising in Hamburg suppressed.
17 June-8 July 1924	Fifth World Congress of the Comintern. Swing to left, bolshevization of Communist parties.

December 1924	Stalin announces doctrine of socialism in one country. It implies absolute support for the Soviet Union.
January 1926	Third Congress of PCI in Lyons. Victory of Gramsci-Togliatti group over Bordiga's ultra-leftists.
December 1927	Failure of Communist uprising in Canton led by Comintern.
17 July-1 September 1928	Sixth Comintern congress. Nearly complete victory of Stalin's "Left" force over Bukharinite "Right." Forty member parties with 1,600,000 members. Social Democrats denounced as "Social Fascists." In reaction to failure in CPCh-Kuomintang cooperation, denunciation of all cooperation with the "bourgeoisie" in developing countries.
October 1930	Thorez becomes PCF leader. Final bolshevization of PCF.
July 1934	Unity of action pact between French Socialists and Communists.
January 1935	Mao Zedong takes over CPCh leadership. Party begins gradual emancipation from Moscow.

25 July-20 August 1935	Seventh Comintern Congress. Turn to Popular Front tactics with new views on bourgeois democracy, social democracy, fascism. Sixty-one member parties with 3,100,000 members.
February 1936	Spain: Popular Front parties, including Communists, win election.
May 1936	PCF gives parliamentary support to Socialist-led government in Popular Front alliance.
July 1936	Outbreak of Spanish Civil War.
August 1939	Hitler-Stalin pact; CP's confused and demoralized.
15 May 1943	Stalin decrees dissolution of Comintern.
1944	Doctrine of "national" special ways to socialism for Eastern and Western Communism first propagated.
1945	Members of Western European CP's (including PCI, PCF) taken into government.
May 1947	PCI and PCF excluded from government.
September 1947	Founding of Information Bureau of Communist and Workers' Parties (Cominform), Szklarska Poreba.

	Participants: CPSU, CP's of Bulgaria, Czecho-slovakia, Hungary, Poland Romania, Yugoslavia, PCI, and PCF. Zhdanov's "two camp" theory calls on all CP's to renounce "special roads," support Soviet policy uncondi-tionally.
July 1948	Exclusion of Yugoslav party from Cominform for "nationalism" and "anti-Sovietism."
5 March 1953	Death of Stalin.
May 1955	Khrushchev trip to Bel-grade for reconciliation with Tito.
14-25 February 1956	Twentieth CPSU Party Congress. Khrushchev's secret speech condemns Stalin's personality cult. Revision of impor-tant dogmas: "inevit-ability of war" gives way to "peaceful coexis-tence;" new views on Third World; variety of ways to socialism.
April 1956	Cominform dissolves itself.
May 1956	PCI chief Togliatti speaks of "degeneration" of Soviet system. PCI rejects concepts of "leading party" in Com-munist movement, asks for "polycentrism" in world Communism.

August 1956	Japanese CP first raises territorial question of Kurile islands with CPSU.
October 1956	Victory of Gomulka, nationalist and reform-minded, over Stalinists in Poland reluctantly accepted by CPSU.
October-November 1956	Victory of reforms under Nagy in popular democratic movement in Hungary. USSR suppresses popular uprising by force.
December 1956	PCI Seventh Party Congress upholds "Italian way to Socialism."
14-19 November 1957	First world Communist conference, Moscow; divided into inner circle 12 ruling CPs and wider council of 64 CPs. Former sets forth binding ideological-political declaration, latter general "peace manifesto." "Increased authority of CPCh because of CPSU loss of authority.
March 1958	Differences sharpen between Moscow and Belgrade when LCY "revisionist" program becomes known.
March 1958	Problems of Peace and Socialism (English version: World Marxist Review) founded in Prague as multi-lingual Soviet-

	directed organ of ideological coordination.
1 January 1959	Castro comes to power.
10 November-3 December 1960	Second world Communist conference in Moscow. Present: 81 CPs, including Chinese but not Yugoslavs. Drafts declaration that reveals growing differences between CPSU and CPCh. Recognizes full autonomy for all CPs.
June 1963	Chinese CP "Proposal on the General Line of the International Communist Movement." CPCh accuses CPSU of revisionism, capitulation to United States, lack of support for national liberation movements, great-power chauvinism.
Spring 1964	Japanese CP breaks with CPSU in protest over Soviet policy on peaceful coexistence (atomic test treaty).
August 1964	Deaths of Togliatti and Thorez. PCI publishes Togliatti notes prepared for talk with Khrushchev. "Yalta memorandum;" criticizes USSR, underlines PCI autonomy, pleads for "unity in diversity" in Communist movement.
1965	Under strong influence of Guevara, Castro develops a special mili-

	tant model of revolution for Latin America.
1966	Japanese CP breaks with CPCh during "cultural revolution," and because of Mao's refusal to co-operate with USSR in Vietnam war.
March 1966	CPSU-CPCh relations broken off.
May 1966	Finnish CP enters government.
24-26 April 1967	Conference of European CP's. in Karlovy Vary. Present: 24 parties. Missing: Yugoslavs, Romanians. Issues declaration on peace and security in Europe.
21 August 1968	Military intervention of USSR and Warsaw Pact states in CSSR. Strong protest by autononmist CP's. CPSU develops "Brezhnev doctrine" on limited sovereignty of socialist states.
March 1969	Border clashes on Ussuri river between Soviet and Chinese forces.
April 1969	De facto split in Finnish CP between reformist majority and traditionnalist minority.
5-17 June 1969	Third World Communist conference in Moscow. Present: 75 CP's. Absent:

CP's of China, North Ko-
rea, North Vietnam, Yugo-
slavia, Japan. Issues
"Main document" to
which some parties (PCI)
agree only in part.

October 1970   Allende Unidad Popular
government including
Communists comes to pow-
er in Chile.

June 1972   French Socialists and
Communists agree on
"Common Program of Gov-
ernment."

September 1973   Allende government over-
thrown by coup d'état in
Chile.

April 1974   Portuguese dictatorship
collapses. PCP joins
new government.

Summer-Fall   PCP tries to take over
1975   the revolution. Excluded
from government, opts for
militant but constitu-
tional opposition.

November 1975   PCF leader Marchais goes
Rome. With PCI chief Ber-
linguer signs declara-
tion on CP autonomy,
democratic strategy, re-
cognition "bourgeois li-
berties." Together with
similar PCI-PCE state-
ment July 1975, declara-
tion gives rise exten-
sive comment on funda-
mental change inside
Western Communism, called
"Eurocommunism."

March 1976	Japanese CP at Thirteenth Congress publishes "Manifesto for Peace and Democracy" with Eurocommunist ideas.
29-30 June 1976	Conference European CP's in East Berlin. Present: 29 parties, including LCY. In final document CPSU makes verbal concessions on "new internationalism."
August 1976	As part of "historic compromise," PCI begins support series Christian Democratic governments. March 1978-January 1979 backs five-party coalition as part parliamentary majority, but is not allowed join government.
2-3 March 1977	Eurocommunist summit Madrid: Berlinguer, Marchais-Carrillo. Cannot agree on common regional strategy; different views on "real socialism."
October 1977	PCE included in "Moncloa Pact" for economic and political stabilization in Spain.
October 1977	PCF provokes break in Union of the Left with Socialists.
1978	After Left defeat in elections, PCF begins reconciliation with Moscow.

1978	After Tito visit Beijing August 1977, LCY/CPC resume relations. Chinese party begins return to role in Communist movement.
December 1979	Normalization JCP-CPSU relations. Disagreement persists on Kurile islands.
27 December 1979	Soviet intervention in Afghanistan. Strong criticism on "hegemonism" by CPC, "great power chauvinism" by JCP, "sphere of influence activism" by PCI.
Spring 1980	Chilean CP advocates use violence ("counter-violence") to overthrow Pinochet. Disagreements on violence divide anti-Pinochet forces.
12 and 14 March 1980	Berlinguer meets West German, French Socialist leaders Brandt, Mitterrand at European Parliament. Abandonment of "Eurocommunism" for "Euroleft" strategy.
April 1980	Berlinguer visits Beijing. CPC resumes party relations with PCI, first renewal with Western CP.
29-30 April 1980	Rump conference 18 European CP's Paris on peace and disarmament. Absent: Yugoslavs, Romanians, Italians, Spaniards.

June 1981	After Mitterrand elected president of France, PCF enters Mauroy government as junior partner.
11 December 1981	Soviet-inspired suppression <u>Solidarnosc</u>. Sharp criticism by various CP's. PCI declares propulsive force Soviet system is exhausted.
November 1982	Carrillo forced resign as PCE leader after severe electoral defeat. Schisms accelerate in PCE.
July 1984	PCF leaves French government, resumes polemics against Socialists.
19-24 November 1985	Seventeenth Congress of JCP. Program denounces Soviet and Chinese hegemonism.
25 February-6 March 1986	Twenty-seventh CPSU Congress. Gorbachev counters his dogmatists, speaks against "hierarchy and uniformity" in the Communist party system. No party has "monopoly of truth."
16 March 1986	Dramatic PCF losses in parliamentary elections, worst since 1924: 9.8%.
9-13 April 1986	Seventeenth PCI Congress. PCI declares itself "integrating part of ⟨West⟩ European Left."
June 1986	Finnish CP splits.

Fall 1986	Chinese party resumes relations with Polish, East German parties.
November 1986	Failure of talks on resumption JCP-CPC ties.
December 1986	Gorbachev calls idea of new world Communist conference currently unrealistic. CPSU reckons Communist party system has 100 parties on all five continents, 15 in "world socialist system," some 85 nonruling parties.

Appendix Two:
Strengths of Communist Parties

The International System of Communist Parties, 1980-1986

1. **Total Membership:** official data for 1984/85 MB 6/1985

Ruling parties: 15, with approximately 75,000,000 members.
Nonruling parties: circa 85, with approximately 5,000,000 members.
Total: circa 100 parties; approximately 80,000,000 Communists.

2.**Ruling Communist Parties** (according to Soviet designation)

CCP	(PR China)	40,000,000	RR	25/ 9/85
CPSU	(USSR)	19,000,000	Pr	26/ 2/86
RCP	(Romania)	3,400,000	Sc	20/11/84
KWP	(North Korea)	3,200,000	STP	3/86
SED	(GDR)	2,304,221	ND	18/4/86
YCL	(Yugoslavia)	2,167,860	PFS	9/86
PUWP	(Poland)	2,115,400	hor	6/86
CPV	(Vietnam)	2,000,000	NhD	17/12/86
CPC	(CSSR)	1,700,236	RPr	12/3/87
BCP	(Bulgaria	932,055	RD	7/4/86
HSWP	(Hungary)	871,000	MTI	25/3/86
CuCP	(Cuba)	524,000	U	5/2/86
TAWP	(Albania)	140,000	hor	11/85
MPRP	(Mongolian PR)	88,000	PFS	8/86
LRPP	(Laos)	47,000	PFS	10/86

3. Non-Ruling Communist Parties: Regional Distribution

Western Europe	3,000,000	MB	6/86 (for 1984/85)
Asia, Australia, and Oceania	1,340,000	MB	6/86 (for 1984/85)
Africa	70,000	MB	6/86 (for 1984/85)
America, total §	460,000	MB	6/86 (for 1984/85)
Latin America § (§ both excluding Cuba)	440,000	BIOst	86*
North America (U.S. and Canada)	20,000	BIOst	86*

*Figures marked with an asterisk are estimates; all others are official party statistics. Figures are for the year noted, except where otherwise indicated.

---

4. Membership: Selected Latin American and Asian Communist Parties

PSU	Mexico	40,000	hor	20/ 83
PPP	Panama	36,000	ND	7/5/82
CP	Brazil	30,000	ND	9/7/86
CP	Columbia	25,000	hor	49/80
CP	Bolivia	20,000	hor	11/82 (for 1980)
CP	Japan	466,000	A	25/11/85
CP	India	445,195	PFS	12/86
CP	India (M)	270,000	B	4/83

Abbreviations

A: Akahata, Tokyo; B: Beitrage zur Geschichte der Arbeiterbewegung, East Berlin; BIOst: Bundesinstitut, Cologne; BT: Berlingske Tidende, Copenhagen; C: Communisme, Paris; H: l'Humanité, Paris; hor: horizont, East Berlin; MB: Marxistische Blätter, Frankfurt; MTI: Magyar Tavirati Iroda, Budapest; NhD: Nhân Dân, Hanoi; ND: Neues Deutschland, East Berlin; PFS: Probleme des Friedens und des Sozialismus, Prague; Pr: Pravda, Moscow; RD: Rabotnicesko Delo, Sofia; RPr: Rudé Pravo, Prague; RR: Renmin Ribao, Beijing; Sc: Scinteia, Bucharest; STP: Sozialismus, Theorie und Praxis, Moscow; U: l'Unità, Rome; US: Uusi Suomi, Helsinki; UZ: Unsere Zeit, Düsseldorf; YICA: Yearbook on International Communist Affairs, Stanford.

5. Membership: Western European Communist Parties

PCI	Italy	1,544,000	U	11/11/86
PCF	France	608,000	H	14/10/85
PCP	Portugal	200,753	ND	16/12/83
PCE	Spain	93,000	hor	2/87
DKP	FR Germany	57,802	UZ	9/5/86
KKE	Greece	40,000	BIOst	1985
SKP	Finland	33,052	US	5/11/83
CPN	Netherlands	20,000	hor	3/84
KPÖ	Austria	16,000	PFS	6/81
VKP	Sweden	16,000	U	6/4/86
CPGB	Great Britain	15,000	BIOst	85
AKEL	Cyprus	15,000	hor	2/87
DKP	Denmark	11,000	C	11-12/86
KKE-I	Greece	10,000	BT	17/11/83
PCB/KPB	Belgium	10,000	YICA	1985 (for 1984)
PdA	Switzerland	9,000	C	11-12/86
PCPE	Spain	4,500	YICA	1985 (for 1984)
SEW	West Berlin	4,500	YICA	1985 (for 1984)
AB	Iceland	3,000	YICA	1985 (for 1984)
TCP	Turkey	3,000	C	11-12/86
NKP	Norway	2,000	BIOst	1985 (for 1984)
PCSM	San Marino	1,098	hor	5/86
PCL	Luxembourg	600	YICA	1985 (for 1984)

Bibliography

Accornero, Aris; Mannheimer, Renato; Sebastiani, Chiara.
L'identità comunista: I militanti, le strutture, la
cultura del PCI. Rome: Editori Riuniti, 1983.
Adams, T. W. AKEL, the Communist Party of Cyprus. Stanford:
Hoover Institution Press, 1971.
Adereth, Maxwell. The French Communist Party. A Critical
History (1920-1984) from the Comintern to "the colors
of France." Manchester: Manchester University Press,
1984.
Adler, Alexandre, et al. L'URSS et nous. Paris: Editions
Sociales, 1978.
Albright, David E., ed. Communism and Political Systems in
Western Europe. Boulder: Westview Press, 1979.
Amendola, Giorgio. Il rinnovamento del PCI. Intervista di
Renato Nicolai. Rome: Editori Riuniti, 1978.
Arbeitsbereich Geschichte und Politik der DDR am Institut
für Sozialwissenschaften der Universität Mannheim.
Ziele, Formen und Grenzen der "besonderen" Wege zum
Sozialismus. Vol. 2. Mannheim: 1984.
Ardant, Pierre. "L'AKEL, parti communiste de Chypre." Est
et Ouest 30: 16-18.
Aspaturian, Vernon V.; Valenta, Jiri; Burke, David P., eds.
Eurocommunism between East and West. Bloomington:
Indiana University Press, 1980.
Barnouin, Barbara. "Dissonant Voice in International Commu-
nism." In The End of an Isolation, edited by Harish
Kapur. Dordrecht: Nijhoff, 1985.
Bell, David. Eurocommunism and the Spanish Communist Party.
Brighton: Sussex European Center, 1976.
Berlinguer, Enrico. La "questione comunista" 1969-1975.
Rome: Editori Riuniti, 1975.
_____. La Politica internazionale dei comunisti itali-
ani, 1975-1976. Rome: Editori Riuniti, 1975.
Berner, Wolfgang. "Sowjetische Aussenpolitik und Aussenbe-
ziehungen der Partei auf dem XXVII. KPdSU-Kongress."
Beiträge zur Konfliktforschung 16: 121-145.
Berton, Peter. "The Japanese Communists' Rapprochement
with the Soviet Union." Asian Survey 20: 1210-1222.

_____. "Japan: Euro-Nippo-Communism." In Eurocommunism between East and West, edited by Vernon V. Aspaturian, Jiri Valenta, and David P. Burke. Bloomington: Indiana University Press, 1980.

_____. "Japanese Eurocommunists: Running in Place." Problems of Communism 35: 130.

Beyer, Hermann. "Finnlands Kommunisten vor grossen Problemen." Osteuropa 34: 353-364.

Bialer, Seweryn, and Afferica, Joan. "The Genesis of Gorbachev's World." Foreign Affairs 64: 605-644.

Blackmer, Donald L. M., and Tarrow, Sidney, eds. Communism in Italy and France. Princeton: Princeton University Press, 1975.

Boeninger, Edgardo. "The Chilean Road to Democracy." Foreign Affairs 63: 812-832.

Boffa, Giuseppe. "L'internazionalismo del PCI." Critica Marxista 19: 519.

Boggs, Carl. The Impasse of European Communism. Boulder: Westview Press, 1982.

Bon, Frédéric, et al., eds., Le communisme en France. Paris: Armand Colin, 1969.

Borkenau, Franz. World Communism. A History of the Communist International. Ann Arbor: Michigan University Press, 1962.

Brahm, Heinz. "Der chinesisch-sowjetische Konflikt." In Sowjetunion: Aussenpolitik 1955-1973, edited by Dietrich Geyer. Cologne and Vienna: Böhlau, 1976.

Braunthal, Julius. History of the International. Vol. 2. New York: Praeger, 1967.

Brunner, Georg. Das Parteistatut der KPdSU 1903-1961. Cologne: Wissenschaft und Politik, 1965.

Buton, Philippe. "Les effectifs du Parti communiste français 1920-1984," Communisme 7: 5-30.

Carrillo, Santiago. Le communisme malgré tout. Entretiens avec Lilly Marcou. Paris: Presses Universitaires de France, 1984.

_____. Eurocomunismo y Estado. Barcelona: Editorial Grijalbo, 1977.

Central Committee of the Italian Communist Party. The Italian Communists. Foreign Bulletin of the P.C.I. Rome (bimonthly).

Central Committee of the Japanese Communist Party. Sixty-Year History of the Japanese Communist Party. Tokyo: Japan Press Service, 1982.

_____. Bulletin: Information for Abroad.

Childs, David, ed. The Changing Face of Western Communism. London: Croom Helm, 1980.

Claudín, Fernando. The Communist Movement. From Comintern
to Cominform. New York: Monthly Review Press, 1975.
_____. Eurocommunism and Socialism. London: NLB, 1978.
Clissold, Stephen, ed. Yugoslavia and the Soviet Union
1939-1973. London/New York/Toronto: Oxford University
Press, 1975.
Communist Party of China. The Polemics on the General Line
of the International Communist Movement. Beijing:
Foreign Language Press, 1965.
Communist Party of Spain. Manifiesto Programa del Partido
Comunista de Espana. Paris: Coleccion Ebro, 1975.
Cunhal, Alvaro. Kurs auf den Sieg. Die Aufgaben der Partei
in der demokratischen und nationalen Revolution. East
Berlin: Dietz, 1981.
Degras, Jane. The Communist International 1919-1943. Docu-
ments. Vol. 1-3. London: Oxford University Press,
1965-1971.
Devlin, Kevin. "The Challenge of Eurocommunism." Problems
of Communism 26: 1-20.
_____. Radio Free Europe Research background reports on the
world Communist movement, 1967-1986.
Donath, Margarete. "Die Kommunistische Partei Japans
zwischen Peking und Moskau." Berichte des Bundesin-
stituts für ostwissenschaftliche und internationale
Studien 28 (1975).
Donneur, André. L'Alliance fragile: Socialistes et Commu-
nistes français. 1922-1983. Montreal: Nouvelle Op-
tique, 1984.
Ellison, Herbert J. "United Front Strategy and Soviet
Foreign Policy." Problems of Communism 34: 45-64.
Esser, Klaus. "Die chilenische Revolution." Berichte des
Bundesinstituts für ostwissenschaftliche und interna-
tionale Studien 39 (1971).
Fajon, Etienne, ed. L'Union est un combat. Paris: Editions
Sociales, 1975.
Fauvet, Jacques. Histoire du Parti communiste français.
Paris: Fayard, 1977.
Focà, Anna. "Zyperns Kommunisten und die zypriotische
Gesellschaft." In Die kommunistischen Parteien Süd-
europas, edited by Heinz Timmermann. Baden-Baden:
Nomos, 1979.
"Foreign Contacts of the Communist Party." Beijing Review
27: p.19.
Friend, Julius W. "After Eurocommunism." Studies in Com-
parative Communism 19: 55-65.
_____. "The Roots of Autonomy in West European Commu-
nism." Problems of Communism 29: 28-53.

Furci, Carmelo. The Chilean Communist Party and the Road to Socialism. London: Zed Books, 1984.

Fuwa, Tetsuzo. Stalin and Great Power Chauvinism. Tokyo: Japan Press Service, 1984.

Gärtner, Heinz, and Trautmann, Günter, eds. Ein Dritter Weg zwischen den Blöcken? Die Weltmächte, Europa und der Eurokommunismus. Vienna: Verlag für Gesellschaftskritik, 1985.

Goldenberg, Boris. Kommunismus in Lateinamerika. Stuttgart: Kohlhammer, 1971.

Griffith, William E., ed. The European Left: Italy, France, and Spain. Lexington: D.C. Heath & Co., 1979.

Grlickov, Alexandr. "National und International." Sozialistische Theorie und Praxis 4: 3-38.

Guerra, Adriano. Gli anni del Cominform. Milan: Mazotta, 1977.

_____. Il Giorno che Chruscev parlò. Rome: Editori Riuniti, 1986.

Hajek, Milos. Storia dell' Internazionale Comunista (1921-1935). Rome: Editori Riuniti, 1975.

Hermet, Guy. The Communists in Spain. Study of an Underground Political Movement. Westmead: Saxon House, 1974.

Hodgson, John H. "Finnish Communism and Electoral Politics." Problems of Communism 23: 34-45.

_____. "Il comunismo finlandese nei governi di coalizione. Dallo stalinismo all' eurocomunismo." Il Mulino 31: 31-51.

Hough, Jerry. "Gorbachev's Strategy." Foreign Affairs 64: 33-55.

Iivonen, Jyrki, "State or Party? The Dilemma of Relations between the Soviet and Finnish Communist Parties." Journal of Communist Studies 2: 5-30.

Ilardi, Massimo, and Accornero, Aris, eds. Il Partito comunista italiano: Struttura e storia dell'organizzazione 1921-1979. Milan: Feltrinelli, 1982.

Institut für Marxismus-Leninismus beim ZK der KPdSU, ed. Die Kommunistische Internationale. Kurzer historischer Abriss. East Berlin: Dietz, 1970.

Internationale Beratung der kommunistischen und Arbeiterparteien Moskau 1969. Prague: Verlag Frieden und Sozialismus, 1969.

Isenberg, Veronika. "Die Kommunisten Spaniens und Portugals und die Europäische Gemeinschaft." In Die Kommunisten Südeuropas und die Europäische Gemeinschaft, edited by Heinz Timmermann. Bonn: Europa Union Verlag, 1981.

Jacob, Alain. "La lente réinsertion de la Chine dans le

monde communiste." Politique Etrangère 3: 63-73.
Juquin, Pierre. Autocritique. Paris: Grasset, 1985.
Kellmann, Klaus. Pluralistischer Kommunismus? Wandlungs-
tendenzen eurokommunistischer Parteien in Westeuropa
und ihre Reaktionen auf die Erneuerung in Polen.
Stuttgart: Klett-Cotta, 1984.
Kernig, Claus D., ed. Die kommunistischen Parteien der Welt.
Freiburg: Herder,1969.
Kriegel, Annie. Les Communistes français 1920-1970. Paris:
Editions du Seuil, 1985.
_____. Le Système communiste mondial. Paris: Presses Uni-
versitaires de France, 1984.
Kusin, Vladimir V. "Gorbachev and Eastern Europe." Prob-
lems of Communism 35: 39-53.
Lange, Peter, and Vanicelli, Maurizio, eds. The Communist
Parties of Italy, France, and Spain: Postwar Change
and Continuity. Casebook Series on European Politics
and Society, vol. 1. London: George Allen & Unwin,
1981.
Langer, Paul F. Communism in Japan: A Case of Political
Naturalization. Stanford: Hoover Institution Press,
1972.
Lavau, Georges. A quoi sert le parti communiste?. Paris:
Fayard, 1981.
Leonhard, Wolfgang. Eurocommunism. Challenge for East and
West. New York: Holt, Rinehart, and Winston, 1979.
Li Ji, and Guo Quinshi. "Principles Governing Relations
with Foreign Communist Parties." Beijing Review 26:
15-19.
Lian Yan. "The CPC's Relations with Other Parties." Bei-
jing Review 29: 22-25.
Löwenthal, Richard. Chruschtschow und der Weltkommunismus.
Stuttgart: Kohlhammer, 1963. English title-
World Communism, the Disintegration of a Secular Faith.
New York: Oxford University Press, 1964.
_____. Weltpolitische Betrachtungen. Göttingen: Vander-
hoeck und Ruprecht, 1983.
Luccioni, Xavier. "Pékin et l'unité dans la diversité."
Le Monde diplomatique 27: 4.
Marchais, Georges. Le défi démocratique. Paris: Grasset,
1973.
_____. L'espoir au présent. Paris: Editions Sociales,
1980.
_____. Parlons franchement. Paris: Grasset, 1977.
Marcou, Lilly. "Le Grand virage du communisme chinois." Le
Monde diplomatique 33: 12.

_____. L'Internationale après Staline. Paris: Grasset, 1977.

_____. Le Kominform. Le communisme de guerre froide. Paris: Presses de la Fondation nationale de sciences politiques, 1977.

_____. Le Mouvement communiste international 1945-1976. Paris: Presses Universitaires de France, 1980.

_____. Les Pieds d'argile. Le communisme mondial au présent 1970-1986. Paris: Editions Ramsay, 1986.

_____, ed. L'URSS vue de gauche. Paris: Presses Universitaires de France, 1982.

Martelli, Roger. 1956: le choc du vingtième congrès du pcus. Paris: Editions Sociales, 1982.

_____. Communisme français. Histoire sincère du PCF 1920-1984. Paris: Editions Sociales, 1984.

McLeod, Alex. "Portrait of a Model Ally: The Portuguese Communist Party and the International Communist Movement." Studies in Comparative Communism 17: 31-52.

Meyer, Thomas; Klär, Karl-Heinz; Miller, Susanne; Novy, Klaus; Timmermann, Heinz, eds. Lexikon des Sozialismus. Cologne: Bund-Verlag, 1986.

Middlemas, Keith. Power and the Party: Changing Faces of Communism in Western Europe. London: André Deutsch, 1980.

Miller, Robert F., and Féhér, Ferenc, eds. Khrushchev and the Communist World. London and Sydney: Croom, 1984.

Mlynar, Zdenek. "Leninistische Partei und pluralistische politische Demokratie." Forum ds 4: 107-114.

Mujal-León, Eusebio. Communism and Political Change in Spain. Bloomington: Indiana University Press, 1983.

_____. "Decline and Fall of Spanish Communism," Problems of Communism 35: 1-27.

_____. "The PCP and the Portuguese Revolution." Problems of Communism 26: 21-41.

Napolitano, Giorgio. In mezzo al guado. Rome: Editori Riuniti, 1979.

Pajetta, Giancarlo. Le crisi che ho vissuto: Budapest, Praga, Varsavia. Rome: Editori Riuniti, 1982.

_____. La lunga marcia dell'internazionalismo. Intervista di Ottavio Cecchi. Rome: Editori Riuniti, 1978.

Partito Comunista Italiano. La politica e l'organizzazione dei comunisti italiani. Rome: Editori Riuniti, 1979.

_____. Organizzazione-Dati-Statistiche. Rome: Editori Riuniti, 1986.

Pohl, Manfred. Die Kommunistische Partei Japans. Hamburg: Institut für Asienkunde, 1976.

Ponomarev, Boris. Die lebendige und wirksame Lehre des Marxismus-Leninismus. Frankfurt am Main: Verlag Marxistische Blätter, 1978.

Poulantzas, Nikos. Die Krise der Diktaturen: Portugal, Griechenland, Spanien. Frankfurt am Main: Suhrkamp, 1977.

Priester, Karin. Hat der Eurokommunismus eine Zukunft? Perspektiven und Grenzen des Systemwandels in Westeuropa. Munich: C.H. Beck, 1982.

Ragionieri, Ernesto. Palmiro Togliatti. Rome: Editori Riuniti, 1976.

Ranger, Jean. "Le déclin du Parti communiste français." Revue française de science politique 36: 46-63.

Reale, Eugenio. Nascita del Kominform. Verona: Mondadori, 1958.

Rosenberg, Arthur. Geschichte des Bolschewismus. Reprint. Frankfurt: Europäische Verlagsanstalt, 1966.

Rubbi, Antonio, et al. I partiti comunisti dell'Europa occidentale. Milan: Teti Editore, 1978.

Sassoon, Donald. The Strategy of the Italian Communist Party. London: Frances Pinter, 1981.

Schüssler, Georg, et al. Der demokratische Zentralismus: Theorie und Praxis. East Berlin: Staatsverlag, 1981.

Schwab, George, ed. Eurocommunism. The Ideological and Political-Theoretical Foundations. London: Aldwych Press, 1981.

Siebenundzwangzigster Parteitag der KPdSU, März 1986. "Sowjetunion zu neuen Ufern?" Dokumente und Materialien. Düsseldorf: Brücken Verlag, 1986.

Sigmund, Paul E. "Chile: Two Years of 'Popular Unity.'" Problems of Communism 21: 38-51.

Spieker, Manfred, ed. Der Eurokommunismus: Demokratie oder Diktatur? Stuttgart: Klett-Cotta, 1979.

Spriano, Paolo. I comunisti europei e Stalin. Turin: Einaudi, 1983.

Spring, Seija, and Spring, D. W. "The Finnish Communist Party: Two Parties in One." In The Changing Face of Western Communism. Edited by David Childs. London: Croom Helm, 1980.

Steinkühler, Manfred, ed. Eurokommunismus im Widerspruch. Analyse und Dokumentation. Cologne: Wissenschaft und Politik, 1977.

Strbac, Cedomir. "Zeitgenössischer Sozialismus und Internationalismus." Internationale Politik 34: 23-27.

Strübel, Michael. Neue Wege der italienischen Kommunisten. Baden-Baden: Nomos, 1982.

Tannahill, R. Neal. The Communist Parties of Western
   Europe. A Comparative Study. Westport and London:
   Greenwood Press, 1978.
Tiersky, Ronald. Ordinary Stalinism: Democratic Centralism
   and the Question of Communist Political Development.
   Boston: Allen & Unwin, 1985.
_____. French Communism 1920-1972. New York and
   London: Columbia University Press, 1974.
_____. "Das Problem des demokratischen Zentralismus." In
   Die kommunistischen Parteien Südeuropas. Edited by
   Heinz Timmermann. Baden-Baden: Nomos, 1979.
Timmermann, Heinz. "Aspekte der innerparteilichen Struktur
   und Willensbildung bei den Eurokommunisten." In Sozi-
   alismus in Theorie und Praxis. Festschrift für
   Richard Löwenthal. Berlin and New York: de Gruyter,
   1978.
_____. "The Cominform Effects on Soviet Foreign Policy."
   Studies in Comparative Communism 18: 3-23.
_____. "La conférence des partis communistes européens à
   Berlin." Politique Etrangère 41: 507-519.
_____. "The Controversy between the CPSU and the Italian
   Communist Party on the Polish Question." In The Soviet
   Union 1982-83. Edited by the Bundesinstitut für
   ostwissenschaftliche und internationale Studien. New
   York and London: Holmes and Meier, 1985.
_____. "The CPSU and the Western Communist Parties in the
   1980s." International Journal 37: 241-262.
_____. "Eurocommunism: Moscow's Reaction and the Implica-
   tions for Eastern Europe." The World Today 33: 376-
   385.
_____. "The Eurocommunists and Soviet Policy toward Wes-
   tern Europe." In The Soviet Union 1978-79. Edited by
   the Bundesinstitut für ostwissenschaftliche und
   internationale Studien. New York and London: Holmes
   and Meier, 1980.
_____, ed. Eurokommunismus: Fakten, Analysen, Interviews.
   Frankfurt: Fischer, 1978.
_____. "The Fundamentals of Proletarian Internationalism."
   In The Present State of Communist Internationalism.
   Edited by Lawrence L. Whetten. Lexington: D. C. Heath
   & Co., 1983.
_____. "Die genetischen Mutationen der KPI." Die Neue
   Gesellschaft 30: 449-455.
_____. "Gorbatschow zeigt aussenpolitisches Profil. Kurs-
   korrekturen oder Konzeptionswandel?" Osteuropa 36:
   3-21.

_____, ed. Die kommunistischen Parteien Südeuropas: Länderstudien und Queranalysen. Baden-Baden: Nomos, 1979.

_____. "Reform Communists in West and East: Conception, Cross-Connections, and Perspectives." In Soviet Foreign Policy and East-West Relations. Edited by Roger E. Kanet. New York: Pergamon Press, 1982.

Tökés, Rudolf L., ed. Eurocommunism and Detente. New York, New York University Press, 1978.

Togliatti, Palmiro. "Nove domande sullo stalinismo." Nuovi Argomenti, no. 20, June 16, 1956.

_____. "Promemoria sulla questione del movimento e della sua unità." Rinascita 20: 1-4.

Togliatti, Palmiro; Longo, Luigi; Berlinguer, Enrico. Il PCI e il movimento operaio internazionale. Rome: Editori Riuniti, 1968.

Urban, George R., ed. Communist Reformation: Nationalism, Internationalism, and Change in the World Communist Movement. New York: St. Martin's Press, 1979.

_____, ed. Eurocommunism. Its Roots and Future in Italy and Elsewhere. London: Maurice Temple Smith, 1978.

Urban, Joan Barth. Moscow and the Italian Communist Party. Ithaca and London: Cornell University Press, 1986.

Vaner, Semih. "Chypre: Petite ile, grandes puissances." Politique Etrangère 50: 157-171.

Wagner, Ulrich. Finnlands Kommunisten: Volksfrontexperiment und Parteispaltung. Stuttgart: Kohlhammer, 1970.

Waller, Michael. Democratic Centralism: an Historical Commentary. Manchester: Manchester University Press, 1981.

Whetten, Lawrence L., ed. The Present State of Communist Internationalism. Lexington: D. C. Heath & Co., 1983.

Whetten, Lawrence L. New International Communism, The Foreign and Defence Policies of the Latin European Communist Parties. Lexington: D. C. Heath & Co., 1982.

Wilson, Frank L. "French Communism on the Defensive." Problems of Communism 34: 77-84.

Zänker, Christian. "Die entgültige Spaltung der finnischen Kommunisten." Die Neue Gesellschaft/Frankfurter Hefte 34: 83-88.

Zagladin, Vadim, ed. Triebkräfte des revolutionären Weltprozesses. East Berlin: Dietz, 1983.

_____, ed. Die internationale kommunistische Bewegung. East Berlin: Dietz, 1984.

Zimbler, Brian L. "Partners or Prisoners? Relations between the PCF and the CPSU." Studies in Comparative Communism 17: 3-29.

Index

178-179
Renovica, Milanko
72(n3)
Republican Left, Spain
180
Resistance, France,
155
Revolutionary tide,
ebbs by 1920, 14
Right-opportunist
"revisionism," 79
Rigout, Marcel, 161-
162
Rochet, Waldeck,
162, 164
Rome, 135
Romania, 56, 112-113
Romanian Communist
party, 93, 110
Romanov, Georgi, 188
Rosenberg, Arthur, 14,
19, 28, 31
Rubbi, Antonio,
11(n5)
Rusakov, Konstantin,
67

Saarinen, Aarne,
188-189
St. Etienne, 158
Salazar-Caetano regime
195, 197
San Francisco Treaty,
232
San Marino Communist
party, 93
Sanchez Montero,
Simon, 178
Sandinistas, 221
Sartorius, Nicolas,
183(n25)
Scala mobile, 133
Second International,
3-4, 14, 80, 137
Secret ballot in
CP's, 89

Seine-Saint-Denis,
158
Sejm, 85
SFIO, 153. See also
French Socialist
party
CNT, 212. See also
Chilean National
Workers' Commando
Self-Defense Forces,
Japan, 225
Semprun, Jorge, 176
Servin, Marcel, 160
Shevarnadze, Eduard,
233
Shiga, Yoshio, 111,
226
Shikotan, 232
El Siglo, 215
Sinisalo, Taisto 189,
191-192
Sinocommunism, 106
SKP dogmatists, "Com-
mittee of the SKP
Party Organiza-
tions for Unity,
against Schism,"
191
SKDL, 189-190
Sklarska Poreba, 25
SKP, 87, 185-192
SKP, formal split of,
185, 188
SKP-CPSU, 187
Soares, Mario 199
Social fascism, 18,
21, 154
"Socialism in one
country," 15, 28
"Socialism in the
colors of France,"
162
Socialist Action
party, Spain, 180
Socialist Interna-
tional, 5, 54,